JAN SHIPPS

A Social and Intellectual Portrait

JAN SHIPPS

A Social and Intellectual Portrait

How a Methodist Girl from Hueytown, Alabama, Became an Acclaimed Mormon Studies Scholar

Gordon Shepherd and Gary Shepherd

GREG KOFFORD BOOKS
SALT LAKE CITY, 2019

Copyright © 2019 Gordon Shepherd and Gary Shepherd
Cover design copyright © 2019 Greg Kofford Books, Inc.
Cover design by Loyd Isao Ericson
Unless noted, all images are courtesy of Jan Shipps and Tony Shipps

Published in the USA.

All rights reserved. No part of this volume may be reproduced in any form without written permission from the publisher, Greg Kofford Books. The views expressed herein are the responsibility of the authors and do not necessarily represent the position of Greg Kofford Books.

ISBN 978-1-58958-767-0 (paperback); 978-1-58958-768-7 (hardcover)
Also available in ebook.

Greg Kofford Books
P. O. Box 1362
Draper, UT 84020
www.gregkofford.com
facebook.com/gkbooks
twitter.com/gkbooks

Library of Congress Cataloging-in-Publication Data

Names: Shepherd, Gordon, 1943- author. | Shepherd, Gary, 1943- author.
Title: Jan Shipps : a social and intellectual portrait : how a Methodist girl from Hueytown, Alabama, became an acclaimed Mormon studies scholar / Gordon Shepherd and Gary Shepherd.
Description: Salt Lake City : Greg Kofford Books, 2019. | Includes bibliographical references and index.
Identifiers: LCCN 2019018973| ISBN 9781589587670 (pbk.) | ISBN 9781589587687 (hardcover)
Subjects: LCSH: Shipps, Jan, 1929- | Religion historians--Biography. | Mormon Church--Study and teaching. | Church of Jesus Christ of Latter-day Saints--Study and teaching. | LCGFT: Biographies.
Classification: LCC BX8611 .S455 2019 | DDC 289.3092 [B] --dc23
LC record available at https://lccn.loc.gov/2019018973

For Jan

Sometimes we ask people if they pray, and they say different things.
It's the different things they say that tell us something about who they are.
We asked a ninety-year-old woman historian of religious studies fame if she prayed.
She said yes.
She prays out loud every night before bed, because her ninety-year-old skeptic, librarian husband wants to hear her words of comfort and say amen.
Why doesn't *he* pray?
He believes in his wife's prayers, that she can say for him what he can't say for himself.
It makes him sleep better at night.
She prays for protection.
She prays that their home will be protected from fire, because his childhood memories of smoke and flame in his bedroom have never been extinguished.
She prays for immigrants, because she fears for their safety in a calloused country that no longer welcomes their aspirations.
She prays for her born-again son, who prays for her redemption; and she prays for her grandchildren's children and their generations to come.
She prays for her country.
She prays for the protection of many but not for herself.
More forbearing than fearful, her faith is simple.
She believes in a just God and in herself.
She sleeps at night without her husband's prayers in her ears.

Contents

Preface and Acknowledgements	ix
1. Growing Up Through the Great Depression and World War II, 1929–1946	1
2. College, Marriage, and Motherhood in Post-war America, 1946–1960	15
3. Discovering the Mormons and Acquiring Academic Credentials, 1960–1966	31
4. Engagement with the Mormon Scholarly Community, 1967–1974	51
5. Becoming a Renowned Mormon Studies Scholar, 1974–1985	79
6. Major Intellectual Influences and Turning Point Events	113
7. Career Comparisons with Fawn Brodie and Juanita Brooks	143
8. Personal Views on Religion and Feminism	185
Epilogue: Concluding Reflections on Jan Shipps's Legacy	207
Appendix: Jan Shipps's *Curriculum Vita*, 2001	209
Bibliography	223
Index	233

Preface and Acknowledgements

How did Jo Ann Barnett—a Methodist girl born and raised in Hueytown, Alabama, during the Great Depression and World War II—come to be Jan Shipps, a renowned non-Mormon historian and scholar of The Church of Jesus Christ of Latter-day Saints? Our objective in writing this book is threefold. First, we want readers and scholars of Mormon Studies to understand and appreciate the improbable story of how Shipps not only became an important and trusted authority in a field that was at the time predominantly made up of Mormon men, but also the crucial role she played in legitimizing Mormon Studies as a credible academic field of study. We tell this story in Chapters 1 through 5. In Chapter 6 we pull together, summarize, and analyze the biographical strands narrated in the previous chapters.

As part of our second objective, we pose an arbitrary but interesting question: What are the three most important books to date written about Mormon history? That is, what three books have had the greatest impact on the way key aspects of Mormon history are viewed, studied, and written about? Consensus among qualified scholars undoubtedly would be difficult to achieve. Over the years an increasing number of very good books on important Mormon topics, essential to our understanding of Mormon history and institutional development, have been published.[1] Of these, many stand out as truly consequential works that have altered the way other scholars in the field think and write about their subject matter.

Nevertheless, a strong case can be made that the three most consequential books to date about Mormon history are Fawn Brodie's *No Man Knows My*

---

1. A comprehensive bibliography of scholarly works on Mormonism and the LDS church published in the twentieth-century is provided by James B. Allen, Ronald B. Walker, and David J. Whittaker, eds., *Studies in Mormon History: An Indexed Bibliography*. For more recent books on The Church of Jesus Christ of Latter-day Saints and its history, see the catalogue listings of the University of Illinois Press, Oxford University Press, The University of Utah Press, The University of North Carolina Press, Harvard University Press, and Yale University Press, all of which have published important books on Mormon topics. For brevity and clarity this volume regularly employs "LDS Church," "LDS," and "the Church" in lieu of the full name of The Church of Jesus Christ of Latter-day Saints. "RLDS" is used occasionally when referencing persons or themes affiliated with the Reorganized Church of Jesus Christ of Latter Day Saints before it was renamed Community of Christ.

History: The Life of Joseph Smith, Juanita Brooks's *The Mountain Meadows Massacre*, and Jan Shipps's *Mormonism: The Story of a New Religious Tradition*. We attempt to make this case in Chapter 7. Both Brodie and Brooks have had well-deserved biographies written about them and their work. As of yet, Jan Shipps has not.[2] While not in any true sense attempting to write a full-fledged biography, we focus on the shaping social and intellectual influences in Shipps's life that led her, a non-Mormon woman, to become a distinguished scholar of Mormon history and Mormon Studies generally. In the process, we compare and contrast Shipps's scholarly contributions with those of Brodie and Brooks, both to substantiate our judgment of their preeminent standing and to understand how and why they were able to accomplish what they did.

Finally, our third objective in writing this book is a further outgrowth of the first two. As Shipps's reputation and active prominence in scholarly circles grew, so also did her thoughts and actions regarding issues ancillary to Mormonism come into clearer focus. Her response to these issues is important for understanding her approach to studying Mormonism. Two ancillary issues we find most pertinent to explore are the evolution of her personal religious orientation, as well as her attitudes toward modern feminism. We lay out the way in which both of these concerns have helped shape her work and professional identity in Chapter 8.

***

In a 2016 interview with us, Shipps reflected on her improbable emergence as an important figure who helped bring Mormon Studies into mainstream academia. She modestly concluded that the most important factor was serendipitous change taking place in the LDS Church and Mormon culture at the time of her graduate training in the mid-1960s. Her subsequent academic career moved in parallel fashion with Mormonism's transformation from a relatively provincial faith and insular culture to a worldwide, institutional church. She was in the right place at the right time. Her graduate research on nineteenth-century Mormon politics dovetailed with her participation in a rapidly expanding LDS intellectual community, supported by the inauguration of Mormon professional associations (the Mormon History Association and John Whitmer History Association) and their respective journals, as well as the emergence of

---

2. As of this date, Philip Barlow, former Professor of History and Arrington Director of Mormon Studies at Utah State University, is cataloging Jan Shipps's personal papers with the intent of writing a full-scale biography of her life. In the meantime, both Barlow and Klaus Hansen have published essays that summarize significant aspects of Shipps's life and scholarly career. See Phillip Barlow, "Jan Shipps and the Mainstreaming of Mormon Studies," 412–26, and Klaus J. Hansen, "The Long Honeymoon: Jan Shipps among the Mormons," 1–28.

other, scholarly oriented periodicals like *Dialogue: A Journal of Mormon Thought* and *Sunstone* that had no official ties with the LDS Church.³

All of this is pertinent to understanding how Shipps established her role in Mormon Studies. However, this is not a role she simply stepped into; she had to exercise great personal initiative in order to take advantage of the opportunities the times afforded. If Shipps was in the right place at the right time, she was also the *right person* at the right place and time. *How* Jan Shipps became the right person is the overarching question we attempt to address in this book.

***

A brief comment on our documentary sources is in order. In part we have relied on previously published information, such as Shipps's 1982 "Personal Voices" essay in *Dialogue*;⁴ her introspective and semi-autobiographical book, *Sojourner in the Promised Land: Forty Years among the Mormons*, published in 2000; and two unpublished oral history interviews conducted for the LDS Historical Department in 1983 and 1986 by Maureen Ursenbach Beecher and Gordon Irving, respectively.⁵ However, our primary source of information—especially for the first three chapters dealing with Jan's childhood and marital years prior to commencing her academic career at Indiana University-Purdue University Indianapolis—comes from personal interviews we conducted with Shipps at her home in September and October of 2016 and subsequent Skype conversations with her from November 2016 through the fall of 2017. Neither our personal interviews nor Skype conversations followed a formal protocol. We formulated a set of open-ended questions to frame our conversations but allowed discussion to emerge spontaneously as

---

3. The Mormon History Association was founded in December 1965; its biennial journal, the *Journal of Mormon History*, began publication in 1974. The John Whitmer Historical Association was organized by scholars of the Reorganized Church of Jesus Christ of Latter Day Saints (subsequently the Community of Christ) in September 1972; its official journal, the *John Whitmer Association Journal*, was inaugurated in 1981. Preceding either of these two publications as outlets for the New Mormon History, *Dialogue: A Journal of Mormon Thought*, commenced publication in the spring of 1966. *Sunstone* magazine was launched in 1974 by Mormon graduate students, and its first issue was printed in November 1975. In 1979, *Sunstone* began sponsoring an annual symposium in Salt Lake City and subsequently has conducted regional symposia in other cities throughout the United States. All these events helped fuel the New Mormon History movement and coincided with Jan Shipps's early interest in the study of Mormon history and her scholarly development as an authoritative exponent of Mormon Studies.

4. Jan Shipps, "An 'Inside-Outsider' in Zion," 138–61.

5. Shipps was interviewed first by Maureen Ursenbach Beecher (October 15–16, 1983) and subsequently by Gordon Irving (May 6, 1986).

Gordon Shepherd (left) and Gary Shepherd (right) interviewing Jan Shipps, 2016. Photo courtesy of the authors.

we engaged in follow-up queries. Often our follow-up probes would stimulate fresh recollection of events and anecdotes, further fleshing out Shipps's social and intellectual development. When drafting our biographical sketches for the first three chapters, we sent Shipps copies to double-check for the factual accuracy of names and dates or any topical items that we might have misconstrued based on our interview notes.

Those chapters in which we describe some of the foundational and turning point events in Shipps's life, both personal and professional, are, of course, narrated from her point of view. Other individuals participating in the same events, such as family members and colleagues, might very well remember things differently. This is an inherent problem in any oral history or study that relies on recollections provided by the subject. We assume that all individuals, including Jan Shipps, are self-interested in the interpretation of their own experience—that they routinely provide accounts of themselves that are biased and self-vindicating.[6] The problem of objectivity in studies of this kind can only be ultimately remedied by the accretion of numerous other documentary

---

6. The self-vindicating character of memoir and autobiographies is explored at length by Erich Goode in *Justifiable Conduct: Self-Vindication in Memoir*. See also Gordon Shepherd, "Memoir Construction," 44–65.

sources that are weighed and balanced in the conscientious and unbiased construction of a complete biography—something that we trust other scholars will attempt in the future with regard to the noteworthy life of Jan Shipps.

We have not talked extensively with Shipps merely to draw an idealized or self-aggrandized portrait. We are not interested in writing a hagiography. In our interviews we asked focused questions and follow-up questions to spotlight what, in our professional judgment, represented the things in Shipps's life that would help explain her intellectual development and scholarly achievements. The chapters following the biographical sketch are all based on comparative, conceptual, and interpretive analysis of her scholarly contributions, for which we alone are responsible. In addition to these chapters, we also have included Jan Shipps's curriculum vitae as an appendix, which will reinforce and broaden readers' appreciation of her work and scholarly career.

From this point forward, we identify Jan more informally by her first name (which is actually a contraction of her given name, Jo Ann) rather than continually referring impersonally to her as Shipps, her married name as the wife of retired Indiana University librarian, Dr. Anthony W. Shipps.

A final comment on our sources and quotations taken from them. Unreferenced quotations by Jan are all from our oral interviews with her. All other quotations obtained from sources other than our interviews are referenced in the notes. In Chapter 4 in particular we rely heavily on Beecher's oral history interview recorded for the LDS History Department in 1983, which focuses on Jan's personal history in becoming an active member and leader of the Mormon History Association. For our narration of Jan's childhood and early adult years in Chapters 1 through 5, however, we relied primarily on our own interviews. Any readers who would like to see our 2016–17 interview notes with Jan are welcome to contact us for copies.

Acknowledgements

We are most indebted to Jan for her remarkable hospitality and candid openness to our oral interviews over the course of many conversations—some conducted in person at her Bloomington home and many more on Skype. We are also indebted to Jan's husband, Tony, who complemented her interviews with snippets of information that eluded Jan and otherwise enlivened our visits with his inimitable sense of humor. Jan and Tony's son, Stephen, provided additional helpful support for our project, as did close family friends Liane Johnson, and Linda and Ed Stevenson.

Philip Barlow has been particularly helpful to us since the very inception of our idea to write this book. As a mentee of Jan's and a subsequent collaborator of hers in various scholarly activities, Phil has been generous with his insights, suggestions, provisioning of documents, and overall encouragement. Sarah Barringer Gordon, Jan's longtime friend and collaborator, has likewise encouraged and facilitated our work. We also have received helpful critical comments and suggestions from Elbert Peck, Armand Mauss, Nancy Ross, and Paul Edwards, which have improved the clarity of our writing and strengthened our analysis. Finally, both Liz Dulaney and Kathryn Daynes contributed helpful insights derived from their longtime friendship and scholarly collaboration with Jan.

Holly Hansen Rogers took on the task of creating an index within a constricted time frame and, as she has done for us in the past, produced a tool that serious readers will find quite useful in squeezing the most out of our book.

Lastly, we are indebted to Loyd Isao Ericson, our editor, who has been a virtual one-man band in meticulously pushing this book through every step of the publication process.

None of the people singled out above for our thanks have, at this point in time, ultimate responsibility for whatever errors of fact or interpretation may remain unwinnowed from our text. We alone are responsible for these, if any there be.

CHAPTER 1

Growing Up Through the Great Depression and World War II, 1929–1946

On October 24, 1929, three weeks after her birth, Jan Shipps was christened Jo Ann Barnett in the Hueytown, Alabama, Methodist Church. (As a college freshman, she began going by Jan to avoid being confused with a dozen other classmates whose first names were also Jo Ann, Joann, or Joanne.) Jan's mother, Thalia Jenkins Bell Barnett, was a lifelong Methodist. Her father, William McKinley Barnett,[1] grew up in a fundamentalist Baptist church but later joined the Methodist Church when he married Jan's mother and consented to their children being baptized into Thalia's faith. Jan's Methodism would become one of several important influences that shaped her early intellectual development in the process of becoming an adult.

Hueytown and the Depression

On the same day of her christening, the New York Stock Market crashed, ushering in the Great Depression. The economic fortunes of American families across the country were severely upended, especially in rural areas and blue collar industrial cities like Birmingham, Alabama, where steel mills and manufacturing plants were forced to close, and workers like Jan's father lost their jobs by the tens of thousands.[2]

---

1. To his friends, William was "Bill," but to Thalia he was always "McKinley."
2. According to Matthew L. Downs, "Alabama's industrial sector, centered in the Birmingham District, had expanded in the late-nineteenth and early-twentieth centuries, and its collapse during the Great Depression devastated the state's economy even further. Of nearly 3,000 mines and mills operating in the state in 1929, only half were still in operation in 1933 as an abrupt decline in national demand and international trade led to a drop in production. Employment in iron and steel industries fell by 28 percent from 1929 to 1931. Of 100,000 wage and salaried workers in Birmingham, 25,000 were jobless, 60,000 were working part time, and only about 15,000 were working full time by June 1932—an unemployment rate of 25 percent. When city leaders announced that 100,000 people in Birmingham (out of a total population of 260,000 or nearly 40 percent) received some kind of economic aid in 1934, President Roosevelt called the city the 'worst hit town in the country.'" See Matthew L. Downs, "Great Depression in Alabama."

Hueytown was located on the outskirts of Birmingham and emerged in the early twentieth-century as a "line-town" that served primarily as a residential community for workers who were employed either by the Tennessee Coal, Iron and Railroad Company (TCI) or the Bessemer Steel Company.[3] Linked to the sprawling, industrial area around Birmingham, Hueytown nonetheless provided a small-town environment with its own schools and local merchants. Because of the predominantly blue-collar employment in town, Jan and other children growing up in Hueytown did not think of themselves as "farm kids"; instead, she and other "town kids" looked down on children living in rural areas just a few miles outside of Hueytown as unsophisticated hayseeds.

Jan's parents, Thalia and William, were introduced by a mutual friend who taught school with Jan's mother. They were married in 1926 in Dadeville, Alabama, and later moved to Hueytown where William found employment with TCI. Thrown out of work when TCI closed one of its Birmingham steel-making operations, William relied thereafter on his entrepreneurial talents and jack-of-all-trades construction and mechanical skills to help support Thalia and their four children: Jan, her older sister Sue, and her two younger brothers, Billy and Bernard. In contrast to Williams's irregular earnings, the family depended substantially on Thalia's salaried employment as a "home demonstration agent," funded through the federal government's Works Progress Administration (WPA), where she "taught country women" in Alabama's Jefferson County "principles of nutrition and home economics" and assisted in the implementation of nutritious lunch meals for children in the county's public schools.[4] In addition to her government employment, Thalia was a licensed public school teacher—a profession she practiced most of her adult working life.

Thalia had a bachelor's degree in home economics from the Mississippi State College for Women—a traditional Southern women's college.[5] In con-

---

3. For a history of the rise and decline of the coal and steel industries in the Birmingham region, see Ethel Armes, *The Story of Coal and Iron in Alabama*.

4. The Roosevelt administration's efforts to provide nutritious lunchroom meals to hungry schoolchildren during the Great Depression were initiated in 1933 through the newly established Federal Emergency Relief Administration (FERA). In 1935, FERA programs were reorganized under the WPA, which employed women like Thalia with college degrees in home economics. For a history of lunch school programs and government agencies in the United States, see Susan Levine, *School Lunch Politics: The Surprising History of America's Favorite Welfare Program*.

5. Established in Columbia, Mississippi, in 1884 as the "Industrial Institute and College for the Education of White Girls," the school's name was changed in 1920 to the Mississippi State College for Women in order to reflect an emphasis on collegiate, rather than vocational, education. It was during this period of educational change that

trast, William had only a high school education and never attended any college. Although Thalia was better educated, Jan recalls her father having a kind of "natural intellect" for figuring things out: "Daddy may have been smarter than Mother. He was very smart; he could do anything." Fresh out of high school, William worked for the Navy shipyard in Mobile, Alabama, during World War I installing asbestos in ships. This employment, along with smoking, contributed to his development of lung cancer in later life and his early death at 58. Nevertheless, as a young man, work in the war industry kept William free of the military draft.

Thalia's two sisters had also attended the Mississippi State College for Women and become school teachers, passing on to Jan a relatively rare family value for that era: the importance of women's education. With her mother and aunts as examples, Jan simply took it for granted that she would wind up going to college as well. Her mother and aunts were important role models of smart women who did not regard themselves as intellectually inferior to men and were actively involved in community affairs. Jan's Aunt Sue (for whom her sister Sue was named) was a particularly significant adult in Jan's childhood. Aunt Sue married a wealthy widower and subsequently lived in a plantation-style home in Century, Florida, on the northwestern edge of the Florida panhandle bordering Pensacola. Among other indicators of Southern gentility, Sue's home featured a black cook, black maids, and a black butler. Jan refers to her Aunt Sue as "my rich aunt," whom she admired for her apparent self-confidence and sophistication. Among other things, Aunt Sue paid for Jan's and her sister's Easter outfits, their dance lessons, and later for Jan's advanced piano lessons in Birmingham.

As children, Jan and her sister, Sue, developed a close but sometimes competitive sibling relationship. Jan describes Sue as "daddy's favorite" and "the pretty one" (graceful, athletic, and popular, with dark, wavy hair and a dark complexion like their father) and herself as "the smart one" and an "ugly duckling" (awkward, towheaded, straight haired, and plain). Jan never thought of herself as pretty or attractive growing up: "I only learned I was attractive after meeting Tony [her husband]." Jan was respectful of her father but much closer to her mother, who took obvious, vicarious pride in early signs of Jan's scholastic talent and musical ability. While only a year apart in age, and despite their differences, Jan looked up to her older sister. In childhood and adolescence, they were a complementary pair who served as each other's closest playmate and best friend.

Jan's mother and sisters enrolled as students. In 1974 the school's name was changed again to the Mississippi University for Women. The history of the school is reviewed in Bridget Smith Pieschel, "The History of Mississippi University for Women."

Encouraged by her school teacher mother and aided by Josephine—a black woman who was hired to perform domestic chores and watch after Jan and her siblings while Thalia was working for the WPA—Jan began learning to read before she was five. She recalls Josephine "teaching me my letters" by pointing to labels on consumer items in the kitchen while she was ironing. Sue started school in the first grade, a year ahead of Jan, and began sharing her school books and take-home assignments with her younger sister. The following year, when Jan turned six, she tested at a first-grade level and was quickly promoted to the second grade with Sue. From that point forward, Jan and Sue were always in the same grade.

Schoolwork came easily for Jan, but Sue was dyslexic and struggled with reading and spelling. Although Thalia was ambivalent about Jan helping Sue with her schoolwork (which she always did anyway), she wanted each girl to develop her own abilities and admonished Jan to not think she was smarter than Sue; Jan was to be grateful, not prideful, for her intellect. More important, Thalia emphasized that *both* of her daughters had gifts, and that Sue's were simply different than Jan's. For instance, both girls were expected to help make their own clothes; while Jan's efforts looked amateurish and homemade, Sue's creations were elegant. Bringing their talents together, Sue would make lovely baskets from pine boughs to give as gifts, and Jan would make candy to put in them.

Thalia and William's different educational backgrounds informed their parental roles. Thalia would talk with the children about their schoolwork and ask questions about the books they were reading. She was a good writer and would review her children's letters to relatives and essays for school assignments (plausibly implanting in Jan an early appreciation for the importance of editing written work). In contrast, William emphasized practical learning. (One result of this emphasis, predictably seen in retrospect, was that Sue excelled to a far greater degree than Jan in acquiring their father's skills for "fixing things.") Furthermore, William didn't like hearing excuses or seeing his children give up: "We were expected to take initiative and responsibility and always try our best before asking for or receiving any help." As a child, Jan internalized her parents' values of personal responsibility and do-it-yourself initiative, which, as an adult, would surface in her untiring efforts to educate herself as a nontraditional student seeking academic credentials and scholarly recognition.

Thalia was also eager for her daughters to acquire cultivated as well as practical talents. She enrolled both Sue and Jan in tap-dancing lessons at an early age (subsidized by their "rich Aunt Sue"). According to Jan, Sue excelled and continued to excel into adulthood: "She could dance like a dream." In contrast, Jan characterizes her own dancing ability as "horrible." At piano, however, it was Jan who excelled. A local woman offered Jan and her siblings free lessons in exchange for use of the family's old upright piano to teach other Hueytown children. Of the Barnett children, only Jan, who began at age five, persisted with her lessons. She became the local teacher's star pupil, and the teacher arranged (again, with Aunt Sue's financial assistance) for Jan to take monthly lessons at the Birmingham College of Music.[6] As a young girl, Jan paid a ten-cent fare to ride the bus by herself to her lessons in Birmingham, while dressed up and wearing white gloves.

Jan continued studying piano as a teen until she entered college, practicing at least two hours a day. As she recalls, "Piano was a lot of my childhood. In those days many people didn't have radios or record players." Jan's growing proficiency with the piano put her in high demand at school dances and other venues, which gave Jan a credential for socializing with her popular sister and their Hueytown friends. During this time Jan was also the pianist for the local Methodist Church, which, along with her good grades, earned significant adult recognition of her talents.

Jan (seated) and Sue in front of their home in Hueytown, Alabama

Thalia and William were not inclined to routinely use physical punishment to discipline their children. Occasionally, though, Jan and Sue would receive a light switching for misbehavior deemed too egregious. On one such occasion that stands out in Jan's memory, she and Sue had acquired tap shoes for dancing lessons and impulsively tried them out on top of a neighbor's chicken coop because of the vibrant sound their taps made on the metal roof. The loud clattering frightened the chickens roosting on eggs below, and the

---

6. The Birmingham College of Music was originally known as the Birmingham Conservatory of Music and was established in downtown Birmingham in 1895. In 1940, the conservatory moved to the campus of Birmingham-Southern College (at a time when Jan was still taking piano lessons), and in 1953 it was fully merged into BSC's music department, as the Birmingham-Southern College Conservatory of Fine and Performing Arts. For a brief overview of this history, see Jim Bennett, "Ever Wonder What Happened to Birmingham's Forgotten Colleges?"

alarmed hens frantically "flew the coop," causing an uproar and ruining some of the eggs. A switching swiftly ensued.

In 1938, when Jan was nine, the Barnett family was forced to move from their comfortable "valley house" in Hueytown to the top of a local mountain, two miles out of town. The move was largely to help relieve her brother Billy's severe asthma from Birmingham's noxious industrial haze that would settle over Hueytown and constitute a growing threat to his health. Mounting financial stress as a result of the Depression may have also been a factor in the move. The home they left behind was "a very nice house" with an electric stove in the kitchen, a big dining room, and three bedrooms.

Before the move, Jan's family occupied what she perceived as a "middle class status" in the Hueytown of the 1930s. They didn't have a lot of money, but "we never went hungry." As a child, Jan had a conception of "rich people" but didn't see her family as living in poverty. More than disposable income, middle class status for the Barnetts during their Hueytown years was indicated by such markers as possession of books, a piano, music and dance lessons for Jan and Sue, hiring of a housekeeper, a telephone (that neighbors frequently came over to use), an electric stove, silverware, nice china, and a new Chevrolet—as well as Thalia's college degree, government job, and participation in a book club.

While still residing in the valley house, Jan remembers people coming by, looking for food, and she credits both her parents with modeling a compassionate attitude toward people in need. It was common during the Depression in the South to give food to hungry people who came to the back door. But Jan's friends "thought it was weird" that her parents invited people (mostly strangers, both black and white), "who were desperate for food," to come inside and eat at the kitchen table. Her mother always had oatmeal, biscuits, corn bread, homemade butter, and vegetables from the garden to share with those in need. While Jan was made aware of her parents' more considerate treatment of strangers, compared to her friends' parents, she also notes that the hungry were not allowed to eat in the *dining room*, implicitly acknowledging a kind of moral condescension on her parents' part in helping less fortunate people, rather than harboring feelings of genuine social equality. And while Jan emphasizes "how good my father was to people of all races who were in need," he was nevertheless steeped in the racial prejudices and mores of the old South and "always used the N-word when talking about black people." These caveats notwithstanding, it's fair to infer that both her parents' compassion and generosity were latent influences on Jan's emerging interest in and empathy for people different than herself.

In contrast to their valley home, the "mountain house" to which they moved from town was constructed by William from scrap materials he obtained from nearby Fairfield, a former company town whose homes for workers (now unemployed and dispersed because of the Depression) were being torn down by the Tennessee Coal, Iron and Railroad Company. Jan remembers the children helping their father construct the floor by holding boards in place while he nailed them together. Initially, the makeshift mountain home lacked running water and electricity and was relatively isolated in a wooded area. Later, ever confident of his ability to fix anything, Jan's father wired the house for electricity and installed a water pump. Jan describes the house as "five rooms and a path," meaning there were no indoor toilets and, when nature called, one had to beat a path to the outhouse. The Barnett children were no longer close to their friends in town, but they loved roaming and playing outdoors. At the same time, with finances becoming tighter and less certain, everyone had to work, including the children. "We were all expected to do more after moving to the mountain house." But Jan and Sue also complained that it was unfair for the boys to do outside chores while theirs were largely confined to domestic chores inside the house, involving much of the work done previously by Josephine (whose services the family could no longer afford).

Jan credits both her parents for their attitudes of personal independence and self-sufficiency. During the Depression, "Daddy was absolutely opposed to being on relief. He would do any kind of work." "I can take care of my family," Jan recalls him insisting as he pridefully refused any government assistance, "He wouldn't let his family go on welfare." Her father's handyman skills and self-confidence made him marketable for most any kind of job. Among other things, he had good sales ability ("He could sell a glass of water to a drowning man") and sold *Compton's Pictured Encyclopedia* (a home and school encyclopedia first published in 1922) door to door. Jan recalls him selling a set of encyclopedias to a man who couldn't read and then, displaying his compassionate side, returning to give the man reading lessons.

For a while, during the early years of the Depression, William and a black partner also operated a "one-horse-mine," employing a cart and a borrowed horse to dig coal from a nearby abandoned mine shaft, which they then sold to local Hueytown households in need of heat during the winter. "One-horse-mine" was the term William used in describing how he and his partner would (beginning around four o'clock in the morning) dig, load, and pull small loads of coal in carts from the abandoned mine shaft. William's partner, an unemployed black miner, would sell and deliver coal in black neighborhoods, while William would do the same in the white section of town. For a white man to partner in this way with a black man during that time and place was highly unusual, even potentially dangerous, and it illustrates Williams's tenaciousness, inventiveness, practicality, and flexibility in trying to provide for his family. As he saw it, partnering with a black man was simply a pragmatic way to maximize sales by selling to customers of both races. Jan was old enough to absorb significant, taken-for-granted lessons regarding practical tolerance and self-sufficiency from observing this arrangement. It seems plausible to speculate that it helped lay an early foundation for establishing her own attitudes regarding race, work, and independence that were subsequently enlarged upon by additional parental inputs and related circumstantial experiences during her childhood.

Jan says her father was likewise good at buying scraps of land and re-selling them for small profits. He also purchased a cow, which contributed milk and butter for his family and for selling to Hueytown neighbors. While virtually everyone Jan knew struggled financially during the Depression, relative to others in the community, the Barnetts did all right. Unlike some, they were never desperate or without means; they always had enough to eat and came up with sufficient finances to pay for necessities.

Just below the mountain where the Barnetts had moved was a blacks-only cemetery that Jan, Sue, and her brothers would explore. During this time, a child of a fondly regarded black janitor at the white Hueytown school died and was buried in this cemetery. Jan and Sue experienced this death and burial as sad and sobering events that further humanized their perceptions of black people and increased their empathy with them as human beings. They knew where his grave was located and placed flowers on the headstone when walking from school back up the mountain.

Black families, including that of their former housekeeper, Josephine, lived at the foot of the mountain where their homes were clustered around a black church. Walking to the school bus stop, Jan and her siblings passed Josephine's house every day and would stop to get drinks of water and talk. They thought of Josephine as part of their family and brought her presents for Christmas. Jan and Sue also got to know black children their age who lived nearby. While waiting for the bus (black children were bussed to a segregated school on the opposite end of town), they talked with each other about their different schools, teams, and favorite games. According to Jan, she and Sue didn't think of these children as black: "They were friends, just kids." Furthermore, Jan's parents didn't strenuously object to their casual contact with black children, which deviated significantly from the racially rigid rules enforced by most white parents in the heyday of the Jim Crow South during the first half of the twentieth century.

In the fifth or sixth grade, Jan began playing piano for the Methodist Church after the adult pianist became ill. As church pianist, Jan attended and had to pay attention to the main service in the sanctuary every Sunday. As a result, she "learned to listen to the sermon." According to her, the Hueytown Methodist Church had "good preachers—not Baptist preaching." These were preachers who, for the most part, expounded social gospel principles rather than engaging in emotional exhortation and always included an intellectual content to their sermons. Religious balance was maintained by the Methodist bishops periodically assigning new ministers and alternating these assignments between liberal and conservative pastors. Their chapel was under construction for years while Jan was growing up, its financing largely dependent on meager donations and labor from members who were struggling to make ends meet. Assistance came from an unusual degree of religious cooperation offered by the Hueytown Baptists in sharing their church facilities, especially during revivals, which Methodists as well as Baptists regularly conducted. According to Jan, these shared activities provided a way of "melting religious differences," especially for the young people: "The Baptist kids couldn't dance, but all of them could play football and sports together."

Although Thalia was active in the Methodist church as a Sunday school teacher and president of the local Missionary Society (now the United Methodist Women), Jan recalls Thalia not being especially pious or publicly devout: "She was an activist, she had a gift to teach. . . . Her main moral admonition was to be a good Christian through actions that helped others." William was even less pious and saw church mainly as "a place people could go to for comfort." At the same time, William did maintain adherence to certain Baptist doctrines that differed from her mother's Methodist beliefs. Jan remembers her parents occasionally discussing doctrinal differences that "sometimes became heated arguments." For the most part, however, the two fundamentally agreed that "church was primarily a place to help people" and emphasized practical religious morality to their children.

Thus, as a child, Jan was made aware of different religious points of view supported by the arguments of significant adults while simultaneously learning that kindness and generosity were religious mandates that superseded abstruse doctrinal differences. It may be plausibly inferred that, growing up, Jan acquired a relatively open-minded attitude toward religion fostered by her parents' tolerant practicality at home, Methodist social gospel preaching at church, and the sustained Methodist-Baptist cooperation she witnessed in the Hueytown community during the Depression. As for her own religiosity, Jan says that while growing up she wasn't especially pious either. She doesn't recall experiencing religiously induced feelings of guilt or resorting to personal prayer to obtain comfort or supernatural aid; she simply assumed, in a taken-for-granted manner, the ultimate beneficence of her inherited Methodist faith.

In addition to her church-related activities, Thalia also belonged to a ladies' book club, which met regularly to discuss the books that they shared and to keep each other informed of local news and gossip tidbits. Because of this, books were a familiar and emphasized part of Jan's life that helped her become an avid reader who made weekly visits in the summer to the Hueytown library.

Although Jan and Sue were admonished by their mother to be friendly with everyone, regardless of their social standing, as young girls they had few friends to socialize with on the mountain and didn't go to town much outside of school and church. When Jan was in the eighth grade, Thalia took a teaching job in Oak Grove, a rural community "out in the country." According to Jan, "Oak Grove was where *poor* people lived; it was the poorest section of the county." She often accompanied her mother to Oak Grove and "got acquainted with the country kids," eventually socializing with them more than with the kids in Hueytown.

By early adolescence, having a boyfriend became an important objective among Jan's peers, including her sister Sue, but Jan "wasn't one to have boyfriends." It was in Oak Grove that Jan met her only high school quasi-boyfriend—a 15-year-old country kid nicknamed "Lucky," who chose Jan as his partner at a school dance. This was not a serious romance, and it did not advance much further than occasional note exchanges and country school dances ("spin-the-bottle kind of stuff," where boys would walk the girls around the block). The friendship did, however, afford Jan a brief interlude in which she didn't have to compete with Sue for male attention. Further reducing pressure to compete for boys, Jan began playing pop music (swing and boogie-woogie) for Sue and her friends at dances back in Hueytown.

Hueytown and the War

Beyond its pedestrian, small school curriculum, Hueytown High School was a unifying institution for the community. Its academics, extracurricular activities, and civic functions centered the inhabitants of a linear line-town (who otherwise were dispersed along a narrow state highway) and generated a sense of shared pride and identification. Because of the Second World War (which commenced for the United States in 1941, when Jan was in the seventh grade, and ended in 1945, when she was about to start her "senior year" in the eleventh grade), the school curriculum was restructured in such a way that it was possible to complete one's graduation requirements by the end of the eleventh grade. During the war years, Jan describes a keen sense of patriotism at the high school; everyone was preoccupied with the war effort. All the boys wanted to enlist, and most did as soon as they graduated. Thus, having already been accelerated in school by skipping the first grade, Jan graduated from Hueytown High School in 1946 at the tender age of fifteen.

Despite his practical competence, William had drinking (and gambling) problems that Thalia tried to conceal from the children while they were growing up. He was never mean or abusive, and Jan only became fully aware of her father's alcoholism when she was a teenager.[7] The impact of her father's behavior on the family's finances became clearer to Jan when she had to withdraw from college after the first semester because of her father's gambling losses. Looking back, Jan cannot recall her father articulating any remorse or regret, and she only remembers him trying to make amends by constantly fixing things around the house and working on home improvements. Instead, she thinks more about what her father's lapses did to her *mother*. For example, it seemed unfair to Jan, even as a child, that her mother would always have to milk the family cow when her father called to say he wouldn't be home because he had been drinking while playing dominos with his buddies. (According to Jan, Thalia would not teach her how to milk the cow, because if she did not learn she would not have to do it to cover for her father—an implicit aspersion of resentment toward her truant husband.)

Generally speaking, however, Jan's mother was longsuffering and stoical, not just tolerating her husband's occasional binges and accompanying gambling losses but taking the responsibility to recover what he had lost: three times her father put the house up for collateral to pay off debts, and each time her mother paid off the loans to get the house back. Despite this, she never threatened to leave him. "Mother," according to Jan, "was probably more tolerant of him than any woman should have been." But she "believed in marriage for life." Similarly, Williams's drinking and gambling did not seem to change Jan's basic affection for him, but it did prompt "the realization that life wasn't always going to be wonderful." As Jan got older there was a dawning realization of "how complicated my family's situation was," and how unfair it often was for her mother.

During the war years, William saw an opportunity to make money in the expanding war economy by leasing a truck to haul war-related supplies and materials between various production centers in Texas and the central-Georgia boomtown of Warner Robins, which was situated next door to a large US Army air depot undergoing rapid construction by the War Department.[8] For

---

7. Like their father, Jan's brother Billy became an alcoholic in later life; also like their father, her brother was a functioning alcoholic who was never abusive to his wife or children and always apologized for his drinking lapses, resolving to do better and make amends. Billy completed an engineering degree at Georgia Tech University and pursued a successful career as an engineer working on federal government projects.

8. Selected by the War Department as the site for a major Army Air maintenance and supply depot, Warner Robins was founded in 1942 from the sparsely inhabited, rural community of Wellston, Georgia. Situated twenty miles south of Macon, the new town was named after Army Air Force General A. Warner Robins. For a brief history of the rapid construction of the Warner Robins Army Air Depot (today,

approximately four years (1941–45), William alternately rented a room in Warner Robins and made quick stopovers in Hueytown to see his family while hauling loads back and forth between Texas and Warner Robins. Jan recalls that "Daddy was in and out all the time" during this period, which coincided with her adolescence and high school years. Consequently, during those years Thalia was also the de facto parent in charge of raising the children and managing their household affairs.

After the war, at the beginning of 1946, Jan's mother moved with Jan's younger brothers, Billy (age thirteen) and Bernard (age eleven), in tow to Talladega, Alabama, to be closer to relatives. (Talladega is a little over fifty miles east of Birmingham and approximately two hundred miles northwest of Warner Robins, Georgia). Jan and Sue, however, stayed behind in Hueytown, living together in the basement of some family friends as they finished their final semester at Hueytown High. In retrospect, Jan says she doesn't really know why her mother moved when she did: To preserve her marriage? Take advantage of better employment prospects? Provide better schooling opportunities for the boys? Whatever the reason, as Jan says, "the war disrupted many people's lives . . . [and] our family was dispersed."

During this time of upheaval and uncertainty, Jan avoided getting too involved in the family's disarray and never talked to her brothers about what was happening with their parents. Despite the familial challenges, both brothers in Talladega became active in the school band and excelled in school. Back in Hueytown, the sisters performed in high school talent shows, with Sue dancing and Jan playing piano pieces. Jan also performed her high school piano graduation recital in the Methodist Church before a large audience of admiring friends, neighbors, and relatives. According to Jan, at this stage in her life, everyone assumed she would go on to become a professional musician.

When the war ended in the summer of 1945, William leased a gas station in Warner Robins, Georgia, and Jan's mother and brothers joined with him to reunite the family. It seemed as though everyone was on the move and that lives were suddenly and simultaneously fraught with new prospects and uncertainties. Consequently, after graduating from high school, both Jan and Sue also moved to Warner Robins and worked for their father as cash register clerks at the service station. Jan recalls that she routinely referred to black male customers at the station as "Mr.," which displeased her father, who thought it was bad for his business with white customers. "You can do what you want, I'm going to call them Mr.," Jan retorted. Although William was unusually racially tolerant for a Southern white man of his time and was a

---

Robins Air Force Base) following the Japanese attack on Pearl Harbor, see William Head, "History of Warner Robins, Georgia."

significant role model in this regard for Jan and Sue, he nevertheless retained certain culturally ingrained prejudices about black people and, according to Jan, continued to use racial slurs throughout his life.

Sue was far more outspoken than Jan regarding the ubiquitous racial discrimination openly practiced and legally sustained throughout the region. As an adolescent, Sue worked summers as a lifeguard and tanned darkly. She made a practice of sitting in the back of public buses with black passengers, which angered the white bus drivers. Jan admired this in her sister—that Sue deliberately sat with black passengers to *provoke* the drivers. Sue and Jan's early, affectionate relationship with their family's domestic helper Josephine, their childhood friendships with black children waiting for the school bus, and their parents' generosity to people of all races in need during the Depression appear to have contributed significantly to Jan and her sister's racial tolerance and emerging sense of social justice.

CHAPTER 2

College, Marriage, and Motherhood in Post-war America, 1946–1960

The Alabama College for Women

In the fall of 1946, both the sixteen-year-old Jan and seventeen-year-old Sue enrolled in the Alabama College for Women, located in Montevallo, about forty miles south of Birmingham, following the examples for higher education set by their mother and aunts.[1] According to Jan, both her parents supported their college enrollment (even though William may have resented Thalia's education and degree, which gave her formal credentials and salaried employment opportunities as a public school teacher). As to their choice of the Alabama College for Women, it was simply the cheapest, closest option.

Throughout her childhood, Jan had received high praise for her musical talents, but college quickly made her realize the limits of those talents: "Other music majors were a lot better than I was." Jan had difficulty properly executing "four against five" pieces (playing four-four time with one hand while playing five-eight time with the other hand), and she didn't especially care for her music professor, a Polish immigrant, whose English was hard for her to understand. She still enjoyed playing for entertainment (and occasionally for money), which got in the way of her school work. "I was too young to go to college," she recalls. Instead of studying and practicing classical piano, she spent much of her time playing popular tunes at dances and in the student recreational hall for her classmates. Jan also spent time learning to play organ, which she enjoyed (so much so that she regularly sneaked through a window at the music building at two in the morning to practice).

Jan recalls that during this time she and Sue "were disturbed that [Southern] women's colleges didn't enroll black female students." She and her sister would meet with black female students from Tuskegee for chats at night

---

1. What was known as the Alabama College for Women when Jan enrolled as Jo Ann Barnett in 1946 has undergone several name changes over the course of its institutional history. Founded in 1896 as the Alabama Girls' Industrial School, it gradually developed into a traditional degree-granting institution, becoming the Alabama State College for Women in 1923. In 1956, the school became coeducational and shortened its name to Alabama College. Finally, in 1969, the college was renamed the University of Montevallo. See Rosemary H. Arneson, "University of Montevallo."

on the roof of their dormitory in Montevallo.[2] Word of these clandestine get-togethers came to the attention of the college president, who circulated an admonishing letter prohibiting Alabama Women's College students from any such gatherings. This was not an era of student protest or defiance, and the meetings were instantly halted.

For the most part, Jan and Sue—still in their teens—depended on their parents for financial support to attend college. After only one semester, however, they learned that some recent gambling losses by their father had depleted the family's scant savings, and that only one of the girls could continue being supported. Thalia informed Jan that a fourth-grade substitute teaching position had become available in Talladega, and Jan left school to take the job. Though Sue was her academic inferior, Jan does not recall feeling any resentment or unfairness that Sue remained in school while she dropped out. This may be because Jan was much better equipped academically than Sue to get the teaching job and saw it as a good opportunity to make some money. Consequently, Jan moved to Talladega and stayed with her mother.

As a substitute teacher at age sixteen, Jan was particularly effective at teaching fourth-grade spelling and arithmetic and "kept the students in pretty good order." The principal expressed disappointment when she did not continue teaching at the school when the term ended. As she did in college, to earn a little extra cash, Jan moonlighted playing the piano on weekends with a local Talladega dance band.

While Jan was teaching, Sue found college increasingly difficult because of her dyslexia and dropped out after her second semester to start her own dance school in Warner Robins.[3] Subsequently, she moved to New York with aspirations of becoming a professional dancer—a dream that never materialized. She ended up working with troubled young people at an institution in Westchester County, a few miles north of New York City. "She could handle problem kids like no one else," says Jan. Sue also became politically active and eventually became intensely involved in the nuclear disarmament movement.

---

2. Tuskegee is the home of Tuskegee University—a private, historically black college/university. First known as the Normal School for Colored Teachers, then as the Tuskegee Normal and Industrial Institute under the leadership of Booker T. Washington (later shortened to Tuskegee Institute), Tuskegee University is located approximately one hundred miles southeast of Montevallo. For a brief history, see Shannon Gary, "Tuskegee University."

3. This enterprise didn't last long. The local Baptist congregation built a church next door to Sue's dance studio, then successfully complained to the city that dancing shouldn't be allowed so close to the church. Ironically, Sue was at that same time also serving as head of education for the local Methodist Church, which did not frown upon dancing.

Despite her youthful popularity with boys, Sue only had a brief, unsuccessful marriage in New York, never remarried, and, as much as she loved children, never had any of her own.[4]

After substitute teaching for a semester (following her dropping out of school in Montevallo), Jan was encouraged by her mother to re-enroll at the Alabama Women's College in the hope, perhaps, of earning a teaching degree. (By this point Jan fully realized she wasn't destined to become a concert pianist.) Back in school, Jan took classes in world history and sociology—which she found more interesting than her music classes—but she also confesses that she still wasn't a diligent student, again spending much of her free time playing dance music for friends rather than studying. In high school she got straight A's with little effort, but the same minimal effort in college was now earning her B's and C's. Her money ran out once more, and once more her mother advised her of a teaching opportunity, this time as a piano teacher at the Academy for the Blind in Macon, Georgia, where she received room and board and quickly "learned to read Braille with my eyes."

Macon, Georgia, and Tony Shipps

While living in Macon, Jan's father visited often. He was making a modest but regular income running the automobile service station in nearby Warner Robins, where Thalia eventually rejoined him, again employed as a school teacher. Jan says she always felt relieved when her father was at home and getting along with her mother, but from this point forward, Jan never again lived with her parents.

Despite her initial challenges in college, Jan wasn't worried about the future: "There were always two things present in my life as a young person that kept me optimistic: First, music, and second, I knew I was smart." Even though she had become disillusioned about being a music major, Jan thought of herself as a musician with sufficient talent to fall back on should the need arise. She also knew she had the ability to make good grades in school if she applied herself, which, at minimum, could lead to teaching jobs, as it had for her mother and aunts. (An advanced degree and future in the rarified world of academic scholarship was not even a blip on Jan's radar screen at this time and would not emerge in her thinking as a realistic possibility for another fifteen years.)

It was in Macon, Georgia, that Jan met Anthony (Tony) Shipps in the fall of 1948. Three years older than Jan, Tony was back home from the Navy,

---

4. Jan calls Sue's short-term husband "the crazy monk." He was a former Catholic brother who left a silent order and, after not being allowed to talk for so long—according to Jan—couldn't stop talking following his marriage to Sue and was socially incompetent in general.

having served as a pharmacist's mate on the USS Endicott during the last six months of World War II. Tony's family had been socially prominent in Macon; among other things, his maternal grandfather (Olin J. Wimberly) had helped found Mercer University's law school.[5] After he became a widower, however, Olin placed his youngest daughter Mary Wimberly (Tony's mother) in a convent for her education, and she ended up forsaking her family's Episcopalian faith and converting to Catholicism.

After getting married, Mary persuaded her husband, Harrold Southerland Shipps, to convert to Catholicism, and together they had four children in rapid succession—three sons and a daughter. The successive pregnancies and childbearing took a toll on Mary's health (she lost a kidney and weighed a scant ninety pounds), and her doctor told Mary that she would likely die if she were to get pregnant again. However, Harrold, strongly supported by their parish priest, insisted that they have more children. Mary refused and sought a civil divorce. The divorce judge awarded custody of Tony and his younger brother Stephen to his mother, but his older brother (named after his father) was given to Harrold, who then had him placed in a Catholic orphanage. Anne, Tony's sister, was the oldest of the four and, of legal age, chose to live with her mother. Mary decided to go back to school to get her bachelor's degree and placed Tony and his younger brother Stephen in foster care. Subsequently, a judge wanted the foster parents to adopt the two boys, but this recommendation was successfully resisted by Tony's influential Macon relatives, who wanted the children to remain part of the family; they provided the boys with financial support while they were in foster care. The couple who foster-parented Tony and his brother Stephen were kind and caring people, and Tony developed a genuine attachment to them. Nonetheless, his parents' angry domestic conflicts, their unpleasant divorce, and his subsequent separation from his mother and older brother at such an early age were traumatic, leaving Tony with ambivalent feelings of abandonment and insecurity.

When he was twelve, Tony and his younger brother rejoined their mother in Macon who had recently earned her library degree with Phi Beta Kappa honors and could support them on her own as a public-school teacher.[6] At that point in his life, Tony felt far closer to his foster parents, who took care of him and his brother Stephen for seven years.[7] His relationship with his

---

5. Founded in 1873, Mercer University School of Law is one of the oldest law schools in the American South, and the first one in the state of Georgia accredited by the American Bar Association. See J. C. Bryant, "Mercer University."

6. Mary would eventually become the rare books librarian at the University of South Carolina.

7. Tony remained close to his foster parents, who knew Jan's mother in Talladega through the Methodist Church. When Tony and Jan began dating it was important to

mother and father was permanently strained, and Jan's supportive encouragement many years later was required to help heal the breach with his mother.[8]

During the war, Mary opposed Tony joining the service and prevailed upon his aunt to provide the necessary tuition money for Tony's enrollment as a pre-med student at Oxford University College in Oxford, Georgia. At the end of his freshman year, however, and to his mother's great dismay, Tony joined the Navy. After the war, he enrolled at Mercer University in Macon, changed his major from pre-med to English, and took a job working as an attendant at a private adult care center.

Tony's return to Macon overlapped Jan's own move there to teach piano at the Macon School for the Blind. Not long after, the ever-popular Sue—now living with her parents in nearby Warner Robins—was invited to a party in Macon. Sue had other plans for that night and recommended that her would-be date take her sister Jan instead, since Jan's residence was close to the party's location, and she was available. Arrangements were made, and Jan accompanied the unknown young man as a substitute for Sue. However, when the party concluded, Sue's jilted date claimed he had a "sore foot" and asked his friend Tony Shipps to walk Jan home.

The happenstance romance that quickly ensued took on a kismet quality. Tony escorted Jan home from the party, they talked for two hours, and Tony kissed her goodnight. Jan's instant conviction when Tony left was: "This is the man I'm going to marry." Tony called her the next day, and, as Jan recalls, it was indeed a case of "love at first sight. . . . We both immediately concluded we had found our marriage partner." At the same time, Jan's self-doubt caused her to question how Tony could be attracted to or interested in her, because she considered herself to be "fat" and not very pretty. Nevertheless, Jan thought she was the "luckiest person in the world to have him: Tony was

---

Tony that Jan meet his foster parents—even more so, perhaps, than meeting his biological parents. Both liked Jan and preferred her to Tony's high school girlfriend. Tony stayed in contact with his foster parents until they died. On visits home after leaving to pursue education and careers in the North, Jan and Tony would spend one day with Jan's parents, one day each with Tony's mother and father, and one day with his foster parents. This became the standard pattern for their vacation trips home as a married couple.

8. Jan's periodic efforts to help reconcile Tony with his mother coincided with her own reactivation in later life as a practicing Methodist. Jan reports that she had not been religiously active for decades until Tony's mother visited them in Bloomington, Indiana, in 1981. Renowned religious historian Martin Marty—by then one of Jan's valued colleagues—was scheduled as a guest speaker by the Bloomington First Methodist Church. Jan naturally planned to attend his talk and determined to invite Mary as well, who was duly impressed by Jan's scholarly connections. From that point forward, both Jan and Tony became increasingly involved in the Bloomington Methodist community.

so much smarter and better educated," with a college degree and prominent relatives in Macon.

After a brief three-and-a-half month engagement, Jan and Tony decided to elope for "practical reasons" involving mutual family issues. Tony's parents were divorced, and Jan's parents' marriage was marred by her father's alcoholism, which they were afraid might cause an embarrassing scene at a formal wedding. Tony's father, Harrold, *also* had problems with alcohol, which compounded the likelihood of embarrassment. (Even though wary of alcoholic men, Tony would occasionally drink beer with Jan's father and respected him for his practical skills, which his own father lacked.) At the same time, Jan liked Tony's mother, Mary, who unexpectedly complimented her looks. Jan's father and brothers in turn were impressed by Tony's education and intelligence. Thalia, however, frostily disapproved of Tony, in large part because of a deep attachment to her youngest daughter in whom she had invested her own aspirations. According to Jan, "she didn't want to give me up." All things considered, then, Jan and Tony decided against having a church wedding to avoid awkwardness and potential family conflicts. They were married, without family or friend knowledge, on May 25, 1949, by a justice of the peace. Jan was nineteen and Tony was twenty-two.

Upon hearing news of Jan's elopement with Tony, Thalia's immediate response was to ask her, "Did you *have* to get married?" alluding to her concern that Jan was already pregnant. She initially had a hard time accepting that Jan and Tony were in love and truly committed to each other after such a brief courtship. Thalia's withholding of approval caused conflicts between her and Tony for the first four years of Jan and Tony's marriage. The tension between them ended when the death of one of Tony's aunts—with whom he had become very close—prompted Thalia's compassionate character to prevail over her ambivalence about him. She reached out to console Tony, and the two subsequently developed and maintained a close relationship.

Jan and Tony's marriage occurred at a hopeful point in US history. The economic devastation of the Great Depression and social dislocations of World War II were rapidly receding in the thinking of most young, white Americans. Jan and Tony joined millions of other post-war newlyweds who optimistically anticipated a return to domestic normalcy. Demobilization at the end of the war brought many changes. Marriage and birthrates soared, producing the "baby boom" generation, which stimulated a huge demand for new housing and schools to accommodate the country's sudden population bulge.[9] Concomitantly, millions of women who had joined the workforce

---

9. See Steven Gillon, *Boomer Nation: The Largest and Richest Generation Ever, and How It Changed America*.

during the war were displaced by returning fathers, husbands, and boyfriends. Messages in popular culture and the mass media encouraged women to give up their jobs and return quietly to domestic life as wives and mothers. Marketing campaigns for advertising consumer goods or household appliances targeted women customers, emphasizing the value of using them to attract men or please their husbands. The superiority of traditional gender roles for maintaining a healthy society, in which men made a living and provided civic leadership while women cared for the home and supported their husband's career, was idealized and normatively reasserted in 1950s America.[10] This was the historical and cultural context in which Jan and Tony commenced their marriage, and to a significant degree they accepted uncritically those prevailing gender definitions.

At the time of his elopement with Jan, Tony had graduated from Mercer with a bachelor's degree in English. He immediately accepted an improbable offer, beginning that September, to serve as the principal of a small-town school of sixty students, spanning grades one through twelve, in Pittsview, Alabama, on the Alabama-Georgia border. In the meantime, Jan spent the first part of the summer of 1949 living with her "rich Aunt Sue" in Century, Florida, to raise additional income for their anticipated move. Jan's other aunt, Rebecca, who lived in nearby Pensacola, knew the owner of a neighborhood bar who was willing to pay Jan five dollars on weeknights and ten dollars on Saturday night to play the piano for bar customers, who would request popular tunes for Jan to play by ear.

Thalia came to Pensacola to visit Jan during this time, and Jan suggested they go to a nearby beach for a swim. They went out too far into the ocean, and Thalia began to flounder. Jan, who had received lifeguard training at Girl Scout camp as a girl, was able to swim her exhausted mother safely back to shore. My "mom was so grateful," Jan recalls, "she kept saying, 'If you hadn't been there, I would have drowned.'" This incident both strengthened and altered Jan and Thalia's relationship, giving Jan equal status in her mother's eyes as a competent adult to whom she could turn for help when needed.

Jan returned home in late summer of 1949 and was encouraged by Tony to enroll for a term at the Georgia College for Women in Milledgeville (where

---

10. Normative pressures on women and girls to conform their role activities to domestic and feminine stereotypes following World War II and during the 1950s Cold War era are explored in Elaine Tyler May, *Homeward Bound: American Families in the Cold War Era*; Eugenia Kaledin, *Mothers and More: American Women in the 1950s*; Virginia Nicholson, *Perfect Wives in Ideal Homes: The Story of Women in the 1950s*; Jessamyn Neuhaus, "The Way to a Man's Heart: Gender Roles, Domestic Ideology, and Cookbooks in the 1950s," 529–55; and Susan J. Douglas, *Where the Girls Are: Growing Up Female with the Mass Media*.

Tony was finishing his employment at an adult care center) to earn credits toward a teaching degree. She consequently enrolled and took courses in American history and psychology. Now married to a college man who was about to become an educator, Jan was highly motivated to be a successful student and this time excelled in her courses. Interestingly, Jan and Tony didn't share a residence until Tony started his job in the fall as the Pittsview school principal. Until then, Jan continued living in a small, rented room, and Tony kept his room and board at the care center. The Depression years were long over, but Jan and Tony Shipps were starting married life living on a shoestring.

Pittsview, Alabama

On the first of September, at the onset of the 1949–50 school year, Jan and Tony boarded a Greyhound bus for Pittsview, Alabama, each carrying two suitcases of clothing plus an ironing board— the sum of their worldly possessions. To get a hotel room that night, Tony had to purchase a dime store ring for Jan (who still didn't have a wedding ring) to "prove" they were a married couple. They moved into the Methodist parsonage in Pittsview for three months but had to vacate it before Christmas so that the newly married pastor could move in with his bride. They then rented a tiny, two-room house with no indoor plumbing on the single highway out of town that originally had been built for highway construction workers. At his new job, Tony (with no previous teaching or administrative experience) not only served as a twenty-three-year-old school principal, but he was also (having never played basketball) the coach of the boys' basketball team. While Tony labored at the school, Jan made a little extra money teaching local children to play piano, although she was often paid in kind with chickens, eggs, and produce. Jan says she taught piano to practically "every child in town," but this meant only the white children. Pittsview was a highly racialized, segregated town, and it was unacceptable for the new principal's wife to teach black children.[11]

Regular church attendance was also expected of the school principal and his wife. Pittsview was pastored by three itinerant ministers of different Protestant faiths. Consequently, the entire town attended church every week, rotating among Baptist, Methodist, and Episcopal meeting houses, depending on whose minister was providing services. Neither Jan nor Tony were particularly religious at this point in their lives—especially Tony, who had been

---

11. In Pittsview, Alabama, in 1907, a respected black man was shot to death in broad daylight by a white crowd on the main street of the business district because his son allegedly had disrespected a white woman. See Jeffrey Toobin, "The Legacy of Lynching, On Death Row," 47. Three decades later, the parents or grandparents of some of Jan's piano students may very well have observed this crime. According to Toobin, Pittsview today is still a racially divided and segregated town.

baptized Catholic as an infant but, like Jan, had been raised Methodist by his foster parents. Notwithstanding his foster parents' positive influence, Tony maintained a jaundiced view of religion as the prime cause of his parents' divorce. Nevertheless, while living in Pittsview, he and Jan conformed pragmatically to the town's religious norms. For Jan, it again meant exposure to a small-town community where religion was of taken-for-granted importance, but also where denominational boundaries—at least within the Protestant faith tradition—were not rigidly drawn.

Tony loved books (a passion shared by Jan) and was educationally ambitious. He wanted to move on to graduate school and pursue a scholarly career in higher education. Rather than concentrating on admission to reputable nearby schools in the deep South, such as Mercer, Emory, Auburn, or the Universities of Georgia or Alabama, Tony looked north and was delighted by his acceptance as a PhD student of the highly regarded English Department at Northwestern University in Evanston, Illinois, a northern suburb of Chicago.[12] Financially strapped but not deeply in debt, he and his young bride eagerly anticipated the ascetic existence of graduate school life north of the Macon-Dixon line. Thus, after a year in Pittsview, Alabama, and having grown up and lived their lives in the insular and conservative heartland towns of the American South, Jan and Tony Shipps prepared to turn their faces north and pursue their academic destinies in the sprawling urban confines of Chicago, the boisterous melting pot of Carl Sandburg's City of the Big Shoulders.

Chicago

In retrospect, Jan says it "became a big deal for Tony and me to be a separate family unit"—not just an appendage to the *Barnett* family. Despite her family's problems during the war (many of them a result of her father's drinking), Jan had maintained a strong attachment to her family. She was especially close to her mother and, growing up, her single most important significant other had been her sister, Sue. In contrast, as Jan puts it, "Tony's family situation growing up had been so hard." Tony's relationship with his parents had been fractured and scarred, leaving him with insecurities about getting close to others and trusting in the permanence of his and Jan's commitments to each other. According to Jan, for the next ten years of their

---

12. Like other American research universities, both undergraduate and graduate enrollments surged at Northwestern following the end of World War II. This escalation was fueled in large part by the G. I. Bill that made it financially possible for tens of thousands of veterans like Tony Shipps to further their education, thereby transforming both the demographic character and academic nature of American higher education. See Daniel A. Clark, "'The Two Joes Meet—Joe College, Joe Veteran': The G. I. Bill, College Education, and Postwar American Culture," 165–89.

married life in the Midwest, a big concern for Tony was the question of Jan's primary loyalty: Was it to Tony (later including their son, Stephen) or to the Barnetts? Craving affirmations of loyalty, priority connection, and stability in intimate relationships, Jan says she "needed to reassure Tony that my first commitment was to us." Tony needed to believe that Jan was an integral part of his life, that he was more important to her than her own family. To do so, Jan recalls that she "distanced myself from my family to reassure Tony. I had to prove to Tony that he was my most important commitment." Sue, whose life had coincided so closely with Jan's growing up, receded to the margins of Jan's priority concerns. They remained in touch through occasional cards or letters, and when Jan and Tony's only son Stephen was a teen, he spent Christmases with Sue in New York while playing the violin in holiday orchestras at Carnegie Hall. According to Jan, "Sue was grateful for the time Stephen gave to her; how much it meant to her—she was crazy about him." With new lives operating in different directions, the two formerly inseparable sisters now pursued distinct lives in separate worlds.[13]

Looking back, Jan concludes that their marital adjustments would have been much greater if she and Tony had not moved out of Georgia—away from both of their families—to Alabama the first year of their marriage and especially *away from the South*, to Illinois, for Tony's schooling the following year. While this decisive departure from home was ultimately a consolidating factor in their marriage, it was also hard on Jan, who anxiously depended on Tony's reciprocal support in pursuing their life together in a strange new world. In their new life together away from family, friends, and trusted social connections, Jan and Tony quickly developed a strong sense of unity and shared commitment in overcoming the challenges of a new environment on their own as a married couple.

Young married couples coping with the deprivations and adversities of graduate school life in an alien city and region of the country face a distinct challenge to strengthen and consolidate their marriage and future. Under these conditions, there is significant potential for marital discord and dissolution rather than unification and solidarity. In Jan and Tony's case, however, they were fortunate to share additional sustaining attributes, including compatible social values and intellectual sensibilities, a love of books and learning, and a mutual interpretation of their complementary roles as husband and wife. For

---

13. When Jan's *Mormonism* book came out, she recalls that Sue "was very proud and showed it to all her friends." When Sue was terminally ill with cancer shortly following publication of Jan's book, Jan spent a sabbatical summer in 1986 attending to Sue and residing in a hotel near Sue's residence in New York. Sue bequeathed $3,000 to Jan and Tony upon her demise, and the Shipps subsequently used this money to purchase a baby grand piano.

Jan, this meant most importantly supporting Tony through graduate school and his subsequent academic career.

At first, Jan and Tony lived in dormitory housing for graduate student couples, shared a bathroom and refrigerator with a dozen other couples, and cooked their meals on a hotplate. Tony worked six nights a week as an assistant manager of a neighborhood food store. (The owner was an alcoholic who wanted somebody he could trust to close the store.) Jan worked as a sales clerk in a local department store and also sold clothes at the Three Sisters Clothing Store.[14]

In 1952, two years after their arrival in Illinois, Jan gave birth to their only child. Tony had been hoping that their child would be a boy so they could name him after his younger brother Stephen, who had been killed in a motorcycle accident several years earlier. Tony got his wish, and their new son was named Stephen. Although she understood the reason for Tony's wish, Jan says it took her a long time to realize just how close Tony had been to his brother, with whom he had shared his foster home experience. Stephen's actual birth was preceded by what turned out to be a somewhat providential false alarm. When Jan first began experiencing labor pains, Tony drove her thirty miles to a hospital in Evanston. But the labor pains then ceased. The pediatrician who was scheduled to deliver the baby was going out of town for Thanksgiving and invited Jan and Tony to stay in his apartment until the baby came. As repayment, Jan polished the doctor's silver and did other light household cleaning until, five days later, Stephen was finally born.

Both Jan and Tony became doting parents, though their circumstances required some eccentricities in how they raised Stephen in his early years. For example, due to the demands of Tony's graduate school studies, on Saturday nights Jan would play the piano at a neighborhood bar for extra cash, while Tony (with Stephen napping nearby) studied in the back. While this arrangement did not last long, the requirements of graduate school and parenting brought other unique opportunities for their young family.

Graduate student housing was not an ideal place to raise a child, so Jan and Tony were on the lookout for a preferable alternative. They responded to a newspaper ad for house parents at a children's care facility in Lake Bluff, Illinois, twenty-five miles north of Evanston on the western shore of Lake Michigan, where they could live and work while Tony was continuing his coursework. After Jan and Tony were hired, their young family moved into

---

14. The Three Sisters Clothing Store was located on famous Michigan Avenue between 111th and 112th Streets in the Roseland neighborhood of Chicago's South Side. Bereft of a family car, both Jan and Tony relied entirely on public transportation to get back and forth from school and work.

the Methodist Children's Center in Lake Bluff. There, they were paid a salary, plus room and board, to care for orphaned girls who were being supported by the local Methodist Church. Jan derived extra maternal satisfaction in her role as a house parent. According to her, taking care of twelve to sixteen girls in Lake Bluff required rapid development of good management skills. With her own child also to care for, Jan often accompanied Tony to libraries (both the Newbury Library in Chicago where he had acquired part-time work and the University Deering Library on the Northwestern campus) with Stephen in tow. While Tony worked, studied, and did research, Stephen napped and Jan read books—mostly history, especially histories of the South.

A Southerner by birth and rearing but now in the North, Jan was becoming keenly aware of distinctive regional manners and regionally-based perceptions of national life, and she wanted to better understand the peculiarities of her own cultural heritage. Although she seldom read fiction, one exception was novels by Henry James. These books appealed to her because of the way James dealt with his characters' divergent cultural backgrounds and status differences, particularly on what it means for people to be outsiders trying to fit economically and socially into new cultural environments—an experience that Southerners Jan and Tony were now experiencing in the North.

In addition to her own voracious reading and childcare duties, Jan also became a sort of research assistant to Tony. She typed his papers, master's thesis, and later (after moving to Detroit) drafts of his PhD dissertation, learning much about English literature in the process. While she was still years away from beginning her own academic career, helping Tony track down the oldest published essays in the English language initiated Jan's learning to sleuth through historical documents; Tony's punctilious adherence to proper standards of scholarly prose and referencing significantly informed her own later scholarly research and writing habits.

Detroit

In 1954, Tony accepted a faculty position in the English Department at Wayne University in downtown Detroit.[15] He had finished his coursework at Northwestern but was still working on his dissertation, a highly specialized study of the true provenance of quotations commonly attributed to sixteenth-century English writer, Robert Johnson. To support themselves in Detroit, Jan and Tony once again became house parents, this time at Williams House, then an Episcopal residential institution for pregnant and otherwise "at risk" adolescent girls, located just a few miles northeast of downtown on

---

15. In 1956, two years after Tony accepted the position, Wayne University was renamed Wayne State University by the Michigan State Legislature.

East Grand River Avenue in the "Carriage House" of the old Stroh's Family mansion (of beer brewing fame, which now houses the Federation of Youth Services). For the first two years of their six-year stay at the Williams House, their young family occupied a small room with a fold-out-bed couch. While Jan had not been religiously active since her initial year of college in Alabama, she began attending Episcopal services—but more, she claims, "as a kind of sociological interest."

During their time in Detroit, Jan suffered a miscarriage just two months into her pregnancy. Both she and Tony had been hoping to have a girl, especially Tony, and they would not try for another pregnancy again. (Later, in Colorado, Tony wanted to have another child, but by then Jan was in graduate school and focused on pursuing her own career). The pain of the miscarriage was perhaps somewhat eased by the new familial relationships they were building with the young girls of Williams House. Jan says that living in the carriage house with a half-dozen teenage girls was like being part of a big family, which included Stephen as a kind of little brother.

Sympathetic to the girls' plight due to his own childhood experience in foster care, Tony readily assumed the role of a father figure, and Jan insisted that they all eat dinner together as a family. Supper would come from the "big house" (the Stroh's mansion) and would be served by the girls. Tony always sat at the head of the dinner table with Stephen on his left, Jan on his right, and the girls spread around the table. They would have conversations during the meals, and every night Jan would read them a chapter from the works of Dickens and other classics. According to Jan, "The girls *wanted* to read; they wouldn't leave the table until the chapter was finished." At the same time, the girls would argue over whose turn it was to read to Stephen. This nightly custom proved to be educational for Stephen as well, who was starting to read books by age four.

In a defining moment for Jan as a surrogate mother, after Stephen began wearing glasses, one of the girls proclaimed, "Now everyone in *our family* is wearing glasses." Conversely, when Stephen was at the door wanting to come in, he would mimic the girls by calling out, "Mrs. Shipps! Mrs. Shipps!" All of this made Jan feel that they had achieved a sense of family—for the girls as well as themselves—and that their small family was "having a positive impact on girls who had never lived in a close family." This familial relationship enabled the girls to talk openly with Jan, discuss their past, and confide their personal troubles—frequently while smoking cigarettes together. Tony, who had already quit smoking because of mounting medical evidence of its toxic effects, nevertheless encouraged Jan's continued smoking because he felt it aided her in building rapport with the girls. It was another decade before Jan determined to quit smoking herself.

When Stephen started kindergarten and grade school at the private University Ligget School on Cook Road in Gross Pointe,[16] Jan experienced having a good deal more free time, which she says she took advantage of by "just reading all day long for three or four years," again gravitating to American history. Those years of self-directed learning as a wife and young mother not only formed the foundations for an eclectic knowledge base but also exposed her to models of good composition and historical argument. She also became interested in psychology due to a "good psychiatrist assigned to assess the girls" at Williams House, who conversed with Jan and other staff about the girls' evaluations.

In the meantime, Tony continued working on his dissertation while teaching English at Wayne. When asked if she and Tony often engaged in intellectual exchanges during this period, Jan answered "yes and no." For all practical purposes she continued functioning as Tony's research assistant by typing his papers, making spelling and punctuation corrections, and "helping a lot" with his dissertation (but not critiquing or rewriting anything Tony did). While proofreading Tony's dissertation, Jan was impressed by the rigorous standards of his academic research, which involved painstaking intellectual detective work. Using vocabulary flash cards, she also helped Tony study for and pass his mandatory PhD tests in French and German. While French proved relatively easy for Tony, he struggled with German. To help him, Jan and Tony together read *The Way Back* by Erich Maria Remarque (author of *All Quiet on the Western Front*). Tony read every word out loud in German while Jan followed along, reciting the text in English. All of this enabled Jan to absorb an intellectual ethic and academic discipline and gain an appreciation for what being a scholar required.

After four years as a faculty member at Wayne, and while still working on his dissertation, Tony decided he no longer wanted to continue teaching English. Instead, he was increasingly drawn to the possibilities of becoming an academic librarian, a profession pursued by his mother and older brother

---

16. Founded in 1878, the University Ligget School is Michigan's oldest independent day school and enjoys a national reputation for its college preparatory curriculum. Tuition was expensive and consumed a sizable fraction of Tony and Jan's income. Once Stephen started school—and even though their living arrangement at the Williams House for girls drastically cut down on living expenses—Jan and Tony would still typically have only a few dollars left in their bank account by the last few days of each month. Financial tightness was further exacerbated during the year taken by Tony to obtain a master's degree in library science at the University of Michigan in Ann Arbor. Willingness to divert meager resources to achieve educational priorities for themselves (and subsequently their son, Stephen) was always a hallmark of both Jan's and Tony's academic careers.

Harrold, and one that he had sampled for himself working at the Newbury Library in Chicago.[17] Tony began taking evening classes to obtain a master's degree in library science at the University of Michigan while still teaching at Wayne, commuting forty-five miles from Detroit to Ann Arbor on a Greyhound bus. According to Jan, what Tony wanted most was "a job with books."

In 1959, Tony completed his dissertation ("Robert Johnson's Essays, or Rather Imperfect Offers (1601): A Critical Edition") and graduated with a PhD from Northwestern while simultaneously obtaining his master's in library science from the University of Michigan. With these two degrees in hand, he was a highly marketable candidate for a staff position at any university library. He entertained offers from Harvard, Washington University in St. Louis, and Utah State University in Logan, Utah. Remarkably, he chose Utah State. For close to a decade the Shipps had struggled to achieve an academic career for Tony while living in unusual housing arrangements in the urban centers of Chicago and Detroit. Both Jan and Tony were now enticed by the prospects of returning to a small town and family-oriented community, where they hoped to provide their son Stephen, now age seven, with a more conventional upbringing. To this point in his young life, Stephen had mostly lived with his parents in institutional homes for wayward girls and had never experienced growing up in a normal neighborhood with kids his own age. The apparently quirky decision (from a career standpoint) was made: The Shipps were about to meet the Mormons.

---

17. As already mentioned, Tony's mother gained employment as a reference librarian at the University of South Carolina. His brother Harrold later became a librarian at the Air Force Academy library in Colorado Springs.

CHAPTER 3

Discovering the Mormons and Acquiring Academic Credentials, 1960–1966

After eleven years of marriage, Jan and Tony Shipps were not a conventional, bourgeois couple. They both hailed from relatively small communities in the American South where their families had faced their share of dysfunctional problems during the Great Depression and war years of the 1930s and 40s. Breaking away from family entanglements, they migrated north to the booming post-war urban centers of Chicago and Detroit in pursuit of higher education for Tony and a bookish career for him as an academician. During this time they had either lived in student housing or secured room and board as house parents for court-designated "at-risk" girls. Thus, they had never paid a mortgage or owned any real property, and their tangible and intangible possessions were negligible. Tony by interest and education was an intellectual, but so too was Jan. Or, perhaps better said, Jan had *quietly become a latent intellectual*, whose commitment to Tony's academic career as his informal research assistant—along with her own long-established, inveterate reading habits—had helped to discipline and inform a curious mind. Despite Jan's budding interests, Tony's career took precedence in their decision-making as they sought to fulfill the dream of a homeowning, traditional nuclear family.

It was in Logan, Utah, where Tony's budding career as an academic librarian took them next, that Jan found a suitable subject for her curiosity and belatedly commenced her own career as a serious student of Mormon history.

Logan, Utah, 1960–1961

Tony visited Logan before accepting Utah State University's (USU) offer to be assistant head librarian. The USU hiring committee was impressed by Tony's Northwestern PhD, especially when many of their faculty at the time did not have doctoral degrees and had received their educations from local institutions in the Mormon cultural regions of Utah and Idaho. According to Jan, one of the hiring committee members remarked to Tony during his interview that he would discover there were "lots of sons-of-bishops" in Mormon Logan, a quip that Tony initially wasn't sure how to interpret. But the mountain scenery surrounding the picturesque town of Logan was stunning, the well-groomed campus of Utah State University was beautiful, and the welcoming friendliness of his hosts was highly appealing.

In preparation for their westward trip to Cache Valley, Utah, Tony and Jan had to purchase their first car (a Nash Rambler, which they decided on—in predictably studious fashion—after consulting *Consumer Reports*). At the time, neither one of them knew how to drive; for the first ten years of their marriage they had relied on public transportation. They both took driving lessons in Detroit, but subsequently Tony did all the driving, first to visit Jan's family in Georgia and then throughout the cross-country trip to distant Utah, while Jan navigated their journey using service station roadmaps.[1] Along the way, Stephen gradually stopped compulsively identifying the John Deere highway signs they passed traversing the Midwest and instead began announcing the "Watch for Deer" signs that started to appear on the sides of the road when they reached the Rocky Mountains.

Jan describes the last leg of their journey from Bear Lake on the Utah-Idaho border to Logan in rapturous, literary language:

> The beauty is breathtaking. . . . Having never seen elevations of this magnitude before and having never viewed a natural spectacle of such magnificence, I was awestruck. . . . We had managed the heights and were descending past mountain meadows into a canyon from which, in places, the mountains stand virtually perpendicular to the road and to the Logan river that, for many miles, runs alongside. . . . It seem[ed] that we were negotiating a passage through a chasm that was separating us from everywhere we had been and everything we had done before we entered it. . . . [W]hen we reached the mouth of the canyon and the narrow passage through which we had traveled opened out onto an amazing vista, I gazed transfixed. The scene revealed a valley dappled in light and shadow, with the sun's rays reflecting off the stone of Utah State's Old Main tower and the pristine whiteness of the Logan temple. It was enclosed by mountains standing afar, and it seemed to be another world.[2]

---

1. According to Jan, Tony loved driving and liked to call himself Jan's "male chaufferist." He wouldn't allow Jan to drive when they traveled together until later in life when his doctor told him he couldn't drive. Tony didn't like Jan to sleep while he was driving. She had to stay awake to read road signs and books (usually mysteries) for Tony, or they would listen to the radio together. In this respect and in many others, Tony assumed a traditional male role in their marriage, which Jan readily consented to, even though she also quietly asserted her own marital prerogatives when she felt strongly about an issue.

2. Jan Shipps, *Sojourner in the Promised Land: Forty Years Among the Mormons*, 366. Completed in 1884 and constructed of limestone and quartzite, the Logan temple's weathered surface actually displays a greyish hue. What probably struck Jan's eyes upon emerging from Logan Canyon were the large, white weathervane towers that anchor the temple's east and west center towers.

When Jan, Tony, and Stephen arrived in Logan in early August 1960, they moved into a modest rental home near the USU campus. They had no furniture and spent their first few nights sleeping on cots. Their new neighbors were friendly and generous in aiding them to get settled. This neighborliness soon included a set of "ward missionaries" who made visits practically every Wednesday night. (Unlike the full-time LDS missionaries, ward missionaries are members of the local LDS congregation or "ward" who assist the former with service and evangelizing.) Jan had heard of Brigham Young and polygamy (from a school history textbook) but had no idea who Mormon founder Joseph Smith was. She knew virtually nothing about Mormons or Mormon history and assumed the Mormons were just another denominational group in Protestant Christianity. Prior to arriving in Utah, Jan had been interested in Southern history and also had done some reading about Judaism, both topics broadening her interest in and appreciation for cultural differences in American society. Her curiosity now piqued by the almost exclusively Mormon community in which she and Tony found themselves, she quickly discovered that the neighborly ward missionaries were more than willing to talk about Mormonism and Mormon history. Tony was always welcoming to their visitors but, unlike her, had virtually no interest in finding out more about their religion. "In retrospect and in some ways," Jan recalls, "Tony has rued the day ever since." Occasionally Jan would be absent when the missionaries dropped by to visit, and Tony would tell them, "Oh, don't worry about Jan, you'll baptize her in the afterlife."

Jan also quickly learned about the peculiar social divisions in Logan and the local religious labels commonly employed to reference them. Jan and Tony became friends with a couple by the auspicious name of Smith, who were actually non-Mormons and lived on their cul-de-sac. The husband was a member of the USU English department and shared literary interests with Tony. Invited to supper, Jan and Tony were informed by the Smiths that in Logan they were considered "gentiles" (non-Mormons) and, for that matter, so were Jan and Tony. The Smiths also carefully explained that they were not "Jack Mormons" either (members or former Church members who no longer believed or practiced Mormonism's religious mandates, but who retained certain cultural connections to their heritage). However, they learned that several of Tony's library and English associates were, in fact, Jack Mormons.

By this time in her life, Jan had become a thoughtful self-learner with an ingrained habit of exploring library holdings and consulting books to teach herself about new subjects in her expanding universe of interests. Her curiosity was now heightened to discover more about this odd community where she and Tony had unexpectedly landed, and she began a crash-course reading spree on books about and by Mormons, including and especially

USU Professor Leonard Arrington's recently published *Great Basin Kingdom: Economic History of the Latter-day Saints, 1830—1900*.[3]

Once classes began in the fall, Jan and Tony became part of a gentile and Jack Mormon social network in Logan while simultaneously having regular contact with Mormon neighbors, especially including Everett Cooley (a Mormon historian, later to become Jan's academic mentor) and his wife and two children, who were living on the same cul-de-sac. The USU head librarian and Tony's boss, Milton (Milt) Abrams, was a Jack Mormon whose wife had divorced him after he stopped wearing his temple garments.[4] Through this latter acquaintanceship, Jan learned for the first time about Mormon temples and how mysteriously different they were from ordinary church meeting places or chapels with which she was familiar. The Jack Mormons with whom Jan and Tony socialized liked to critically discuss religious and historical books, including Arrington's *Great Basin Kingdom*, which they regarded as genuine scholarship rather than Church propaganda.

At the same time, Jan and Tony could hardly avoid regular contacts with neighbors and colleagues who were faithful Mormons. One of their next-door LDS neighbors was a USU football coach who enjoyed playing catch with Stephen, who in turn was becoming intensely interested in sports. Some of their other Mormon neighbors also had been inquiring about Stephen's interest in attending LDS primary (children's) classes. Jan experienced a dawning realization that Logan, and the tightly knit Mormon community that dominated the town, was very different than any place she had ever been before: it was "a little like entering the Twilight Zone."[5] She was both perplexed and fascinated by this difference. She says it was superficially like other American towns, but beneath the surface it proved to be alien to any of her previous experience. As an overwhelmingly Mormon community, every local institution, including the university, was shaped and affected by LDS culture.

Alternative places of worship were scarce in Logan; in particular there was no nearby Methodist congregation. Jan and Tony sporadically attended

---

3. Leonard J. Arrington, *Great Basin Kingdom: An Economic History of the Latter-day Saints, 1830–1900*.

4. Temple garments are a type of underwear manufactured by the LDS Church for its members who have gone through the LDS temple endowment ritual, where worthy members covenant fealty to the church and its doctrines. The garments signify those religious commitments. Obtaining ecclesiastical clearance to enter an LDS temple and participate in its covenantal rites is based on periodic worthiness interviews and is a prime indicator of one's good standing in the Church. Conversely, subsequent failure to wear one's temple garments may be taken as an indicator of loss of faith or religious standing.

5. Shipps, *Sojourner*, 22.

a Presbyterian church (which, at the time, was the only Protestant denomination in town) ostensibly to "inoculate" their son Stephen from constant exposure to Mormonism as the only valid religion and to provide him some non-Mormon playmates. (Stephen had, in fact, begun attending—with neighborhood kids—weekly LDS primary classes for children under the age of twelve.) During their stay in Logan, however, Jan and Tony never attended a single LDS religious service. This may seem surprising, given Jan's ripening curiosity about all things Mormon, but it also signals her ultimate attachment to her own Protestant faith tradition as a Methodist.

Demonstrating from the beginning the detached, cultural inquisitiveness of a social scientist did not mean that Jan was a religious seeker looking for a new faith to embrace—a fact that later in her career as a Mormon Studies scholar often flummoxed Mormon colleagues who thought that her deep study of Mormonism might naturally lead her to join the LDS Church. Puzzled by her refusal to do so, a frequently reiterated question by LDS friends to Jan over the years has been, "How can you know so much and not believe?" Jan, like many believing Mormon intellectuals and scholars, ultimately remains attached to the religious tradition in which she was brought up. She takes pride in her own religious tradition in the same way many Mormon intellectuals take pride in theirs. This is important in understanding Jan's scholarly work on Mormonism but should not be regarded as a stunning revelation.[6]

Despite Logan's religious homogeneity, Jan says that she and Tony enjoyed their social life in Logan, though it mostly centered in the company of academic Jack Mormons. Jan appreciated these friends, who offered a refreshing contrast to both the pious and renegade religious stereotypes perpetrated in the local culture. She turned to them to better understand the cultural distinctions between devout Mormons and Jack Mormons that intrigued her—questions that would mark the beginning of her own intellectual study of Mormonism: What was it like growing up Mormon? What was it like disavowing belief in Mormon theology and dropping out from active LDS lay involvement while still maintaining certain attachments to one's Mormon heritage, especially in such a devoutly Mormon community as Logan?

Now that Tony had successfully recast his academic career as a university librarian, it seemed like a propitious time for Jan to resume her own college

---

6. In Jan's words, "Despite the fascination with Mormonism . . . I have somehow managed to keep truth questions 'bracketed' through all my years of study. To a significant degree, this has been a conscious scholarly strategy adopted to provide me with enough distance to be analytical. But it is not only that. In all honesty, the matter of whether, in some ultimate sense, Latter-day Saints are or are not correct when they bare their formulaic testimonies that 'Mormonism is true' is simply not on my agenda of things to try to find out." Jan Shipps, "An Inside Outsider in Zion," 143.

education. Encouraged by Tony, Jan registered for classes at Utah State for the Fall 1960 term. At the time Tony and Jan's main concern was for her to finish a bachelor's degree as quickly as possible and obtain a certificate to teach in public schools, so she could contribute to the family's income. She had no thoughts of going on to graduate school or pursuing an academic career.

Virtually all of Jan's undergraduate classes at USU reinforced her sense of cultural differences between Mormons, Jack Mormons, and "gentiles" on campus and their importance to local people in the community. She took a European history class in which her non-LDS, Protestant professor kept unfavorably comparing the modern LDS church to Roman Catholicism during the Protestant Reformation, while all the Mormon male students (Jan was the only female in the class) vehemently challenged what they considered to be an unjust analogy. According to Jan, an American history class on the Civil War consumed most of the academic quarter talking about the 1857–58 "Utah War" and very little about the actual war between the North and the South over issues of union and slavery.[7] Other USU classes Jan took, regardless of subject matter (including a sociology class and education courses), made constant references or allusions to Mormonism in both course lectures and class discussion, unapologetically emphasizing Mormon perspectives and beliefs. All seemed to assume familiarity with Mormon culture and history, which sent Jan to the library in search of more relevant reading material. When she looked for controversial Mormon classics like Fawn Brodie's scathing biography of Joseph Smith, *No Man Knows My History*, and Juanita Brooks' silence-breaking *Mountain Meadows Massacre* in the Logan public library, she was astonished to discover they were kept behind the front desk along with the sex manuals.

With a keen eye for social distinctions and cultural variations, Jan quickly became attuned to the multidimensional diversity of Mormon society. Her early encounters with local culture (including the sharp divisions between Mormons, Jack Mormons, and gentiles, and variegated reading material on LDS history and religion, both apologetic and polemical) produced an ambiguous, "kaleidoscopic" view of the Mormons.[8] Jan wanted to understand her new environment in insular Cache Valley more than criticize it. Rather than simply

---

7. The Utah War (variously known as the Utah Expedition, the Mormon War, or the Mormon Rebellion) refers to the political and military conflict between the Mormons and the United States government in 1857–58 over the issue of theocratic rule in the Utah Territory under the administration of church president Brigham Young. Consequently, Young was deposed as territorial governor and replaced by a non-Mormon appointee, and Salt Lake City was placed under military surveillance until the outbreak of the American Civil War. See William P. MacKinnon, *At Sword's Point, Part 1: A Documentary History of the Utah War to 1858*.

8. Shipps, "An 'Inside Outsider' in Zion," 149.

dismissing Mormons as misguided fanatics and their religion as a pious hoax, "I realized that a persuasive explanation for the differences would have to be at once more subtle and more fundamental."[9] This detached kind of intellectual curiosity about Mormon institutions and culture was not shared by Tony.

At USU, Jan determined to change her music major for mostly practical reasons: she realized how difficult it would be returning to music after such a long time away from both music theory and practice of classical pieces. Other than part-time gigs playing popular tunes at piano bars in Florida and Chicago for extra income, she had not continued serious piano-playing since her marriage to Tony. At the same time, her "paraprofessional social work" with orphaned and semi-delinquent girls in Chicago and Detroit had proven to be a satisfying experience. She had found human beings "in the midst of life" more interesting than piano, and she "wanted to learn about people."[10] Her decision to major in history rather than sociology or psychology was also pragmatic: through previous college work she had more credit hours in history than anything else. With a history major, Jan calculated it would be possible to graduate in one academic year by carrying course overloads every quarter, taking correspondence courses, and earning course credits through examination.

Jan confesses that initially she was anxious about returning to college after an eleven-year hiatus. Older, nontraditional students—especially women—were rare on college campuses in 1960, and Jan worried that she wouldn't fit in, that she wasn't "book smart," and that, most certainly, she would never be as smart or successful scholastically as Tony. Even though she had done well for one semester at the Georgia College for Women in Milledgeville after marrying Tony, earlier she had failed to make exceptional grades at the Alabama College for Women (having a greater interest then in playing dance music than studying), and she still didn't think of herself as a real student. At the beginning of her first academic term at Utah State, Tony endeavored to give Jan reassurance. Putting his arm around her as he walked her to her first class, he said, "Don't worry, honey, it doesn't matter how well you do. All you have to do is pass." At this transitional point in their lives, neither Tony nor Jan were aware of Jan's tremendous intellectual promise and capability for doing highly original work as a scholar.

Despite concerns about her abilities in school, Jan surprised herself by excelling in her classes. "At first I was shocked at how well I did," she recalls, describing the success she found in not only her lower division, general education courses but in her upper division history classes as well, achieving perfect grades in every course. This surprise stands in contrast to her

---

9. Shipps, 145.
10. Shipps, 145.

childhood self-conception of being a smart and outstanding student growing up in Hueytown. However, as an adult in Chicago and Detroit she had assumed the role of a doting mother to an only child and wife to a highly educated academic. In this new arrangement, Tony was designated the smart one with Jan as his dutiful helper. Her unexpected achievements as a nontraditional student, however, began to slowly change her understanding of their reciprocal roles. At the same time, her academic accomplishments at USU tended to be depreciated by Tony (and Jan herself)—"Oh, well, it's just Utah"—in comparison to the presumably more rigorous academic standards at Northwestern University, Wayne State, and the University of Michigan. After leaving Logan it would take a year of unmitigated graduate school success at the University of Colorado before both Jan and Tony were obliged to fully appreciate her exceptional academic capabilities.

As a history major, Jan did *not* take any courses from Leonard Arrington (future LDS Church Historian), who was on sabbatical leave, or George Ellsworth (a founder of *Western Political Quarterly*), the two most eminent Mormon scholars on the USU faculty. (Jan would not meet Arrington, for whom she developed profound respect, until after the Shipps left Logan.) The only *Mormon* history class Jan took at USU was taught by Joel Ricks, a kindly, well-known local historian and traditional Mormon apologist whose grandfather had been one of the early pioneers that helped establish Logan in 1859.[11]

During her second quarter, Jan took a teaching practicum course through Logan High School to obtain a teaching certificate. Ironically, she was assigned to teach nineteenth-century Utah/Mormon history, about which, at the outset, she knew virtually nothing. This required some motivation to learn all she could about the subject matter through a self-directed, crash-reading course on her own initiative. The self-study paid off, and Jan fondly recalls teaching a lesson that included her reference to the considerable number of plural wives acquired by a certain nineteenth-century Mormon patriarch when a student interjected to say, "That's my grandpa!"

The most critically important history class Jan took at USU was a required historiography methods course for history majors that was being taught that year by visiting professor Everett L. Cooley, the Shipps's close neighbor. Cooley had been the Utah state archivist in Salt Lake City but had accepted an appointment as an associate professor of history for the 1960–61 school year to temporarily cover for Leonard Arrington, who was on sabbatical leave. Given the limited USU library holdings at the time, Cooley's insistence that students work with primary source materials meant that his

---

11. For a brief overview of the Mormon pioneer history of Logan, Utah, see Audrey M. Godfrey, "Logan, Utah."

students' research papers would mostly be on LDS topics. Jan chose to write on the nineteenth-century construction of the LDS temple in Logan. The primary source materials for this project came from the Charles O. Card papers, which had recently been donated by the Card family to the USU library. Card was an early Mormon stalwart in the pioneer development of Logan as a commercial and educational center in Northern Utah. He subsequently became the patriarchal founder of the Mormon colony of Cardston, Alberta, Canada, which was established in 1887 as a sanctuary for Mormon polygamist families fleeing from US federal prosecution under the Edmunds-Tucker Act (that mandated harsh penalties for unlawful co-habitation.)[12] Cooley, who had been impressed by Jan as a student in his History of the US Constitution class the previous term (and, no doubt, was also favorably disposed toward her as his neighbor), alerted her to the existence of the Card materials and encouraged her to use them for her project. Consequently, Jan, as an undergraduate student, became the first person to research this collection of historical pioneer documents.

Jan not only studied Card's papers in the USU library but also visited the Cache County Court House to obtain more material on him (where she discovered that the Mormon patriarch had a divorced wife whom local history seemed to have forgotten) and to the Genealogical Society in Salt Lake City—eighty-five miles south of Logan—for additional materials. In recalling this early student exercise in historiography, Jan says that she was motivated by Cooley's encouragement to "pursue a historical task" and not "just write a paper like most students for a grade." Jan's work earned high praise from Cooley, who thought her paper could easily be refined and published. He even wanted Jan to consider editing the Card collection, but at the time she was still primarily focused on getting a teaching certificate rather than pursuing an academic career in history.

More than anything, Jan's outlook on the future was being redirected by Tony's rapidly developing dissatisfaction with his work at Utah State. According to Jan, Tony discovered there were "no books" in the USU library "except about Mormons," and he found it necessary to travel on weekends to the larger library at the University of Utah in Salt Lake City for the books he wanted on old English sources. After living only six weeks in Logan, Tony told Jan, "We have to go," and began communicating with the University of Colorado about a library position in Boulder. By January 1961, Jan knew they would be leaving Logan. She was not eager to move—her own blossom-

---

12. For a biographical sketch of Charles Ora Card, see The Church of Jesus Christ of Latter-day Saints, "Canada's Brigham Young: The Life of Charles O. Card."

ing as a student at USU had been exhilarating—but, for the higher good of Tony's career, she did not oppose a move to Colorado.

In a hurry to finish her degree at USU, Jan increased her efforts and finished two years of requirements for a bachelor's degree in only nine months with perfect grades. Her grades and exhilarating success in Cooley's historiography course did not completely change her self-image as a student, as they were tempered somewhat by her low opinion of the scholarly standards at USU (which was reinforced by Tony's criticism of the school as a provincial backwater). Nonetheless, Jan acknowledges that the positive feedback and encouragement from Cooley were crucial in laying the foundation for her later identity as a scholar, capable of doing original research. The sincerity of the encouragement was further bolstered when Leonard Arrington, who had just returned to campus before the Shipps's departure, was made aware of Jan's success as a student (probably by Cooley) and offered her a position as a student assistant, mistakenly assuming she was going to be back on campus for the next academic year. Although unable to take the position, the offer portended a later and important collaborative relationship between the two.

Boulder, Colorado, 1961–1966

After one academic year at Utah State, with Jan having enrolled as a full-time student, the Shipps's finances were precarious when they arrived in Boulder for Tony to assume his new position as head of the circulation department at the University of Colorado library. They had no home equity, few possessions, and scant savings. Jan was determined to do her part to help but, unfortunately, Colorado would not recognize her Utah teaching certificate, so she was unable to apply for any public school teaching positions. To get a Colorado teaching certification would require her to take approximately thirty hours of required education courses—a depressing prospect for Jan, who had worked so conscientiously to get her degree at Utah State. An alternative was for Jan to bypass taking more undergraduate credits by enrolling in the history department's master's degree program, which consequently would make her more eligible and competitive in the local high school teaching market.

In the meantime, Thalia (Jan's mother) loaned Tony and Jan enough money to make a down payment on a house—their first after twelve years of marriage. Thalia had unexpectedly gained a fair amount of income through dividends from her one-hundred-dollar investment in an oil well venture that belatedly paid off following the end of World War II, providing her with quarterly checks of three thousand dollars that furnished her with financial security for the rest of her life. Jan stayed in touch with her mother primarily through Saturday phone calls, and Tony (who by then had developed a close relationship with Thalia) began writing her a letter every month, along with a check for one hundred dollars to repay the mortgage loan. (Thalia would later say that she was sorry when the loan was paid off, because that ended her monthly letters from Tony.)

Thalia eventually visited the small family in Colorado, and she and Tony got along famously. During the visit, everyone was watching a TV program together in which a white woman moved to Africa to marry a black man. Thalia disapprovingly said she couldn't understand why a woman would do such a thing. Tony's ingratiatingly sardonic rejoinder was "I don't know, it's not any worse than a nonsmoker being married to a smoker." Upon hearing this remark, Jan resolved to quit smoking cold-turkey and never touched another cigarette. Preoccupied with their own concerns, neither Tony nor Stephen noticed, and to their surprise, Jan had to inform them—over a month after the fact—that she had given up the habit.

After her admission to the University of Colorado, Jan's primary motivation continued to be practical and pecuniary: getting a credential for teaching high school with a master's degree in history remained her chief preoccupation. She and Tony had new house payments to make, and Stephen (now eight years old and in the third grade) was showing signs of musical precocity. The school music director informed Jan that her son seemed gifted and, because he was tall for his age, wanted him to try playing the cello (or, if he got tired of that, the tuba). Stephen, however, refused these blandishments. He was drawn instead to the violin and insisted on only playing that.

As a newly enrolled master's student in history, Jan belatedly discovered that there were no courses on the Mormons in the department's Western American history curriculum. This was a disappointment, since Jan's curiosity and interest in Mormon history had been keenly whetted by her undergraduate experience at Utah State, and she had hoped to parlay her initial exposure to Mormon sources into a project for her MA thesis at the University of Colorado. The department faculty knew "little or nothing at all about the Mormons," with the lone exception of Hal Bridges, who was assigned as Jan's advisor. Bridges, a specialist in American thought and society, had particular interests in the Civil War and American mysticism, and was, according to Jan, "a profoundly religious person, a mystic," who was interested in Joseph Smith's prophetic biography. Accordingly, he supported Jan's intention to do her thesis on nineteenth-century Mormonism.[13]

Although both interested in and supportive of Jan's thesis project, Bridges did not function as Jan's primary research mentor. From Bridges Jan acquired rudimentary skill in handling analytical tools for making sense out of history,

---

13. Bridges's books include *American Mysticism: From William James to Zen* and *Lee's Maverick General: Daniel Harvey Hill.*

but it was Everett Cooley to whom she turned for his expertise in Mormon historiography. Cooley had returned to Salt Lake City to become director of the Utah State Historical Society. Through phone calls and letters, Jan stayed in touch with Everett the entire year.

Once again in a hurry to finish so she could become gainfully employed, Jan completed the requirements for her master's degree in nine months. She expeditiously decided to write her master's thesis about Mormons and politics in Illinois during the final years of Joseph Smith's tumultuous public life. This choice of topic was dictated by Jan's preliminary experience researching Mormon subjects at Utah State and her discovery, through Tony, that the University of Colorado Library had a complete set of nineteenth-century Illinois newspapers on microfilm, along with pertinent state legislature reports of that era. Jan had become accustomed to utilizing microfilmed documents while assisting Tony as he worked on his dissertation. This meant that she had ready access to primary source materials for her thesis, which would be based almost entirely on newspaper accounts of the increasingly intractable "Mormon problem" in Illinois state politics during the 1840s. After collecting pertinent data, Jan finished writing her thesis, "The Mormons in Politics, 1839–1844," which she says was written in just "two to three weeks" at the end of the 1962 Spring term "in order to avoid paying summer tuition."

Jan's intention of finding a teaching job in the public schools, bolstered by her newly earned master's degree, had not yet changed. Once commencing her graduate course work, however, Jan began to realize the intrinsic satisfaction she derived from historical study, and, perhaps for the first time, she was beginning to see the faint prospects of becoming an academic historian. It was only after Jan successfully commenced doing graduate work at the University of Colorado that both she and Tony began to acknowledge the fact that she had become a truly outstanding student. "We both were surprised by my academic success at Colorado," she recalls. But the impetus for continuing in the graduate program at Colorado as a PhD student did not come from Tony or Jan's own insistence. It came in the form of an unanticipated university fellowship of $2,500, the bestowal of which had been urged by the Colorado history faculty who were anxious to retain Jan as a highly promising student in their program.

Following the completion of her thesis, University of Colorado policies required Jan to march at the commencement ceremonies to obtain her degree. Jan, who felt she couldn't afford the extra cost of renting graduation regalia, wrote the graduate school asking for an exemption. The dean (who was the former chair of the history department) told Jan that the school possessed a master's cap and gown for "a deserving, indigent graduate scholar." He also advised Jan to apply for the available university fellowship. Before accepting,

Jan asked Tony for his approval, and he responded with a gratifying, "You go ahead." Years later, when she had become an established scholar, Jan says Tony loved to tell the story of how "Jan had to ask her husband to go to graduate school." Tony, however, did have some reservations, and even though he had initially consented, he had second thoughts and asked Jan to decline the university's offer and instead try to have another child. Jan refused, saying she wanted to continue her graduate school education and pursue an academic career. Tony respected Jan's wish and did not demur, even though this decision dashed any remaining thoughts of enlarging their family.

With Tony's support, Jan abandoned her plans to seek a high school teaching position and, at the age of 33, enrolled as a PhD student in history at the University of Colorado for the Fall 1962 term. Already on a fast track, it would take her only three years to complete all the requirements—including her dissertation—for a doctoral degree, awarded in the spring of 1965. When she began, Jan was one of only three female graduate students in the department, and all of the history faculty were men. In those years relatively few women in the country were pursuing advanced degrees in history. By and large, American history was a male preserve in which the subfields of political and military history received priority emphasis. As a student, Jan had to deflect her share of unwanted personal attention and advances made by both male students and a few members of the faculty. To some degree, she still harbored her adolescent conception of self as a homely girl who compensated for her perceived lack of sex appeal by being the smartest one in class. As a married adult woman with a growing seriousness about pursuing a genuine scholarly career, she was unaccustomed to being sexually solicited by colleagues, and she experienced awkward discomfort when it happened. Unfortunately, occasional womanizing attempts directed at Jan as a female academic did not end for her in graduate school. In later years, she was frequently propositioned by male academics at professional meetings; "I had to deal with it a lot," she dryly recalls. The defense line that Jan quickly learned to employ was simply: "No thanks, I'm happily married."[14]

---

14. Jan never told Tony about any of her experiences of sexual harassment by male academics or colleagues. She says this was just part of what it was like for female graduate students and women academics at the time—a taken-for-granted part of the culture, in which men felt free to take liberties with women, who in turn perceived they had little recourse. At the same time, in our interviews with her, Jan didn't seem personally scarred or angry about what she observed and experienced (primarily sexually inappropriate comments or propositions, but never sexual assault). She shrugs it off as something she simply took in stride and was able to cope with, while remaining faithful to Tony. It did not occur to her at the time to reveal or publicly challenge individuals or the sexist culture that sustained such exploitive behavior.

In spite of the fact that nobody at Colorado taught a course on Mormon history, Jan had found it both expeditiously convenient and personally interesting to continue focusing on the Mormons for her master's degree. Now, as a PhD student, she wanted to put her growing understanding of Mormonism into a larger context. Influenced by Lee Scamehorn (another history faculty member who ended up serving as her dissertation advisor), Jan "became committed to the virtues of comparative history" and expanded her reading focus beyond Mormons to include Puritans, Anglicans, and Quakers in the American colonies; the Methodist revolution in England and Methodism's apotheosis in America; the American Civil War; and the politics of Progressivism. At the same time, she never took any survey courses at Colorado on the history of the American West. Recognizing that Mormon history was part and parcel of US Western history (and increasingly puzzled that this fact seemed to be largely ignored by most American history texts at the time, not to mention history faculty at Colorado), Jan took the initiative to find and read relevant sources to better educate herself.

Just as most of Jan's growing knowledge of Mormonism came from her own reading, so too did her comprehension of materials on the American West. Aside from one undergraduate historiography class at Utah State, she had no formal training in Mormon Studies, nor did she receive any in Western Americana as a graduate student at the University of Colorado. Instead, her prideful attitudes of personal competence and self-sufficiency—inculcated while growing up in Hueytown and reinforced while building a life with Tony Shipps—predictably prompted her to synthesize these two literatures on her own.[15]

In the meantime, Tony was preoccupied with his new job at the University of Colorado Library. He had been hired originally to head the circulation department, was quickly moved to the reference department, and within a few years became the head reference librarian. When at home, Tony decreed that evenings were for family time and peaceful relaxation, instructing Stephen to practice his violin and telling Jan she was to study only when he was working at the library. Jan agreed to this stricture, but after Tony fell asleep she would sneak into the bathroom and resume her studying late into the night.

Although Jan had spent considerable time and energy assisting Tony with his graduate writing, Tony was typically too busy with his new work at the library to return the favor. Clearly, Jan's increasingly avid pursuit of becoming a scholar and academic was still seen by Tony as a secondary avocation in the economy of the Shipps's marriage and family life. Superficially, it might also

---

15. Years later as a tenured historian, Jan became an active member of the Western History Association, chairing both its annual conference program and book prize committees in 1982 and 1984 respectively.

appear that Jan's commitment to maintaining a traditional marriage reflected a fundamental docility on her part; however, such a view ignores the resolve, determination, and perseverance that better describe Jan's approach to living life, especially regarding study, learning, and her scholarly work, which were beginning to assume an increasingly larger portion of her adult identity. Even though she embraced her role as a loyal wife, Jan applied her resolve and determination to secure that which was becoming important to her own well-being. As she recalls, "So many of our decisions have been made because I went to Tony and said: *We* need to make a decision" (on issues that Jan had staked out a clear preference of her own).

Tony and Jan's relationship grew along with her developing academic interests. As a tightly knit family unit, Tony, Stephen, and Jan all practiced a highly focused work ethic that was mutually reinforcing. Jan remembers Boulder as an intellectually exciting time: "Tony and I were both doing scholarly work; we were both increasing our knowledge." Once she commenced her PhD studies, Tony began enrolling in Latin and Greek language courses taught by the university's classics department. Tony liked learning languages, even though he initially had struggled to learn German as a PhD student at Northwestern. It was also in Boulder when he actively began pursuing his academic interest in validating the historical provenance of literary quotations for publication and subsequently began publishing answers to quotation queries in a column for the *New York Times* and later for an Oxford University Press periodical, *Notes and Queries*.[16] According to Jan, Tony was fastidiously dedicated to accuracy and would read an entire book to track down a single quotation. Because of this, their house was "getting phone calls day and night for Tony," requesting authentication for a quote. A typical call would go something like: "I'm so and so from Australia calling for Anthony Shipps. My book goes to press tomorrow, and I absolutely have to identify this source."

At the same time, Stephen (who was becoming increasingly knowledgeable about music and music history) began memorizing liner notes from classical music albums to learn about musicians and their work. His precocious ability on violin quickly had achieved local notoriety, and he frequently was asked to play at school events, churches, and women's club meetings.[17] By the time Stephen reached the seventh grade, the school music teacher in-

---

16. Published since 1849, *Notes and Queries* ("devoted principally to English language and literature, lexicography, history, and scholarly antiquarianism") can now be accessed online at https://academic.oup.com/nq.

17. Jan relates a story about Stephen at this time that is reminiscent of Tony's unique brand of punning wit: On one occasion, Stephen was asked by an acquaintance of Jan and Tony's, "Are you pretty good at stringed instruments?" Steven's sardonic reply was, "Oh, I'm pretty good with the yo-yo."

formed Jan and Tony that he had taught Stephen everything he knew and recommended that he take private lessons from a well-known member of the Colorado music faculty. This recommended professor strongly encouraged parents to attend and observe their children's lessons. However, when Jan drove Stephen to his first lesson, he told his mother, "If you're going in, I'm not." Jan happily obliged, since it would give her time to study in the car for her pending PhD comprehensive exams while waiting for Stephen to finish.

While she was working on her PhD, a paper about black Mormons that Jan had written during her first year as a master's student unexpectedly emerged as a significant milestone in Jan's academic development. The paper, "Second Class Saints," was initially inspired by discussions she and Tony had had with their Jack Mormon acquaintances in Logan at a time when the national civil rights movement was attracting headline news.[18] White-Black relationships had become a particularly controversial issue on the USU campus, because recruited black athletes were starting to date white girls in Logan—a situation that no doubt reminded Jan of her experiences of racial tensions in the segregated deep South during her growing up years. Hal Bridges, who was on the editorial board of the *Colorado Quarterly*, was impressed with Jan's paper and urged her to submit it for review. She did, and in October 1962 it became her first scholarly publication.[19] Jan was both surprised and pleased. Few if any of her fellow graduate students at Colorado were publishing their work in academic journals at that stage of their professional development. Leonard Arrington (who was interested in the development of young Mormon scholars and made a point of being informed of their work) obtained a copy of Jan's article and congratulated her on publishing the first academic essay dealing with the issue of priesthood and race in the LDS Church.[20]

Bridges, who was still Jan's advisor, had been made acting chair of the history department when the previous chair was designated acting dean of the graduate

---

18. Jan say that she did not closely follow national news concerning civil rights struggles in the South while she and Tony were residing in Chicago and Detroit (involving especially ugly and violent episodes of white resistance to racial integration in areas where both she and Tony had lived in Alabama and Georgia): "I was glad we were away from that; I realized it would take a long time to change attitudes and racial practices in the South." Ironically, massive urban riots and other forms of racial unrest spread to both Chicago and Detroit not long after Jan and Tony left the Midwest to pursue their fortunes in Utah and Colorado.

19. Jan Shipps, "Second Class Saints," 183–90.

20. In the 1966 inaugural issue of *Dialogue: A Journal of Mormon Thought*, Arrington also included Jan's PhD dissertation in his lead essay on contemporary Mormon scholarship in the twentieth century. Leonard J. Arrington, "Scholarly Studies of Mormonism in the Twentieth Century," 15–32.

school. Two weeks after Jan passed her PhD oral exam, Bridges abruptly resigned to take a position at the University of California Riverside. This unexpected departure threw the department into a period of uncertainty and conflict between different faculty factions who had opposed Bridges and were split over who was to become the next chair. Meanwhile, Bridges's students, including Jan, were reassigned to Lee Scamehorn, who was the youngest member of the faculty and who had managed to stay detached from the department's antagonistic divisions. Scamehorn specialized in Colorado history (especially the state's mining industry and economic history) and knew nothing about the history of the Mormons in neighboring Utah.[21] Fortunately for Jan, she had remained in regular contact with Everett Cooley, who had unofficially advised her in completing her master's thesis. According to her, "Scamehorn was grateful that I had a working relationship with Cooley" and was more than willing to allow him to continue mentoring Jan in researching and writing her dissertation—an ambitious extension of her master's thesis on Mormons in politics.

It was emotionally stressful for Jan to be caught up in the history department's dysfunctional squabbling. Colleagues were not speaking to one another and were fighting over which students would be their graduate assistants. Jan was anxious to finish her degree quickly to avoid further faculty conflicts and pushed herself to collect the necessary data for her dissertation from the Utah State Historical Society and Utah State Archives (where Everett Cooley was now the director of both institutions) during the 1964 school year. This required fairly frequent and extended trips by automobile or bus to Salt Lake City on the other side of the Colorado Rockies. The Utah Historical Society, where Jan did most of her research, was just over a half mile from the headquarters of the Church of Jesus Christ of Latter-day Saints. While Jan was researching in Salt Lake, she often would bring Stephen with her. If bored, the twelve-year-old Stephen would practice his violin in their hotel room while Jan was gone to research in the archives or take rides by himself on a tourist bus line that motored to various historical sites throughout the Salt Lake Valley. He soon became friendly with the bus driver and would always ride in the seat behind him. Later in the day, he would report his adventures to Jan, and they would discuss them at supper.

Back home in Boulder, Jan sent draft chapters of her dissertation to both Scamehorn and Cooley, but it was Cooley whom Jan credits as being by far her most influential mentor and guide to relevant sources for her dissertation. Cooley was an authority on both Utah and Mormon history, and Jan continued to be impressed by his integrity and scholarly balance. Cooley returned his

---

21. Scamehorn's books include *Mill and Mine: The CF&I in the Twentieth-Century* and *Albert Eugene Reynolds: Colorado's Mining King*.

draft copy of Jan's dissertation chapters with multiple comments and substantive suggestions on virtually every page. (Scamehorn only made occasional grammatical corrections.) Cooley also introduced Jan to important Mormon scholars like Sterling McMurrin and Brigham Madsen,[22] and he encouraged her to present papers based on chapter drafts of her dissertation at the annual meetings of the Utah State Historical Society, where she met Leonard Arrington and George Ellsworth for the first time, as well as younger scholars like Richard Bushman, Tom Alexander, James Allen, and Klaus Hansen. All of these men later become some of Jan's most influential colleagues and were all part of the intellectual vanguard advocating and practicing the New Mormon History, with which Jan later aligned herself.

Cooley also recruited Jan to help edit the Reed Smoot Diaries that his descendants had given to the University of Utah Press for publication. Smoot was an LDS apostle who famously served as Utah's Republican senator to the United States Senate for five terms, from 1903 to 1930. Nationally, Smoot is primarily remembered as the co-sponsor of the infamous 1930 Smoot–Hawley Tariff Act, which raised US import tariffs to record levels and is regarded by many economic historians to have been a significant factor in accelerating the onset of the worldwide Great Depression.[23] At the beginning of his national political career, Smoot's right to occupy his senate seat was contested because of his ecclesiastical position as an apostle in the Mormon hierarchy.[24]

---

22. McMurrin was trained in philosophy and Madsen in history. Both of these scholars had doctoral degrees from the University of California, Berkeley, and both were political liberals who, in contrast to most LDS Church authorities, strongly supported the Civil Rights Movement of the 1950s and 1960s. Jan speculates that McMurrin and Madsen had an outsized influence on sociologist Thomas O'Dea's view of modern Mormonism, expressed in his highly influential book *The Mormons*. She says she eventually concluded that "O'Dea didn't ask hard questions" about what he was learning from a limited sample of informants and was describing a different, overly liberal interpretation of Mormon theology and culture than what she encountered in her own experience with ordinary LDS members (especially later in Indiana and on research and speaking trips to Utah, where she would attend LDS religious meetings and became better acquainted with "Mormons in the pews"). At the same time, Jan was getting acquainted with younger LDS scholars like Tom Alexander and Richard Bushman, who were critically trained professionals, but also devout in their Mormon faith. Consequently, Jan came to the elementary but important realization that there were different *kinds* of Mormon intellectuals, just as there were different kinds of ordinary Mormons.

23. Douglas A. Irwin, *Peddling Protectionism: Smoot–Hawley and the Great Depression*.

24. Concerning the connection of Reed Smoot's political career to the twentieth-century transformation of the LDS Church, see Milton R. Merrill, *Reed Smoot: Apostle in Politics*, and especially Kathleen Flake, *The Politics of American Religious Identity: The Seating of Reed Smoot, Mormon Apostle*.

Through Cooley, Jan's assignment was to comb through the diaries and identify all individuals mentioned therein with Utah connections and compose footnotes about each one. In the process, Jan discovered that Smoot's son had been financially involved in the Teapot Dome scandal that bedeviled the Harding administration in the early 1920s, and, as it happened, at a time when Smoot was a member and lead investigator of the Senate committee charged with investigating the scandal.[25] From his own diary accounts, Jan learned that Smoot went to New York to borrow money from wealthy banking associates in an effort to keep his son out of legal trouble for his involvement in the scandal. Jan consequently informed the university press of what she had learned. The Press's editor was upset and fearful that if these revelations were publicized, the Smoot family wouldn't let the press continue editing the diaries for publication. The project stalled, and the University of Utah Press never published the diaries.[26] Nonetheless, Jan's opportunity to investigate the Smoot diaries enriched both her experience working with primary source materials and her appreciation of the complex dynamics of Mormon history.

Cooley's support and the opportunities he gave Jan were invaluable to her, and she believes she would never have become a scholar of Mormonism without him. His careful standards of research (reminiscent of Tony's assiduous approach to scholarship) and continued mentoring were important professional examples for her to emulate. Years later, Jan was "thrilled to dedicate my Tanner Lecture at the University of Utah to Everett."[27]

After concluding her primary research, Jan speedily wrote her entire dissertation in two to three months, completed in 1965 with the title, "The Mormons in Politics: The First Hundred Years." With her dissertation behind her, Jan was encouraged by Cooley to expand her scholarly range of expertise about Mormonism. At the same time, the University of Utah Press expressed an interest in publishing her dissertation. Jan, however, didn't think it was

---

25. For an arresting account of the backstage financial/political back-scratching that produced the Teapot Dome scandal, see Laton McCartney, *The Teapot Dome Scandal: How Big Oil Bought the Harding White House and Tried to Steal the Country*.

26. Thirty years later, Smoot's diaries were edited and published in Harvard Heath, ed., *In the World: The Diaries of Reed Smoot*.

27. In 2006, the University of Illinois Press published the first twenty years of the Mormon History Association's Tanner Lectures, which had been initiated in 1980 as a forum for eminent non-LDS scholars, like Jan, to prepare presentations in their own specialties that encompassed some aspect of Mormon history. As a contributor to the Illinois Press collection, Jan was responsible for introducing seven of the Tanner Lectures organized under the rubric, "Mormonism Considered from Different Perspectives." See Dean L. May and Reid L. Neilson, eds., *The Mormon History Association's Tanner Lectures: The First Twenty Years*.

good enough. While her graduate work on the Mormons was original, and she personally had learned a great deal about Mormon history from researching and writing her dissertation, she nevertheless felt that her work simply reviewed and consolidated what Mormon scholars already knew.[28] Even though her motivation to further unravel Mormonism's complicated historical and cultural foundations had been strongly reinforced, Jan concluded that her graduate school research had also revealed her relative lack of familiarity with primary source materials on Mormon topics. Tony, who had not proofread any of her writing, concurred with Jan's rigorous assessment that her dissertation wasn't ready for publication and backed her unwillingness to publish. This decision to turn down the opportunity to have her dissertation published as a book astonished most of Jan's graduate student peers, Tony's library colleagues, and her faculty mentors at Colorado.

Besides concern about her limited understanding of Mormon sources, there was another reason Jan did not want to spend the lengthy time and concentrated effort she perceived would be necessary to elevate her study to the high level of scholarly quality she thought was necessary to merit publication. The priority concern for both Jan and Tony at this crowning stage of her educational metamorphosis was for Jan to secure a full-time faculty teaching position at a college or university within manageable proximity to Tony's work and their home in Boulder. This pragmatically reasonable objective would devolve, however, into a frustrating lapse of eight more years of part-time employment, both in and out of academia, before Jan would find an academic home and a renewed pursuit of Mormon Studies that would finally catapult her to scholarly renown.

---

28. As Jan puts it, "Notwithstanding the respectable amount of worthwhile information in my master's thesis and Ph.D. dissertation, I am aware they were written by a historian who was still very much an apprentice. If the things I wrote during graduate school are by no means conspicuous scholarly contributions, they did turn out to be exceptionally useful exercises for me, providing considerable knowledge of the broad sweep of LDS history." Shipps, *Sojourner*, 2.

CHAPTER 4

Engagement with the Mormon Scholarly Community, 1967–1974

In the two years after being awarded a PhD in American history from the University of Colorado, Jan Shipps searched for academic employment in and around the Boulder area, looking as far afield as Denver (situated thirty miles southeast of Boulder). Full-time, tenure-track positions, however, were nowhere to be found, and Jan eventually accepted a position as a part-time instructor teaching history survey courses at the University of Colorado Denver Center.[1] Jan only taught there for just over a year before being derailed by Tony's decision to, once again, advance his own career—this time by accepting an offer from Indiana University (IU) to become librarian for English at the Bloomington campus. At first glance, this may appear to have been, at best, a lateral move for Tony, since he already was the head reference librarian at Colorado. However, the Indiana University Library was one of a handful of libraries in the country at the time that had designated specialty staff positions, requiring specialized credentials (like Tony's PhD in English literature), making it a relatively prestigious promotion. As in the past, it was still Tony's career that mattered most, and Jan again subordinated her own rising aspirations to his.

Academic Frustration in Bloomington, Indiana, 1967–1971

At first Jan was optimistic that she would find better, full-time teaching opportunities in Indiana. It turned out, however, that there were few openings for either high school or college history teachers in the Bloomington area. The IU history department was not looking for any new instructors to teach either American or Western American history, and the fact that Tony had just been hired as the English Librarian raised concerns about nepotism at the university. It would take Jan another six years of searching before she was able

---

1. What was called the Denver Center when Jan taught there had begun in 1912 as the Extension Center of the University of Colorado. In 1973, Colorado lawmakers amended the state constitution to establish additional CU campuses, transforming the University of Colorado Denver Center into the University of Colorado Denver (CU Denver). See UC Denver, "University History."

to discover a permanent academic position with like-minded colleagues and institutional support for her work.²

During her first year in Bloomington, Jan suffered from severe allergies. Having become accustomed to the high mountain altitudes of Logan and Boulder, this initially was a significant problem for her. Allergy tests indicated she was "allergic to just about everything in Bloomington," including the family cat. Upon being told by her physician that her family would need to get rid of the cat, Jan responded that if she "told that to Tony and Stephen, they might decide to let [her] go and keep the cat." Unwilling to find a new home for their beloved pet and needing respite from her other allergies, Jan was given a series of allergy shots for over a year, including one for the cat. Gradually she adapted to Bloomington's summer humidity and miles of surrounding cornfields, and her allergies ceased to be a bother.

The fact that Indiana University boasted of a world-renowned music department, was, as Jan puts it, "a happy coincidence." Anxious for Stephen (who was now fifteen) to continue his violin lessons, she contacted IU music director Josef Gingold and persuaded him to listen to her son perform.³ Gingold was impressed and arranged for Stephen to take violin lessons from his graduate students.⁴ Still unable to find a teaching job, Jan began practicing piano again to accompany Stephen's frequent violin performances.

---

2. Years later, after Jan had built her reputation at Indiana University-Purdue University Indianapolis, she was queried at a luncheon by the dean of the Bloomington Indiana University graduate school as to why she was at IUPUI instead of IU. Previously this dean had, in fact, been the IU history department chair who turned Jan down for a position. With a tone of gratified vindication in her voice, Jan responded using the exact wording he had used when rejecting her job query: "Well, my dear, positions in this department are very competitive." Upon hearing her retort, Jan says the dean's response was to sink his head onto his dinner plate.

3. According to his 1995 *New York Times* obituary, Josef Gingold was a Russian-born violinist who played under Toscanini and George Szell and "later became one of the two or three most influential American violin teachers." From 1943 to 1946, he was concertmaster of the Detroit Symphony and then "capped his orchestral career by serving for 13 years as concertmaster of the Cleveland Orchestra during its glory days under George Szell. While many of his students gained international reputations . . . he was noted less for the manufacture of virtuosos than for the broader values of musicianship he instilled in master classes and the close guidance he gave to chamber and orchestral musicians." See Alex Ross, "Josef Gingold, 85, Violinist And Influential Teacher, Dies."

4. In retrospect, Jan says Gingold didn't see Stephen as a truly great violinist but as a boy who understood how music worked. Gingold himself was a concertmaster for the NBC Orchestra and a great teacher of violin, which is precisely what Stephen

Playing and practicing with Stephen, who Jan says "was surprised by how well I could play," helped preserve Jan's emotional well-being after arriving in Bloomington. She put her scholarly identity on hold and resumed her old identity as a supportive mother and part-time piano player: "I wasn't doing *anything* related to academics."

Jan's sense of loneliness and disconnection from colleagues who shared her intellectual interests in history and religion increased as the months passed by. She and Tony socialized with his library and IU English department colleagues, but Jan found nobody she could talk to who had the slightest interest in her research on the Mormons. In Jan's words,

> I was terrifically unhappy. I had had status in Utah and in the Mormon history world, and I had had status in Colorado where I did my graduate work. But the fact is that there is nothing so horrible in the world as a woman with a PhD going to a Big Ten school as a faculty wife. . . . I was off in my own world and had nobody to talk to about my work.

Tony was concerned that Jan's graduate studies and focus on Mormon history had drawn her into a realm "that was not a part of his, and I think he would have been happy not only for me to not become a part of the Mormon history world, but also the academic world." Gradually, however, it began to dawn on Tony "that I was really not happy."[5]

Consequently, when Jan received an unsolicited notice in the mail that the Mormon History Association (MHA) planned to sponsor a regional conference on the campus of Southern Illinois University in Edwardsville in the spring of 1968, Tony said, "Why don't you go?"[6] Tony's belated realization of Jan's unhappiness and his supportive prompting that she attend the conference was a turning point in their marriage in Bloomington. Without Tony's positive endorsement, Jan says she would not have made the decision to attend.

The 1968 Mormon History Conference in Edwardsville, Illinois

Edwardsville was a two-hundred-mile trip by car from Bloomington, and Jan had neither driven that distance alone before nor did she have a paper to present or invitation to participate on a discussion panel. She nevertheless chose to go and show up unannounced. To her delight, Jan was "welcomed with open arms."[7] Attendees at the conference included notable Mormon scholars Leonard Arrington, Richard Bushman, Alfred Bush, and Klaus Hansen, all of

---

became as an adult. Today, Stephen Shipps is a professor of violin and chair of strings at the University of Michigan School of Music, Theatre & Dance.

5. These quotes are all taken from Jan Shipps, Oral History interview by Maureen Ursenbach Beecher.

6. Shipps, Oral History, 15.

7. Shipps, 16.

whom Jan already had met in Salt Lake City when she was working on her dissertation and when she had presented her research at the Utah State Historical Society. Bushman gave an invited paper at this conference, summarizing the extant scholarship on the Mormons in Illinois and, coincidentally, approvingly citing Jan's master's thesis on Mormon politics in Illinois during the 1840s. At a later session, Klaus Hansen reviewed and criticized Stanley P. Hirshson's nationally published *The Lion of the Lord: A Biography of Brigham Young* for (among other things) claiming that there were no non-Mormons studying Mormon history. "Of course there are," Hansen counterargued, "Thomas O'Dea, Mario De Phillis, and Jan Shipps."[8] Jan recalls the unexpected surge of ego-bolstering gratitude she felt at unexpectedly being singled out by these men for her student contributions to Mormon scholarship and the warm welcome she had received into their closely knit professional circle: "That made me feel like I had some place where I fit in. In Indiana I was in a world where I didn't really have any status, except being Tony's wife and Steve's mother, and here I was at a scholarly conference and somebody mentioned my work."[9]

Surreptitiously, Jan also checked the holdings at the Edwardsville campus library and was pleased to discover that her dissertation had been catalogued as a microfilm entry. However, the catalogue entry also included a note by Mormon historian Stanley Kimball, who was a member of the Edwardsville history faculty. Kimball, in fact, was the MHA member who had proposed that the 1968 meeting be held on the Edwardsville campus, with a conference focus on the history of the Mormons in Illinois. Kimball didn't know Jan and said in his catalogue note that her dissertation was an example of attempted scholarship on Mormon history by a non-Mormon who didn't know anything about her subject. Despite Kimball's dismissive note, Jan took heart from her warm reception at the conference and also by the mere fact that her dissertation had been catalogued in a relatively small college library. (Years later, after she and Kimball had become well-acquainted, Jan says he "repented" of his rash judgment of her incompetence.)

The Kinsey Institute for Sex Research

A year after the conference in Edwardsville and still frustrated by her lack of success in landing a suitable academic position, Jan applied for and accepted a job as the coordinator of a grant from the National Institute of Mental Health (NIMH) awarded to Indiana University's famous Kinsey Institute for

---

8. Shipps, 5. Klaus's presentation was published as Klaus Hansen, "Reflections on *The Lion of the Lord*," 105–11.

9. Shipps, Oral History, 5.

Sex Research.¹⁰ Rather than an academic appointment, it was primarily a clerical and secretarial position. Nonetheless, full-time work at what Jan likes to call "the Sex Institute" made it financially possible for the Shipps to send Stephen to New York for further violin lessons.¹¹

Jan's contract with the Kinsey Institute may have paid her for essentially doing clerical work, but she characteristically began taking personal initiative in helping the principal investigators carry out basic research tasks for which she had no prior training or experience. Those tasks included developing sexual attitude questionnaires, constructing attitude scales, and formulating sampling strategies for drawing valid statistical inferences about sexuality in designated human populations. Jan aided in pretesting survey questionnaires and doing preliminary analysis of the pretest data. After proving her conscientious skill in managing the NIMH grant, Jan was invited to serve as project director for a second Institute project—this time a comprehensive, annotated bibliography of homosexuality in America. This project drew on Jan's already-practiced editing skills while also reinforcing her appreciation for the importance of careful documentation and fact-checking when preparing a comprehensive bibliography of such magnitude.

Thus, though not the teaching position she aspired to attain, Jan's work at the Kinsey Institute demonstrated again her quick-study capabilities and eager aptitude for serendipitous learning. At the Institute, Jan benefitted from practical exposure to the techniques of survey research methodology, attitude measurement scales, and statistical data analysis—research tools that relatively few historians acquire or appreciate in their professional training. In her later writings as a historian and religious studies scholar, Jan would put these

---

10. The Kinsey Institute for Sex Research was established as a nonprofit research institute at Indiana University in 1947 by entomologist Alfred Kinsey. In 2016 it was merged with Indiana University, abolishing the 1947 independent incorporation. Currently known as The Kinsey Institute for Research in Sex, Gender, and Reproduction, the institute's mission is "to advance sexual health and knowledge worldwide. Research, graduate training, information services, and the collection and preservation of library, art, and archival materials are main activities carried out by The Kinsey Institute." Quoted from Judith Allen, *The Kinsey Institute: The First Seventy Years*, 183.

11. As a teen, Stephen attended summers at the Meadowmount School of Music in Elizabethtown, New York. At Meadowmount each student had his or her own cabin. Every morning for four hours in his cabin, Stephen practiced alone and then, for another two or three hours, he practiced chamber music with other students every afternoon prior to the nightly concert. As an adult, Stephen returned to Meadowmount during the summer as a teacher, where his future wife, Terry, was also employed as a school registrar. For a brief history of the Meadowmount School of Music, see Benjamin Pomerance, "Strings of History."

methods to good use in ways that set her work apart from studies that relied exclusively on conventional historiography and chronological narratives.

At the same time, Jan's three years of work at the Kinsey Institute diluted the promising academic development she had achieved as a graduate student specializing in Mormon history. She again felt adrift and "at loose ends" with her professional life. She and Tony both held fast to their traditional marital bonds and committed parenting roles, even though both were self-made intellectuals who together, through dint of personal ambition, had transcended their modest family origins. But in this transformational process their interests had diverged. Tony had virtually no interest in hearing Jan discourse on the Mormons or in learning of the esoteric knowledge she had gained concerning their complicated history and theology. Jan couldn't find a teaching position within commuting distance and was not a permanent part of any collegial circle of scholars with whom she could share her fundamental intellectual interests in history or Mormon Studies. She felt increasingly isolated and dejected that her graduate education in history had gone to waste.

During this time, Klaus Hansen's review of *Lion of the Lord* (with its reference to Jan's student work) was published in *Dialogue: A Journal of Mormon Thought*. Jan recalls, "I was working at the Kinsey Sex Institute as a glorified secretary, with no real status as a scholar, and that review was a lifeline. Actually, both of those incidents [the review mention and Bushman's conference citation of her thesis] were lifelines that helped me remember I was a scholar."[12]

Despite this recognition from established Mormon scholars, Jan's personal identity and status in everyday life had effectively shrunk once more to being wife of Tony Shipps and mother of Stephen Shipps:

> I had an identity crisis to deal with. . . . [T]he whole painful process was made much easier when the matter of whether I was mainly Mrs. Shipps, one-half of a corporate personality known by Tony's name, or just Jan, person in my own right, was settled by my mainly being Stephen's mother. The identities Tony and I had in those years, whatever else they might have been, were engulfed by an identity which was entirely rooted, as they say, in our biological fate. More and more as time went on, we were simply the parents of a gifted young violinist whose picture also appeared regularly on the sports pages of the local newspapers in conjunction with his tennis exploits.[13]

---

12. Shipps, 5.
13. Shipps, "An 'Inside-Outsider" in Zion," 151. Stephen starred on his high school tennis team. In her interview with us, Jan reminisced about a local paper publishing a big story on Stephen's invitation to play at a New Year's Eve concert at Carnegie Hall in New York. The headline read: "Shipps to Play at Carnegie." According to Jan, many of their Bloomington acquaintances thought "to play" meant tennis.

In 1972, five years after she and Tony had moved to Bloomington, Jan was unexpectedly pushed into making a fateful decision about her future. She had spent the better part of a year tediously helping to organize and draft the *Kinsey Institute Annotated Bibliography on Homosexuality*. Feeling that she was entitled to some official recognition for having done a lion's share of the work, she asked the two principal editors of the volume, psychologist Alan Bell and sociologist Martin Weinberg, if they would consent to including—under their credits on the title page as co-editors—the modest acknowledgment: "With the assistance of Jan Shipps." Weinberg's uncharitable and weaselly response was, "*No*; you make those kinds of arrangements *before* you get involved in any project of this nature."[14] Thoroughly disillusioned and irate, Jan drove to Indianapolis to do final checking of sources in the Indiana University medical library, and on the way, she says she "just got angrier and angrier and angrier. I said to myself, 'I'm not going to live with this anymore. I'm going to try again. I've got to get a teaching job.'"[15]

On the spur of the moment, after completing her work in the medical library, Jan determined to visit IU's Indianapolis extension division and talk to whomever she could find there in the history department. The secretary informed her that plans had been finalized by Indiana and Purdue Universities to jointly sponsor the creation of a new urban campus in Indianapolis to be called Indiana University-Purdue University Indianapolis (IUPUI)[16] and that the person who would be the new history department chair, Donald Kinzer, was currently located at the Purdue extension division across town.[17] Jan drove there without an appointment and knocked on Kinzer's door. When Kinzer came to the door and inquired, "What can I do for you?" Jan says she blurted out, "You can give me a job; I'm tired of sex, and I want to get back to history!"[18] Jan's unheralded and unorthodox announcement clearly succeeded in making a favorable impression, because Kinzer decided to hire her on the spot. (It

---

14. Shipps, Oral History, 7.

15. Shipps, 7.

16. IUPUI was established in 1969 through the merger of the Indianapolis extension programs of both Indiana and Purdue universities. According to Jan, faculty wanted the new school to be named *Indianapolis University*, but both Indiana and Purdue presidents refused. By 1972, IUPUI was a rapidly growing urban campus, with an expanding faculty and opportunities for Jan that were not available at IU. Furthermore, it was within reasonable driving distance from Bloomington (a sixty-mile commute). For a history of IUPUI's founding and subsequent development as a major urban university, see Ralph D. Grey, *IUPUI: The Making of an Urban University*.

17. At that time, the Purdue extension office in Indianapolis was located in a building on 38th Street above a Burger King fast food restaurant.

18. Shipps, Oral History, 8.

turned out that Kinzer already knew of who Jan was through his familiarity with Tony's answers to questions about quotations column in the *New York Times*.) Jan walked out of his office with a contractual agreement that, as an adjunct instructor, she would begin teaching night classes at IUPUI. In later years, Kinzer loved to tell the story of how Jan Shipps materialized at his office door to renounce her sex job and plea for a teaching job instead.

In the meantime, Jan had been contacted by well-known Civil War historian Bell I. Wiley, who was a pioneer in the social history of common people.[19] Jan had met Wiley at the University of Colorado when she was a PhD student and he was a visiting professor on sabbatical leave from Emory University. While at Colorado, Wiley and his wife were pleased to encounter Southern compatriots in Tony and Jan. They quickly became good friends and would socialize and share drinks in the evening while their sons, who were the same age, played sports together.[20]

More importantly, during their friendship in Colorado, Jan had impressed Wiley as an able researcher with a bright academic future ahead of her. Now, half a dozen years later, he suddenly and belatedly phoned Jan out of nowhere to say he wanted to get her on the program as a presenter at the 1973 meeting of the Organization of American Historians. Jan was simultaneously thrilled at being asked and jolted into realizing that she needed to quickly renew her professional bona fides as a working historian: "I had to get back to work and start doing some scholarship, so I could write a paper."

Indiana University-Purdue University Indianapolis and the Mormon History Association, 1972–1980

With her foot in the door as a part-time history instructor at IUPUI and a parallel invitation to prepare a paper for the annual meeting of the Organization of American Historians, Jan's reentry into the world of Mormon Studies began to accelerate with locomotive momentum. In the spring of 1972, shortly after she began teaching night classes at IUPUI, Jan again made a last-moment decision to attend the meeting of the Mormon History Association, this time in Independence, Missouri. This was the first MHA

---

19. Bell I. Wiley's books include *The Life of Johnny Reb: The Common Soldier of the Confederacy*; *The Plain People of the Confederacy*; *The Road to Appomattox*; and *Confederate Women: Beyond the Petticoat*.

20. According to Jan, Wiley tried to talk Tony into going back to Georgia to take a library position at Emory University. Had Tony pursued this lead and been hired at Emory, it seems likely Jan would eventually have had a fair shot at being hired too, in the history department. Had this happened, she would likely not have emerged as the prominent Mormon scholar whose remarkable career transformation we are attempting to comprehend in this volume.

conference conducted as an independent organization outside the Mormon cultural region of Utah and the West Coast, and it was organized to facilitate the collegial participation with historians from the Restored Church of Jesus Christ of Latter Day Saints (RLDS). Previous MHA conferences had all been ad hoc meetings or adjunct sessions of the American History and Western History Associations.[21] Not only had Jan begun to research a paper on changing American attitudes toward Mormons over time for the OAH meeting, she also had been contacted by the *Pacific Historical Review* to review a book on former Utah Governor William Spry by Leonard Arrington.[22] These two projects persuaded Jan that, even though she didn't have a prepared paper for the MHA conference, she needed to attend in order to reconnect with the Mormon historical community.

Since Jan's last contact with the Mormon History Association in 1968, several momentous changes had taken place. Perhaps most significantly, in January 1972, the LDS Church Historian's Office had been transformed into the Church History Department and, for the first time in LDS history, an academic historian rather than an ecclesiastical authority was appointed to serve as official Church Historian. The new Church Historian was none other than Leonard Arrington from Utah State University, who in turn had recruited historians Davis Bitton from the University of Utah and James Allen from Brigham Young University to serve as assistant Church historians. Arrington and his new staff of academic historians presumably had an institutional mandate to open up the Church's historical archives and to professionalize the study and writing of LDS Church history.[23]

In addition to transformative changes occurring in the administrative structure of the LDS Church, there also was considerable intellectual ferment

---

21. According to the Mormon History Association website, "MHA was founded in December 1965 at the American Historical Association (AHA) meeting in San Francisco under the leadership of noted historian Leonard J. Arrington. . . . For the first seven years, until 1972, it operated as an affiliate of the AHA. In 1972 it became an independent organization with its own annual conferences and publications. The *Journal of Mormon History*, the official publication of the association, began publication in 1974. The Mormon History Association is an affiliate member of the American Historical Association and a member of the Western History Association." See Mormon History Association, "About Us."

22. The book by William L. Roper and Leonard Arrington was entitled *William Spry: Man of Firmness, Governor of Utah*.

23. For a memoir review of Arrington's tenure as LDS Church Historian, see Davis Bitton, "Ten Years in Camelot: A Personal Memoir," 11–35. Also see Gregory A. Prince, *Leonard Arrington and the Writing of Mormon History*, especially chapter 10. More recently, Arrington's extensive, personal diaries have been edited by Gary James Bergera and published as *Confessions of a Mormon Historian: The Diaries of Leonard J. Arrington*.

taking place in Mormon scholarly associations outside of the formal strictures of Church authority. Founded under the leadership of Leonard Arrington in 1965, the Mormon History Association had operated for seven years as a relatively small affiliate of the American History Association. Animated by a rapidly growing membership, however, the MHA had become organizationally strong enough to separate itself as an independent association capable of sponsoring its own annual conferences and publications. Thus, two years later in 1974, the *Journal of Mormon History* was launched as the organization's official publication. Parallel to the rapid rise of the MHA, a burgeoning interest in Mormon Studies and the "New Mormon History" professional approach to the study of Mormon institutions was evident in the concurrent publication and continuing success of *Dialogue: A Journal of Mormon Thought* inaugurated in 1966, as well as the startup of *Exponent II* in 1974; *The Sunstone Review* in 1975 (which subsequently morphed into *Sunstone* magazine); the formation of the Mormon Social Science Association (originally named the Society for the Sociological Study of Mormon Life) in 1976; and the Sunstone Symposium in 1979.[24]

All of these associations and publications sponsoring the scholarly exchange of ideas on Mormon topics emerged within a few years of each other and were

---

24. "New Mormon History" refers to an approach to the study and presentation of Mormon history that is in line with the professional standards of contemporary, academic historians—an approach that departs from polemical or apologetic concerns, in which writers' explicit goals are to defend and fortify the faith narrative of a particular religious community. Rather than selectively presenting material to either prove (or disprove) Mormonism's ultimate truth claims, the focus of New Mormon History is to present historical events in a more dispassionate way, and to situate Mormon history in the larger context of both American and world history. This more professional approach to understanding the origins and development of the Mormon faith and its religious institutions has not surprisingly been met with resistance by many LDS ecclesiastical authorities who believe the primary responsibility of church historians is to provide faith-promoting accounts of the church and its history. For analysis and discussion of the New Mormon History, see the following sources: Thomas G. Alexander, "Historiography and the New Mormon History: A Historian's Perspective," 25–49; Leonard J. Arrington, Reid L. Neilson, and Ronald W. Walker, *Reflections of a Mormon Historian: Leonard J. Arrington on the New Mormon History*; Robert Flanders, "Some Reflections on the New Mormon History," 34–41; Marvin Hill, "The 'New Mormon History' Reassessed in Light of Recent Books on Joseph Smith and Mormon Origins," 115–27. D. Michael Quinn, *The New Mormon History: Revisionist Essays on the Past*; Roger D. Launius, "The 'New Social History' and the 'New Mormon History:' Some Reflections," 109–27; Jan Shipps, "Richard Lyman Bushman, the Story of Joseph Smith and Mormonism, and the New Mormon History," 498–516.

independent of formal LDS Church control and supported by an expanding intellectual community of lay Mormons as well as trained scholars. Following the politically and culturally challenging decade of the 1960s, this was the stimulating historical and cultural context in which Jan's return to Mormon Studies transpired.[25]

The 1972 MHA Conference in Independence, Missouri

The first person Jan saw when she arrived at the MHA conference hotel in Independence, Missouri, was Leonard Arrington, whose book on Governor Spry she had just negatively reviewed and sent off to the *Pacific Historical Review*. "He came up and kissed me. I felt like Judas," Jan recalls. She decided that she needed to inform Arrington about her review and said, "Leonard, I've got to tell you what I've done. I've written this negative review of the book about William Spry." To Jan's unmitigated relief, the newly minted Church Historian simply brushed aside her worry about her negative review and engaged Jan with warm, human interest as though, for the moment, she was the most important person in the world. "That's alright," Arrington said. "Maybe it deserves it. What are you doing with your life?"[26]

Reassuringly put at ease, Jan basked in the cordial reception she received from the scholarly acquaintances of her graduate student days, as well as numerous other Mormon scholars whom she knew of but had not met previously (e.g., T. Edgar Lyon, Marvin Hill, Gene Campbell, Robert Flanders, Paul Edwards, and Richard Howard). The latter three were all historian-scholars from the Reorganized Church of Jesus Christ of Latter Day Saints (RLDS), now Community of Christ,[27] with Howard being Arrington's functional equivalent in the RLDS Church. While Jan was well aware of the divisions in

---

25. It should also be noted that the political and cultural upheavals of the 1960s contributed to a conservative backlash and retrenchment of LDS Church doctrinal and policy positions in the areas of centralized, male priesthood authority, traditional morality, family gender roles, and sexual identity. See Armand L. Mauss, *The Angel and the Beehive: The Mormon Struggle with Assimilation*.

26. Shipps, Oral History, 9.

27. The Reorganized Church of Jesus Christ of Latter Day Saints was the second-largest Mormon denomination formed after the death of Joseph Smith, centered on the claim that Smith's son, Joseph Smith III, was to succeed his father. In 2001, under the leadership of President Grant M. McMurray, they were renamed Community of Christ, partly to further distinguish themselves form the Salt Lake City-based Church of Jesus Christ of Latter-day Saints. Histories of the Community of Christ can be found in Paul M. Edwards, *Our Legacy of Faith: A Brief History of the Reorganized Church of Jesus Christ of Latter Day Saints*; Richard P. Howard, *The Church Through the Years*; and David Howlett, John Hamer, and Barbara Walden, *Community of Christ: An Illustrated History*.

nineteenth-century Mormonism following the death of Joseph Smith, she had never known personally or worked collegially with any RLDS scholars. For Jan, this was yet another opportunity to embrace rapid integration into the community of all Mormon historians. Within a short time, she was equally trusted and respected by both LDS and RLDS scholars who were making tentative advances to transcend their theological and ecclesiastical differences (many of them retaining the core religious beliefs of their respective Mormon traditions) in order to mutually benefit from one another's research as academic collaborators in the promising developments of the New Mormon History.[28]

In Jan's words,

> There was a kind of high that was going on for the whole Mormon history group as the RLDS and LDS came together. . . . It was like entering into a new world, a world in which I had a place. People began to say to me, "What are you doing? What are you studying?" And it made me feel like people really cared about my work.[29]

Here was what Jan had been desperately seeking for the past half-dozen years: a community of supportive colleagues who shared her seemingly esoteric interests in Mormon history and were genuinely interested in her scholarship and promise as an outside contributor to the complex interpretation of their tradition in the larger context of American history.

At the conference's capstone banquet, Jan managed to make a compelling impression on the gathering with a public display of spontaneous wit and self-deprecating humor that solidified her emerging status as an "inside-outsider" in the Mormon history community. As she put it, "I was sort of a peculiar bird at the Independence meeting, because, as I remember, I was the only woman there who was working as a historian." And when it was time for the banquet,

> The association was small enough in those days that we went around the tables and everybody introduced themselves. Then I realized how much it was a couples' affair, because so many of the scholars had brought their wives. All around the table people would get up and they would introduce themselves: "I'm So-and so," the scholars would say, "I teach at Graceland"—or BYU, etc.— "and here's my wife." It went this way all around the table. When it came to me I said, "I'm Jan Shipps, and I teach at IUPUI, which in Indianapolis people call 'Ooey-pooey' . . . and I have a husband at home."[30]

This gentle gibe provoked a gale of appreciative laughter from her newly accumulating Mormon colleagues.

---

28. For a Community of Christ scholar's perspectives on these ecumenical developments, see William D. Russell, "History of JWHA."
29. Shipps, Oral History, 11.
30. Shipps, 11.

In what was a male-dominated professional association at the time, the facts that Jan was not only a non-Mormon but also a woman were arguably counterintuitive aspects of her professional appeal and ready acceptance into the Mormon History Association.[31] Eventually, of course, what would matter most was Jan's own determined quest for a community of like-minded scholars and the innovative quality of her scholarly work about the Mormon past, regardless of her gender or religious affiliation.

The 1972 WHA Conference in New Haven, Connecticut

Quickly following the MHA conference in Independence that spring was the Western History Association (WHA) meeting in the fall, convened on the campus of Yale University in New Haven, Connecticut. This was not a Mormon conference per se, and again Jan did not have a paper to present. But she was hard at work on her content analysis of American attitudes toward the Mormons over time as revealed in popular, periodical literature and wanted feedback on her analytical categories. In particular, she wanted to do reliability checks of her reading and coding of these materials in comparison to assessments by knowledgeable Mormon readers of the same materials. For this purpose Jan had recruited LDS historian Tom Alexander to analyze and code a sample of periodicals that she had already coded. Alexander was planning on attending the WHA conference at Yale and could meet Jan there to review the comparability of their findings. Since Jan was now employed by IUPUI, she was this time able to obtain funding to cover the costs of her trip.

The Western History Association was a relatively new but reputable professional association with which the MHA affiliated and sponsored sessions on western history related to Mormon topics.[32] At the 1972 WHA meeting at Yale, an unusually large contingent of Mormon scholars showed up, including staff members of the newly formed Church Historical Department, whom Leonard Arrington wanted to be actively engaged in professional meetings. For Jan, it proved to be an important occasion for expanding her own scholarly network. While there, she also reconnected with Lee Scamehorn (her former dissertation advisor) and Emory historian Bell Wiley about the paper she was scheduled to present the following spring at the Organization for American Historians meetings. At the same time, she was able to concretize

---

31. It was not only the Mormon History Association that was dominated by men, but so too were all of the major professional associations at the time that concerned themselves with history, American studies, or religious studies.

32. The Western History Association (WHA) was founded in Santa Fe, New Mexico, in 1961 and began publication of its journal, the *Western Historical Quarterly*, in 1964. Today, the WHA is hosted by the University of Nebraska at Omaha.

her newly acquired sense of belonging and camaraderie within the Mormon History Association.

The MHA-sponsored session featured papers by Richard Bushman, Leonard Arrington, and Mario DePillis (an American religious history professor from the University of Massachusetts who, along with Jan, was the only non-Mormon scholar at the time doing significant research on the Mormons).[33] One of the commentators for the session was Sydney Ahlstrom, whose 1972 book, *A Religious History of the American People*, won the National Book Award in Philosophy and Religion and was in 1979 named the Religious Book of the Decade by *The Christian Century*. The session attracted such a large number of conference attendees that the original presentation room had to be changed for a larger space to accommodate the overflow crowd.

Retrospectively, Jan says, "In some ways, this was the legitimation of Mormon History as a part of Western History." In narrating her perception of the significance of this particular conference for the emerging professional recognition of Mormon history and its practitioners within the field, Jan's self-reflexive language of "we" and "our" in reference to the Mormon history group is highly indicative of her rapid identification with the Mormon scholarly community. Thus, in her account of the conference, she reports:

> Suddenly the Western History Association realized there was a big Mormon contingent.... I remember we had breakfast away from the hotel, and one of the buses became the "Mormon bus." But, in fact, we couldn't all get on the bus, and then the bus filled with Mormons got lost. So we came in late for breakfast. Someone said [to appreciative laughter], "Here come the Mormons, as always, late!" ... Later we began to make our way into the larger world of the WHA and to say, "Hey, we know a lot about Western history, not just Mormon history." My perception was that, somehow or other, we, as Mormon scholars, made our presence known, en masse, at that meeting.[34]

By the time of the Yale conference, the Mormon History Association itself was jelling as an organization that welcomed all scholars of Mormonism into its ranks—whether LDS, RLDS, or non-LDS—and strongly encouraged their collective research efforts. To this end, an informal conference practice had spontaneously emerged of casual late-night meetings in someone's hotel room for further collegial talk and discussion. "Leonard was always the master

---

33. DePillis followed Jan Shipps as the second non-Mormon president of the MHA from 1994 to 1995. Lawrence Foster, another non-Mormon scholar who earned his PhD in history and sociology from the University of Chicago in 1976, also became active in the Mormon History Association, serving on the editorial board of the Journal of Mormon History from 1977 to 1983 and eventually becoming MHA president in 2002.

34. Shipps, Oral History, 14–15.

of ceremonies. We'd all get together, and he would line us up, and then would say, 'Tell me what you're doing,' one by one, and we would go around, and we would report." Jan recalls her inclusion in this informal enclave at the Yale conference along with Mormon academic luminaries she already knew, like Tom Alexander, James Allen, Richard Bushman, Klaus Hansen, and Alfred Bush, as well as others she was meeting for the first time, including Davis Bitton, Michael Quinn, Dean Jesse, and Ron Esplin.

Jan recalls when it was her turn to report:

> I described my study of American attitudes toward the Mormons enough, I suppose, for people to take some realization, "Well, that's Jan Shipps, and this is a woman, and she's doing this scholarship." See, before that there was Juanita Brooks, who everybody loved, and there was Fawn Brodie, who everybody *didn't* love. . . . But anyway, I was the only woman at that time who was describing scholarship.[35]

Jan increasingly felt accepted as part of an inner circle of Mormon male scholars: "I did not have much relationship to women in this group [wives of Mormon historians] for a long time. My first relationships developed with Mormon men, with scholars. They were scholar-to-scholar relationships."[36]

According to Jan, the 1972 WHA meeting crystalized a significant turning point event in her career as a scholar. Under the bold leadership of Leonard Arrington as the new LDS Church Historian, there was an unprecedented number of Mormon scholars in attendance. It was an historical moment for Mormon academicians in which access to LDS Church documents and exciting new research directions were opening up for professionally trained Mormon historians. Moreover, at this meeting Jan perceived the professional divide that had separated LDS historians and historians of the American West, and she began to recognize her own prospects for occupying an important liminal status as an inside-outsider in Mormon Studies. This realization helped set the compass for her rapidly developing academic career.

The 1973 OAH Conference in Chicago, Illinois

"From Satyr to Saint: American Attitudes toward the Mormons, 1860–1960," the paper that Jan presented to the Organization of American Historians in Chicago in the spring of 1973, was based on the first original research she had undertaken since completing her dissertation in 1965. The

---

35. Shipps, 15.

36. Shipps, 15. Along with Juanita Brooks and Fawn Brodie's work, we will later address the question of Jan Shipps' feminist contributions to the study and interpretation of Mormon history. But this is a question that must be understood in the context of Jan's early, strong identification with the predominantly male Mormon history community of that era. At the outset of her academic career, these Mormon men constituted her primary audience as an active scholar.

intent of her new project was to perform an historical analysis of changing American attitudes toward the Mormons over a hundred-year time span, from 1860 to 1960. However, unlike most historical research being done at that time, it was also a study that depended on survey research sampling methods and statistical data analysis.

Jan operationally defined public opinion about the Mormons as news articles, stories, and commentaries on Mormonism, Utah, and polygamy contained in *Poole's Index to Periodical Literature* and the *Readers' Guide to Periodical Literature*. Since there were well over a thousand such articles appearing during the time period Jan had specified for her study, it was pragmatically necessary to develop a strategy for randomly selecting a representative sample. Furthermore, Jan wanted to *measure* the shift in public attitudes over time by differentiating between positive and negative statements published in popular sources in such a way that other researchers could follow her methodology and reach the same essential conclusions that she did.[37] Since measuring attitudes toward the Mormons in Jan's research required making coding decisions as to whether particular statements in her sample of articles reflected relatively positive or negative judgments, she also needed to measure coder reliability by having someone else code a subsample of the same materials and statistically correlate their results with hers. It was for this purpose that she had met Tom Alexander the previous fall at the Yale conference of the Western Historical Society.

Jan's session at the OAH conference was chaired by the University of Chicago's eminent religious studies scholar, Martin Marty. Marty introduced Jan to the large gathering of over three hundred audience members as an adjunct faculty member at the newly instituted Indiana University-Purdue University Indianapolis (IUPUI)—which few in attendance had ever heard of—and consequently added that she also had been a member of the staff at the Kinsey Institute for Sex Research. The latter revelation produced a titillating outburst of laughter. In explaining her esoteric coding methodology to a group of dubious historians, Jan (who was rapidly becoming adept at improvisational interaction with academic audiences) capitalized on the sexual innuendo provided in her introduction by citing a newspaper article from her research—"a marvelous example from the *New York Times* back in the 1890s, at the height of the polygamy thing." Jan then proceeded to illustrate her methodological point by saying,

---

37. A decade later and unaware of Jan's pioneering work, the two of us developed a similar quantitative methodology for measuring the salience of LDS general conference themes over time. See Gordon Shepherd and Gary Shepherd, *A Kingdom Transformed: Themes in the Development of Mormonism*.

The *Times* said, "The Mormons are very industrious." I pointed out that that's a positive reference. "And they have built a beautiful city on the shore of the Great Salt Lake," That's positive too. "But if you put a big roof over it, it would be the biggest whorehouse in the world." That's negative.[38]

More spontaneous laughter erupted.

As Jan describes it,

> I didn't have that kind of hesitation in my voice that says, 'Women ought not to say this.' The people who heard my paper [almost entirely men] laughed a lot . . . and I drew in the audience. . . . That put me in a sort of different area than women who were still having trouble dealing with personal things in scholarly terms. . . . That made a difference in the way people were relating to me."[39]

Most important on this occasion was the fact that Jan was presenting original, innovative work to major scholars in her field who were largely unversed in quantitative methods. On top of this, Jan exemplified her ability to connect with and even "charm" a largely male audience by incorporating in her talk a form of collegial jesting that is a typical element in the formation of male camaraderie. In doing this, Jan was gaining not only the scholarly respect of her peers but also collegial acceptance in a male-dominated profession.

Despite the praise it received, "From Satyr to Saint" was never published in an academic journal. According to Jan, she decided against submitting it for publication after Tony argued it would be a mistake for her first major publication to be based on statistical methodology. Tony shared the negative bias of other academic humanists (and most historians) toward social science's quantitative pretensions and thought it would hinder Jan's efforts to secure an academic career in history. Much later in her career as a distinguished historian, Jan published her paper as a book chapter in *Sojourner in the Promised Land*.[40]

Prior to presenting her paper, Jan had met with Klaus Hansen, who was scheduled to be the commentator at her conference session. Hansen, whom Jan considered by then to be a good friend, had asked for the meeting to clarify his understanding of some of the technical aspects of her methodology prior to delivering his critique. While Jan and Hansen were going over her paper in her hotel room, Jan received a phone call from James Allen, who at the time was both an assistant LDS Church Historian and president of the Mormon History Association. Jan reports:

> He said, "I need to talk to you." I said, "Come on down, Jim, and have a Mormon drink with us. We've got ice water. Klaus is here." And Jim came down, and we sat there, the three of us, and as always it was great fun to talk about Mormon

---

38. Shipps, Oral History, 18.
39. Shipps, 18.
40. Jan Shipps, *Sojourner in the Promised Land: Forty Years among the Mormons*, 51–97.

history. But after a while Jim said, "I have come for a special reason. We want you to be on the MHA council."[41]

Again, Jan's at-ease, joking demeanor with male colleagues and quick assumption of collegial friendship assisted her rapid acceptance by Mormon scholars into the flagship organization of Mormon historians. Only a single year had passed since Jan had reconnected with the Association in Independence, and now, suddenly, she was being invited to join the organization's governing board as its first female (and also first non-Mormon) member. In Jan's words, "[I]t was like being over the rainbow." Not only was she giving an invited paper at the prestigious meeting of the Organization of American Historians, but she was being courted by Mormon scholars to commit herself to continued activity and shared organizational oversight of the rapidly growing, professional scholarship promoted by the MHA leadership. For Jan, Allen's offer "brought everything together," and she enthusiastically accepted the position.[42] As a non-Mormon, Jan had finally secured a scholarly home with people whom she liked and respected in a field of study for which she had developed a consuming intellectual passion—a field of study in which she was being strongly reinforced by the reciprocal respect of her newly acquired academic network of Mormon peers.

Jan's own perceptions of her rapid ascent and acceptance in both the wider field of American history and the much more specialized field of Mormon history are instructive. While she acknowledges that there were very few women historians in either field at the time, she rejects the idea that it was specifically her gender that made her a kind of token member of the male historical fraternity:

> When I gave that paper at the OAH meeting, there were not very many women on professional meeting programs. Affirmative action hadn't really started. . . . I think I was one of two or three women on the whole OAH program. But in that case my being a woman was not as important as being a *quantifier* [referring to her unique contribution of statistical content analysis].

With respect to the Mormon History Association, Jan likewise concluded:

> And my being a woman in Mormon history, I'm convinced, was not as important in the Mormon history world as my being a *non-Mormon*. . . . They were not looking for a woman. They were looking for a non-Mormon.[43]

In Jan's opinion, the MHA leadership at that time had concluded that recruiting a credible non-Mormon scholar for the MHA leadership would help elevate the growing respectability of Mormon Studies as an important

---

41. Shipps, 17.
42. Shipps, 17.
43. Shipps, 17.

but underappreciated field of study in American history. Moreover, Jan concludes, "They needed a non-Mormon who wasn't dangerous"—that is to say, a serious scholar who was not a critic or debunker of the Mormon faith tradition who would upset LDS ecclesiastical authorities and therefore undermine the efforts of MHA leaders to professionalize the study of Mormon history.

While a case can be made for the relative influence of all of these factors—her gender (combined with her ability to cultivate rapport with male colleagues); her relatively novel, quantitative approach to historical analysis; and her non-Mormon status as an objective, outside scholar—the single most important factor in Jan's rapid acceptance by both Mormon and non-Mormon historians was, in fact, the evident quality of her scholarship. Pressed on this point a decade later by Maureen Beecher, Jan responded,

> You don't get ahead because you're a woman. You get ahead because you're a scholar. You do your work and it stands out there representing you. Once it gets past you and out of your hands, it could come from a man or a woman. . . . That has been my whole basis for working in history. It's not because I'm a woman. It's not because I'm a gentile. [Your work is] good or it's not good.[44]

In addition to her pivotal linkage with MHA leaders at the OAH conference, Jan also encountered and impressed non-Mormon scholars, such as Bell Wiley and Martin Marty, who had respectively urged her to attend the conference and introduced her during her session. Wiley subsequently recruited Jan to be on the Advisory Board of *American History Illustrated*, a glossy magazine dedicated to promoting popular appreciation of the American experience through historical essays, stories, paintings, and photography. In this capacity she also became well-acquainted with Brown University's Gordon Wood, a highly regarded historian of Colonial America and the American Revolution.[45] On top of all this sudden attention, Jan also had been approached prior to the OAH conference by representatives of the John Whitmer Historical Association (JWHA)—the RLDS counterpart to the LDS Mormon History Association—to become a member of their organizational council.

Finally, as if to add a confirmatory exclamation point to her coming-out performance at the Chicago OAH meeting, the following Monday Jan got a long distance call on her new office phone at IUPUI: "It was an offer of a job at Case Western Reserve. Not someone saying, 'Would you like to be a candidate?' It was an offer of a job." Someone from Case Western had attended

---

44. Shipps, 59.
45. Gordon S. Wood was awarded the Bancroft Prize in 1970 for *The Creation of the American Republic, 1776–1787*, the Pulitzer Prize in 1993 for *The Radicalism of the American Revolution*, and the National Humanities Medal in 2010.

Jan's session and was impressed enough to urge the history department to make Jan an immediate offer of full-time employment. IUPUI administrators responded by making Jan a speedy, tenure-track counteroffer, which Jan says she was happy to accept:

> Remember I was still teaching just part-time at IUPUI. Since my son [Stephen] had just been appointed to the Cleveland Orchestra, it was conceivable to the people at IUPUI that I might go. So by the end of the week I had a job offer in hand from IUPUI, but it was a job offer that put me half in religious studies and half in history—a joint appointment.[46]

Looking back, Jan acknowledges the subsequent importance of this joint appointment for her career:

> It was very important, because it put me into religious studies and reoriented the way I was doing Mormon history. So it had great significance, I think, even for the [Mormon History] Association, in the sense of bringing the interdisciplinary approach to the Association.[47]

For Jan, 1973 was shaping up as a watershed year: she had presented a well-received paper at the Organization of American Historians, accepted an invitation to join the Mormon History Association council, was invited to be both a member of the John Whitmer History Association council and sit on the advisory board of *American History Illustrated*, and, eight long years after receiving her PhD, she finally had obtained a tenure-track appointment in history and religious studies at newly founded IUPUI. All in all, it was a heady year. But 1973 wasn't over yet, and there was still more to come.

The 1973 JWHA Conference in Nauvoo, Illinois

The John Whitmer History Association had been organized the previous year as an independent, scholarly organization to promote research relevant to the RLDS Church and its history while also seeking to cultivate scholarly connections with the Mormon History Association as part of the New Mormon History movement.[48] Their first annual meeting was planned for September in Nauvoo, Illinois, four months after Jan's appearance at the OAH conference in Chicago, and Jan was invited to deliver one of the keynote addresses.[49] Thus, on the heels of her "Satyr to Saint" paper presentation,

---

46. Shipps, Oral Interview, 19.
47. Shipps, 19.
48. The history of the John Whitmer History Association is summarized in Russell, "History of JWHA."
49. In addition to seeking outlets for her own pursuit of Mormon history scholarship, Jan was simultaneously motivated by her anxious desire to promote the name of IUPUI in general and its nascent religious studies program in particular through association with external scholarly conferences and organizations.

Jan was under the gun to produce yet another substantial piece. Her response for this occasion focused on Joseph Smith: "The Prophet Puzzle: Suggestions Leading toward a More Comprehensive Interpretation of Joseph Smith." Jan subsequently submitted her paper to MHA's new *Journal of Mormon History*, and it was published as the lead article the following year.[50]

After giving her keynote address, Jan met with several of her colleagues in the MHA council (made up of both LDS and RLDS scholars) to plan their next conference, which was to be held in Nauvoo, Illinois. Even though she was just resuming her Mormon connections and was a virtual neophyte to the leadership structure of the Association, Jan felt she had already bonded with both LDS and RLDS colleagues, who shared her passionate interest in the Mormon past. Thus, instead of demurely yielding to other planning committee members' ideas for the conference, Jan confidently asserted herself:

> We were sitting there talking about what we wanted to do, and I made a suggestion. We would be in Nauvoo, and we were going to the different sites and have papers at different sites. . . . I said, "It doesn't make sense for us not to have a paper at the temple site. We must invite Marvin Hill to give a paper on religion in Nauvoo." I will tell you there was dead silence. Then there was a kind of sputtering, and Mark McKiernan [an RLDS historian who oversaw the restoration of RLDS historic sites in Nauvoo], who was on the committee, said, "I'm not sure that's a good idea."[51]

Jan, of course, knew that both the LDS and RLDS churches managed separate historic sites in Nauvoo that were central to both denominations' history, but at the time she did not know how deeply divided they were over the historical and theological meanings of the Nauvoo Temple. Although construction on the temple had begun in 1841 in conformity to Joseph Smith's directions, it was not completed for worship purposes until 1846 (approximately two years

---

50. Jan Shipps, "The Prophet Puzzle: Suggestions Leading Toward a More Comprehensive Interpretation of Joseph Smith," 3–20. In 2006, Mormon historian Michael Quinn published an essay entitled "Biographers and the Mormon Prophet Puzzle," which he begins by quoting Jan's article and crediting her, "[a]s a non-LDS scholar," for lamenting "'the schizophrenic state of Mormon history, with its double interpretative strand of Joseph Smith as a man of God and Joseph Smith as a kind of fraud who exploited his followers for his own purposes.'" Quinn considers Shipps's critique to set the proper parameters of a scholarly analysis of Smith's life and prophetic career as Mormonism's founder (which, in his opinion, has never been fully realized by contemporary biographers of Joseph Smith). Quinn writes of Shipps: "She challenged her listeners and future readers to research and write biographies that 'might allow us to reconcile enough of the inconsistency to reveal, not a split personality, but a splendid, gifted—pressured, sometimes opportunistic, often troubled—yet, for all of that, a larger than life whole man.'" See D. Michael Quinn, "Biographers and the Mormon 'Prophet Puzzle,'" 226–45.

51. Shipps, Oral History, 20.

after Smith's assassination) under Brigham Young's leadership. In 1848 the temple was partially destroyed by an arsonist's fire, and two years later it was totally demolished by a tornado.[52] For those in the Salt Lake City-based LDS Church, the Nauvoo Temple was designed by Joseph Smith as a sacred structure for the performance of religious ordinances intrinsically connected to the realization of humankind's salvation and eternal life. For them, temple worship and its associated saving rites represent the apogee of Smith's prophetic theology. For their RLDS cousins of the Community of Christ, however, LDS temple theology and its accompanying ritual ordinances represent later aspects of Smith's developing theology that they previously denied and do not accept—particularly the practice of plural marriage, which became a major source of conflict in Nauvoo that ultimately led to Smith's death.[53]

According to Jan,

> McKiernan took the role of protecting the RLDS, and I was so dumb that I didn't understand that the RLDS did not accept the temple. I knew about polygamy, but I did not know about the temple ordinances. . . . Well, we left the meeting with a distinct coolness between Mark McKiernan and me. . . . My suggestion was based on a Protestant desire to figure out how to separate out the religion from the rest of the culture in Nauvoo. Anyway, after Mark McKiernan and I corresponded, and after we had a cup of coffee together [the Community of Christ does not strictly proscribe coffee the way the LDS Church does] at Fort Worth at the Western History Association meeting and talked at great length, we made up in a way, and we scheduled [Hill's paper] at the temple site.[54]

Meeting Mark Hoffman

A year earlier, Jan made contact for the first time with the Mormon community in Bloomington, Indiana. While she always thought it was important for religious studies scholars to observe how ordinary members of a religious community actually practice their religion, until then she had been too preoc-

---

52. In conjunction with separate LDS and RLDS Nauvoo restoration projects in the twentieth-century, the temple site subsequently became an iconic tourist attraction. Holding legal title to the temple site property, the LDS Church rebuilt and rededicated the Nauvoo Temple for regular use in 2002.

53. The conflation of LDS temple or celestial marriage with Mormon polygamy was ended by official declarations in 1890 and 1904, which repudiated church sanction of plural marriage, leading to the church's contemporary embrace of the sanctity of monogamous marriage between a man and a woman. See Kathleen Flake, *The Politics of American Religious Identity: The Seating of Reed Smoot, Mormon Apostle*; D. Michael Quinn, "LDS Church Authority and New Plural Marriages, 1890–1904," 9–105; George D. Smith, *Nauvoo Polygamy: But We Called It Celestial Marriage*; and Richard S. Van Wagoner, *Mormon Polygamy: A History*.

54. Shipps, Oral History, 20.

cupied looking for work to take initiative in connecting with local Mormons the way she had in Logan. Serendipitously, however, one of Stephen's music major friends at IU was Mormon, and Jan was invited through him to an LDS open house in Bloomington. There she encountered Doug Alder, whom she previously had met in Logan. Alder taught history at Utah State, but at the time was taking a sabbatical leave and participating in an IU program designed to groom academic administrators. In addition to his academic credentials, Alder was a devout Latter-day Saint and had previously been a bishop of his ward. "Jan Shipps, what are you doing here?" the surprised Alder exclaimed when Jan materialized at the open house (an indication of how disconnected Jan had been from the local LDS community in Bloomington up to that time). Alder invited Jan to speak at a local LDS church gathering and, subsequently, Jan became a frequent guest and speaker at Mormon-sponsored meetings and events in the Bloomington Area.[55] In the meantime, Alder and Jan quickly became close friends, united by their shared interest in Mormon history and undergraduate teaching. As Jan puts it, "I was looking for somebody to talk to . . . and we started talking. We talked that whole year, constantly. . . . It was the first time I'd had anybody who knew about Mormon history close by."

When Alder finished his IU sabbatical, he invited Jan to be a guest speaker at Utah State University in Logan, Utah, giving Jan a chance to return to her undergraduate alma mater for the first time in over a decade. During her 1974 visit, Jan spoke about her JWHA address, "The Prophet Puzzle," in which she identifies a number of Smith's actions and concludes that depending on a person's perspective, "you've got two Joseph Smiths here—prophet and fraud—both of whom can be plausibly inferred from historical evidence." According to Jan, Mark Hoffman, an undergraduate student in one of Alder's classes, was sitting in the back of the room. He found Jan's thesis intriguing and stayed after class to ask her questions about Smith's early history as a

---

55. During the year that Alder resided in Bloomington, local Mormons held regular afternoon discussion meetings with interested IU faculty and staff. Alder invited Jan to speak at one of these gatherings. One attendee was the chairman of the Department of Astronomy, who also happened to be Mormon and in fact was the president of the LDS Bloomington Stake. He apparently already knew something of Jan's early scholarly work on Mormonism but thought the name Jan Shipps must be a pseudonym (perhaps because of the then-rarity of women scholars of Mormonism). Subsequently, the Bloomington LDS ward has invited Jan to speak at religious services numerous times. Currently, Jan's main local Mormon connection is Martha Taysom, PhD in American Intellectual History, earned from Indiana University, who, from 2009–2016, served as editor of the *Journal of Mormon History*. Over the years, Jan has donated surplus Mormon materials (books, journals, etc.) to the Bloomington LDS Institute of Religion.

treasure digger in upstate New York: "Could he have done X, or Y, or Z?" Jan affirmatively answered Hoffman's specific queries concerning Smith's plausibly twofold motives and actions. In retrospect, Jan worries that her talk and after-class discussion may have reinforced or even provided Hoffman with ideas on what to include when he began to forge historical documents concerning early Mormonism—forgeries that would later result in Hoffman using explosives to kill two individuals in a failed attempt to avoid being caught.[56]

The 1974 MHA Conference in Nauvoo, Illinois

Prior to Jan's visit at Utah State, however, she and Alder arranged with Klaus Hansen and Alfred Bush to meet in Indianapolis and then make the eight-hour drive together to the May 1974 MHA conference in Nauvoo. Along the way the four engaged in an uninterrupted talk-a-thon about Mormon theological topics and historical controversies. Unorthodox as this free-flowing exchange in a cramped car may have been, it was precisely the sort of intellectual engagement that Jan had longed for and thrived on. Upon arriving in Nauvoo, Jan and Alder also hooked up with Paul Edwards, an RLDS intellectual and scholar who was one of the principal founders of the John Whitmer History Association. Jan already knew and admired Edwards from meeting previously with JWHA scholars.[57] According to Jan, "Doug and Paul and I just sort of coalesced as friends." The religious-intellectual symmetry of their friendship was emblematic of both the efforts by LDS and RLDS historians of that time to forge scholarly ties, despite their religious differences, and of Jan's emerging status as an outsider who could bridge the cultural divide between them.

LDS and RLDS efforts at rapprochement among their academic historians were tested and strained at the Nauvoo conference, and the value of Jan's emerging role as mediator was made even more evident. Her program

---

56. Carefully documented sources on Hoffman's nefarious history as a document forger and murderer in the 1980s can be found in Linda Sillitoe and Alan Dale Roberts, *Salamander: The Story of the Mormon Forgery Murders*, and Richard E. Turley, *Victims: The LDS Church and the Mark Hoffman Case*.

57. In her 1982 *Dialogue* article Jan reports, "When I first met Paul Edwards I was intimidated. His lineage, his bearing, and his skill in argumentation—deriving in part from his training as a philosopher—made conversation with him a real challenge. Our mutual interest in the history of Mormonism and the phenomenology of religion drew us together." See Shipps, "Inside-Outsider," 157. To a significantly greater degree than most historians associated with MHA, Edwards had a critical, theoretical bend regarding religious phenomena, and in their conversations, Jan was forced to think more conceptually and analytically about the origins of Mormonism and the foundations of its appeal to religious seekers. This was the kind of thinking that helped prepare the way for Jan's later thesis of Mormonism's emergence as a new religious tradition.

committee proposal of including a talk by an LDS scholar at the site of the Nauvoo Temple on the subject of religious worship in Nauvoo (and not just keeping a focus on economics, politics, and cultural developments) had first raised hackles. As it turned out, Marvin Hill's paper on the subject was well-received and unoffending to the RLDS contingent. Hill didn't include any mention of temple ordinances in his talk, but, according to Jan, he did finish his talk by saying, "You can't do what Jan wanted me to do" (i.e., separate religion from culture in nineteenth-century Mormonism).

However, the concluding, after-dinner talk by Reed Durham (who was then President of MHA and director of the LDS Institute of Religion in Salt Lake City) caused a provocative sensation that was dramatically enhanced by crashing thunder claps from a storm raging outside as his speech unfolded. Durham detailed the links between Nauvoo Mormonism and Masonry and ended by presenting physical evidence that the original weathervane atop the temple had been a Masonic symbol rather than the Angel Moroni (who, in Joseph Smith's personal narrative, revealed to him the golden plates from which the Book of Mormon was translated).[58] The close connection between the formulation of nineteenth-century LDS temple ordinances and Masonic rites is well-documented in current scholarship, but it was a disputed topic at the time of this Nauvoo conference, raising the contentious issue of the temple's religious purpose for RLDS adherents and casting doubt for LDS Mormons on the divine provenance of the temple ritual.[59] Under pressure from his ecclesiastical leaders in Salt Lake for his controversial presentation, Durham later issued an apologetic letter of clarification and withdrew from future participation in the Mormon History Association.[60]

---

58. Traditional Mormon ecclesiology has always portrayed the Nauvoo Temple with the Angel Moroni (initially in a recumbent position) atop its clock tower as a template for the spires of other LDS temples being constructed worldwide. Rebuilt by the LDS Church in 2002, the Nauvoo Temple today features a standing, gold leaf Angel Moroni with uplifted trumpet, heralding the "restored gospel" as Mormonism's most prominent symbol to the modern world.

59. For a comprehensive review and analysis of the literature on the historical relationship between Mormonism and masonry, see Michael W. Homer, *Joseph's Temples: The Dynamic Relationship Between Freemasonry and Mormonism*, and Joe Steve Swick III and Cheryl L. Bruno, *Method Infinite: Freemasonry and the Mormon Restoration*.

60. Summary references to the 1974 MHA conference in Nauvoo and the fallout from Durham's presidential address on Mormonism and masonry can be found in Davis Bitton, "Taking Stock: The Mormon History Association after Twenty-Five Years," 1–27, and Clara V. Dobay, "Intellect and Faith: The Controversy Over Revisionist Mormon History," 103–16.

According to Jan, the traditional, hotel-room meeting for informal reflection and discussion that night was dominated by "reverberations" of Durham's talk: "It was not light, and it was not airy, and there was not a lot of joking. It was heavy."[61] Leonard Arrington was furious about the incident, which heightened suspicion toward intellectuals and the association among LDS Church authorities. Jan, in fact, believes the episode energized a movement among senior LDS apostles to have Arrington ultimately removed as Church Historian in 1982 and "banished" to Brigham Young University in Provo, Utah, to direct the school's Joseph Fielding Smith Institute for Church History.[62]

Early the next morning after Durham's talk on Masonry and the Nauvoo Temple, Jan, Doug Alder, and Paul Edwards—her two close friends representing both the LDS and RLDS traditions—walked the streets of old Nauvoo, reflecting on the uneasy relationship between the two denominational factions and on Jan's sympathetic role as an outsider who felt comfortable in both camps. As a non-Mormon intellectual, Jan was both fascinated by and acutely curious about the theological and cultural divisions that historically had separated the Mormon community. Unlike adherents of these contending traditions, she had no personal stake in defending the ultimate legitimacy of either's claims. She simply wanted to understand them, without passing judgment, in order to convey an impartial interpretation of their interrelated narratives to serious students of American religious history. Once Jan became actively involved in planning and participating in MHA conferences, the

---

61. Shipps, Oral History, 23.

62. As recounted by both Bitton ("Ten Years in Camelot," 11–35) and Prince (*Leonard Arrington*, ch. 10), the decade-long experiment of replacing ecclesiastical authorities with professional historians to administer the Church history department ended in 1982, when Arrington was superseded by an LDS ecclesiastical official, G. Homer Durham. Conservative critics of the professionalization of Mormon history had become increasingly suspicious that their religion's faith-based narrative was in danger of being compromised by the work of professional historians. Arrington and other academic historians on his staff were reassigned to the Joseph Fielding Smith Institute of Church History on the campus of Brigham Young University in Provo, Utah. Arrington's picture subsequently was removed from the portrait gallery of Church Historians on the grounds that one must be a LDS general authority to be so honored. On a personal note, while on sabbatical leave in 1986, one of us (Gordon) was waiting in line to go through a security check in order to gain admission to the Church library. There ahead of him in line was Leonard Arrington, former Church Historian, patiently displaying his driver's license to the scrutiny of a security guard in order to verify his identity for clearance to use the library. For Arrington's own take on his release as Church Historian, see his autobiography *Adventures of a Church Historian* and his personal diaries edited by Gary Bergera under the title *Confessions of a Mormon Historian: The Diaries of Leonard J. Arrington*.

practice of gathering informally after the banquet for further conversation soon shifted to her hotel room as a kind of neutral ground, where both LDS and RLDS scholars felt free to meet and discuss topics of mutual interest.

As Jan became active in both the Mormon History Association and the John Whitmer Historical Association, she rapidly developed close friendships with different sets of Mormon scholars. Within their professional circles, all of these individuals were familiar colleagues to one another. But it was Jan Shipps, a woman and non-Mormon, who quickly became a key person in numerous overlapping yet distinctive friendship groups, consisting primarily of men. Informally, for example, Jan divided her closest connections with leading LDS and RLDS scholars in several ways. Thus, she always went out to dinner after conference sessions with Klaus Hansen and Alfred Bush. But at conference banquets, she made a point of sitting with James Allen and Tom Alexander, who were typically accompanied by their wives. When it came to after-session conversations about theological issues and LDS/RLDS difference, Jan routinely sought out Paul Edwards and Doug Alder. Through her frequent religious discussions with Edwards, Jan also became good friends with RLDS historians Robert Flanders and William Russel, along with other prominent RLDS scholars, whose work was well-regarded in larger academic circles. If one were to do a formal network analysis, one would see that the relative strength of Jan's ego-networks within both historical associations made her an especially important catalyst in the world of Mormon historical scholarship.[63] By associating with a wide range of different people in different intimate groupings, Jan was able to obtain more nuanced insights about Mormonism from a variety of scholars, while also becoming an important go-between person in the overlapping networks among LDS and RLDS historians of that period.

The label "inside-outsider," which Jan attached to herself, also helped her non-Mormon colleagues—especially at IUPUI—understand the way she defined herself as a scholar of Mormon history. In her 1982 autobiographical article for *Dialogue*, Jan further reflected on this unique role she was able to take on at the time:

> [B]ecoming an "inside-outsider" in a world belonging to another people is something more than a limited fieldwork exercise with a beginning and an end or a clearly defined project using participant observation techniques. Those research methods allow for investigators to remain detached from the objects of their investigations. An "inside-outsider" surrenders that detachment, giving up the emotional as well as professional safety of the so-called "objective approach"

---

63. Mapping ego-networks in social network analysis is a valuable tool for assessing the relative influence of different individuals who interact in overlapping primary and secondary groups. See Stanley Wasserman and Katherine Faust, *Social Network Analysis: Methods and Applications*.

in exchange for the ambiguity and uncertainty that comes with being "in but not of" a strange universe. . . . [T]his is risky business because it can lead to disorientation and almost surely to misunderstanding. The insiders who allow an outsider to enter also take risks since "inside-outsiders" occupy a platform from which to speak that can hardly be gainsaid.[64]

---

64. Shipps, "Inside-Outsider," 153.

CHAPTER 5

Becoming a Renowned Mormon Studies Scholar, 1974–1985

Settling in at IUPUI, 1974-1984

Indiana University-Purdue University Indianapolis was a relatively new public research university when Jan was hired as a tenure track faculty member. The IUPUI School of Liberal Arts included the department of history and a new religious studies program that had just come into existence. Jan was intrigued by IUPUI's offer to teach religious studies, but says she negotiated the joint appointment with history because she wasn't confident at first that the new religious studies program would survive. As it turned out, the department's religious studies faculty members at the time were far more productive research scholars than were the history faculty. In any case, Jan wanted to keep her foot in history and didn't want to relinquish "my historiography course, which I loved"; she also wanted to be able to teach the American Civil War class. While these wishes were granted, the college dean, Joseph Taylor (a former academic sociologist) had other plans for Jan. He strongly supported the development of a religious studies program and told her he wanted a person on the faculty who "was interested in the impact of religious ideas and beliefs on individual behavior and social action" (*a la* Max Weber), in contrast to the "deconstructionist" approach that was rapidly gaining currency in religious studies—an approach that, like academic Marxism, tends to be dismissive of the independent influence of ideas on the course of history.[1] In short, Taylor wanted someone like Jan who understood the underlying human element of religious beliefs and would not discount the importance of understanding the impact of religion in peoples' everyday lives.

In retrospect, Jan says that Taylor's adamancy about channeling her into religious studies was a crucial factor in later shaping her conceptually more developed approach to the study and theoretical interpretation of Mormon history. Traditional historiography is rooted in an "ideographic" philosophy that emphasizes the unique details of particular historical actors, events, and movements that make them qualitatively distinctive. Thus, for example, to

---

1. Max Weber was a German scholar famous for writing *The Protestant Ethic and the Spirit of Capitalism* as a counterargument to Karl Marx's economic determinism approach to the understanding of human history.

truly understand Mormon history from an ideographic view, one must study in exquisite detail the particular facts and experiences of the Mormons themselves, which distinguish their movement and religious culture from other religions. In contrast, religious studies as a field is more open to a "nomothetic" philosophy of human life, an orientation that provides the grounding for most disciplines in the social sciences. This approach strives more for universalistic rather than particularistic understandings of human societies and their basic institutions. Nomothetic analysis is necessarily comparative and requires many cases for study in order to see underlying social patterns and statistical regularities as the basis for making theoretical generalizations. Thus, for example, to study only the details of Mormon life and history apart from the parallel histories of other religious traditions precludes our capacity to identify significant commonalities that, if properly synthesized, can deeply enrich our explanation of Mormonism as a particular historical case.

In short, ideographic studies aim for particularistic accuracy in narrating the facts of a distinctive case. Nomothetic studies aim for theoretical generalizability in explaining the shared patterns in numerous cases. Both are important approaches to the overlapping subject matters of the humanities and social sciences. Jan was already schooled in the ideographic approach emphasized in her graduate training at the University of Colorado. Though exposed to the nomothetic approach to research by her stint at the Kinsey Institute for Sex Research, her agreement to devote herself half-time to religious studies at IUPUI meant she would need to pursue another self-directed, crash-study course in the theoretical literature of the field.

At the outset Jan was worried that she didn't have an adequate background for teaching religious studies, but Taylor correctly ascertained that she was good at connecting with students and reassured her that she would excel in the classroom. In her first year of teaching, Jan says she "was desperate to do well" and barely stayed a chapter ahead of her students while simultaneously familiarizing herself with classic works in the sociology of religion, such as Emil Durkheim's *The Elementary Forms of the Religious Life* and Max Weber's *The Protestant Ethic and the Spirit of Capitalism*, as well as more contemporary works like Peter Berger's *The Sacred Canopy: Elements of a Sociological Theory of Religion*.

The daughter of an Alabama public school teacher, Jan—from her first experience as a substitute fourth-grade teacher when she was sixteen—always loved teaching. It is unsurprising, then, that Jan was not the type of professor at a research university whose teaching took a distant second to the academic imperatives of research and publication. To the contrary, she was deeply committed to excellence in the classroom and viewed conscientious teaching as a way to stay critically current with the relevant literature in one's academic fields of research.

Jan's approach to teaching college students was somewhat reminiscent of the way she had encouraged wayward adolescent girls to read in Detroit, where she read classic fiction to them and discussed it after dinner every night. In typical seminar style (even when teaching larger, undergraduate courses), Jan's teaching approach at IUPUI emphasized the reading of original texts, writing, and class discussion. She would give students the same reading source, require them to write a critical essay about the source, then compare and discuss in class the different ways in which students applied and interpreted the same source. Under Jan's scrutiny of their work, students learned the importance of reading a text carefully. The larger lesson, however, was not simply to ascertain the correct answer; it was to see how the same set of facts may be viewed differently by different readers and, in particular, the importance of making a plausible case for the interpretative validity of one's own interpretation. The satisfaction Jan got from her teaching was intrinsically important, and students reciprocated by flocking to her classes and nominating her for multiple teaching awards over the years. Even more important for her scholarly work, Jan says that lively student discussions concerning the nature of religion and religious experience in her classes invigorated and reinforced her own conceptual thinking about religious history in general and the peculiar history of the Mormons in particular.

Religious Studies Colleagues and Jan's Maturing Scholarship

Today Jan says she is "very pleased" to have been hired and able to build her career at IUPUI rather than at Indiana University. Starting at an aspiring new university that was in the process of creating new programs and departments was exciting and enabled her to be an integral part of these kinds of forward moving developments, which, in turn, created professional opportunities that she doubts would ever have materialized for her at an older and comfortably established university.

The religious studies program that Jan feared might not survive was soon a department chaired by Rowland Anthony Sherrill, who had a prestigious background in religion and English literature as a graduate student from the University of Chicago.[2] As Jan reimmersed herself in Mormon history scholarship, she credits Sherrill with insightful critiques of her work that stimulated greater commitment to incisive writing and historical analysis on her part. In addition to Sherrill, Jan benefitted from discussions with Theodore "Ted" Mullen, a colleague whose specialty area of interest was Biblical studies, par-

---

2. Rowland A. Sherrill is the author of *The Prophetic Melville Experience: Experience, Transcendence, and Tragedy* and *Religion and the Life of the Nation: American Recoveries*. In recognition of Sherrill's standing as the founding chair of religious studies, IUPUI sponsors the annual Rowland A. Sherrill Prize in Religious Studies.

ticularly the Old Testament. Mullen became a major influence on her thinking about early Mormonism as a new religious tradition in Protestant America in ways that were analogous to the emergence of Christianity from its Hebraic roots as a new religious tradition in the Roman Empire. This, in fact, became the basic premise of *Mormonism: The Story of a New Religious Tradition*, published a decade later on the amalgamated theological foundations of early Mormonism that set it apart from numerous other thriving religious sects in the pluralistic religious economy of nineteenth-century America.

In addition to her departmental colleague's influences on Jan's thinking at the time, her reactivation as a practicing Methodist in the early 1980s contributed serendipitously to her emerging interpretation of Mormon origins and its developmental history. The Reverend Ross Marrs, pastor of the Bloomington First United Methodist Church, strongly supplemented Mullen's influence on Jan's thinking about parallels between the development of nineteenth-century Mormonism and first-century Christianity. According to Jan, Marrs "was a real scholar" who got her interested in Biblical studies, especially the Old Testament. Jan took copious notes on Marrs's sermons and engaged him in extensive conversations about Judaism and the emergence of primitive Christianity. These converging conversations with Marrs and Mullen decisively informed Jan's study of early Mormonism.[3]

In contrast to the IUPUI history faculty, all of Jan's religious studies colleagues were actively engaged in scholarship. Under Sherrill's leadership and with the dean's full support, the religious studies department strongly emphasized the importance of maintaining faculty research credentials and was becoming the most well-published department in the college. As a junior female faculty member, Jan was tensely anxious to make the grade. She felt especially pressured to demonstrate she could "hold her own with the boys," a competitive attitude she had long since cultivated as a public-school student in Hueytown, Alabama, as an undergraduate student at Utah State University, and as a graduate student at the University of Colorado. To earn tenure at IUPUI, Jan knew she would have to develop an explicit research agenda and was now committed to doing so in Mormon Studies—at the time, a nebulous subfield of American religious studies and Western Americana. Serious work in this area would require frequent professional trips to Utah for access to

---

3. We should also mention that Tony began attending the Methodist Church with Jan at this time, but not at first as a religious believer. Rather, he became interested in the Bible as a literary document with which he thought educated people should be familiar. Jan says Tony had religious feelings but was not a church-goer during most of their marriage, and that religion was never a personal issue between them. Tony eventually joined the Bloomington United Methodist Church in 1999 to coincide with his and Jan's fiftieth wedding anniversary.

primary source materials. Consequently, Tony, in his sardonically self-deprecating manner, commenced calling himself a "latchkey husband" in reference to Jan's many conference trips and research travels.[4]

The IUPUI religious studies department conducted monthly seminars where faculty members took turns presenting papers they were preparing for submission as articles to scholarly journals, followed by critical discussion and then dinner. As with the informal hotel room gatherings presided over by Leonard Arrington at early MHA meetings, this departmental practice served to reinforce group commitment to staying current in research and also cultivated a sense of collegial solidarity. While Tony seldom if ever attended social events surrounding Mormon history conferences, he frequently accompanied Jan to socialize at her department gatherings in Indianapolis. It turned out that Tony enjoyed doing this with IUPUI religious studies faculty—who Jan says "adopted" him—more than he did with his own colleagues in Bloomington. Tony's subtle, ironic sense of humor and witty wordplay made him well-liked by Jan's colleagues, especially Sherril, who was also a Southerner by birth. Jan, as always, took vicarious pride in Tony's professional standing within the intellectual circles in which they circulated as an academic couple.

In contrast to the religious studies faculty, Jan was virtually the only person among her colleagues in the history department who actively engaged in doing research for publication.[5] Consequently, she became a mentor to younger history faculty members (mainly males again) seeking to publish their work, earning respect from her history colleagues as a productive scholar. Among her erudite religious studies colleagues, however, Jan says her research in Mormon Studies was not at first accorded genuine respect: they "treated my work politely, but they didn't consider Mormonism to be a serious academic topic until the publication of my book."

Turning Points in Jan's Marital and Parenting Roles

As a member of the Mormon History Association program committee, Jan met with other committee members in Chicago to help plan an adjunct Mormon session for the 1974 American History Association meeting in

---

4. Jan Shipps, *Sojourner in the Promised Land: Forty Years Among the Mormons*, 374.
5. Ralph D. Gray, who was not employed by Taylor for the new religious studies program, was a historian with specialty interests in Indiana history and the history of the automobile. Ironically, it was the new religious studies faculty, spearheaded by Jan, that generated an outpouring of published scholarly work. The history department faculty (except for Gray, as noted elsewhere) did not have a strong publication record. Later in Jan's tenure at IUPUI, Gray compiled and edited a book of readings on Indiana history entitled *Indiana History: A Book of Readings* and *IUPUI: The Making of an Urban University*.

Denver. Afterward, Jan and her program committee colleagues turned to discussing plans for the annual MHA conference to be held the next spring in Provo, Utah. In conjunction with the program committee's deliberations in Chicago, Jan recalls,

> There was a kind of turning point in my own life. . . . I had been to Chicago when I worked at the Sex Institute. We had a number of meetings that required me to go to Chicago. There were two men [Alan Bell and Martin Weinberg] that were the co-directors of a project that was going forward at the Sex Institute [an annotated bibliography of homosexuality in America]. We would always go to the airport, fly up, and, when we got back to the airport, the first place they would head for was the bar. And I always felt sort of strange. I was flying with these people and talking about sex research while we were sitting in airport lounges.

In contrast to this, Jan goes on to describe her 1974 experience in Chicago:

> I went back to the airport with Jim Allen and Doug Alder [both members of the MHA program committee]; we went into the cafeteria, we got orange juice, and I thought to myself, "Oh, how healthy this is. I am in a different ballgame, and I am so happy." It was such a funny kind of feeling that I had found where I wanted to be.[6]

From these reflections we may plausibly infer the appeal that Mormonism's wholesome cultural norms had for Jan's Methodist sensibilities, quite apart from the historically interesting ecclesiology and theological peculiarities of the Mormon religion.

Both happy with and challenged by her joint appointment in history and religious studies at IUPUI—and at home among Mormonism's most prominent scholars—Jan felt confidently ensconced in a new status set that offered her the professional credentials she had craved. According to Robert K. Merton, a status set consists of the total number of positions a person occupies in the structure of a social system, defining one's standing, rights, and responsibilities relative to other people. Attached to each status an individual occupies is an array of role expectations—what Merton calls a "role set"—in relationship to other people, which is subject to varying degrees of negotiation. Acquiring new statuses and negotiating corresponding role expectations is closely connected to the construction or reconstruction of personal identity over the course of one's life.[7] For Jan Shipps, her tenure track appointment at IUPUI and acquiring membership status in the Mormon History Association as a non-Mormon, while negotiating her liminal role as an "outside-insider" with both the LDS and RLDS factions of the association, induced a fundamental transformation of her professional and personal identities.

---

6. Jan Shipps, Oral History interview by Maureen Ursenbach Beecher, 33.
7. Robert K. Merton, *Social Theory and Social Structure*, 368–84.

Jan playing the piano, Bloomington, Indiana, 1974

As Jan prepared for the 1975 MHA spring conference, however, her domestic world was forcefully shaken. In late February, Tony was diagnosed with colon cancer at the age of forty-nine. A completely successful surgery was expeditiously performed at the Indiana University Hospital in Indianapolis, and Tony's doctors subsequently determined that follow-up chemotherapy would be unnecessary. In the meantime, however, Jan spent three anxious days and nights with Tony at the hospital. "It was a profoundly disturbing time," Jan recalls.[8] Both Jan and Tony's health had always been relatively robust, and for Jan it seemed far too soon to begin contemplating a life without Tony. Over the years, Jan's steady movement away from merely being Tony's devoted assistant and conjugal champion toward pursuing an independent, professional career of her own had generated occasional tension, but both had remained strongly committed to their marital partnership. Just as Jan and her sister Sue had a close but competitive relationship growing up, Jan and Tony Shipps were a unit in their domestic lives, in spite of Tony's manifest disinterest in her study of the Mormons.

In retrospect, however, Tony's sudden surgery and relatively lengthy convalescence in middle age, especially at a time when Jan's professional star was on the rise, arguably signaled a manifest change in how they had defined their roles in relationship to one another. Jan, however, objects to the notion

---

8. Shipps, Oral History, 34.

that she was becoming a dominant partner in the marriage: "In our relation to each other, dominance was something we never overtly considered. . . . I never felt that I was the dominant partner. . . . There never was a change in our understanding of our particular roles." While dominance may be the wrong word for describing Jan and Tony's marital partnership, the ascendance of Jan's scholarly standing and professional recognition as a Mormon Studies specialist altered both the way Tony regarded Jan and the way she defined herself. Increasingly, *Jan's* professional commitments, and not just Tony's, shaped the way they negotiated their marriage.

Not only had Tony been stricken with cancer, but on the heels of his illness, he and Jan were informed by their son Stephen that he and *Tony's nurse* (Teri) had fallen in love and were planning to get married. Jan says that during her vigilance at the hospital, Tony kept asking, "When is the young master coming?" (At that time Stephen was a 23-year old member of the Cleveland Symphony Orchestra and aspired to becoming a concertmaster.) "When Stephen showed up and looked at Tony, he turned white and almost fainted," Jan recalls. She told Stephen she was going home to get some rest, and that he could stay at the hospital with his father. According to Jan, Tony said that "the first night, both Stephen and Teri attended to his every need, but by the next night, he couldn't get their attention; they had fallen in love." Actually, Jan and Tony were both happy at this unexpected development. When Jan was attending to him before Stephen arrived, Tony, who liked Teri a lot, whispered to her: "I wish Stephen could find somebody like Teri to marry rather than some other musician."

Jan and Tony were worried that if Stephen married a musician it would create the marital problem of managing dual professional careers (that they themselves were struggling with at the time), and that a musician spouse would care more about her music than she did about Stephen. Teri, however, was a nurse who, through training and personal inclination, cared deeply about the welfare of other people. Teri, they perceived, would make Stephen and a family her priority concern. This, of course, mirrored Jan's own overriding commitments to marriage and family, even though she also desperately wanted an academic career for herself. These kinds of contradictions and their associated tensions are scarcely unique to Jan and Tony Shipps' marriage. The increasing cultural challenges to traditional marriage and gender role definitions in the 1970s did not fail to produce some strains in the Shipps' closely connected domestic and professional lives.

Stephen and Teri were married that September. This, of course, meant that Jan was now relinquishing the primacy of her role in Stephen's life to another woman. Stephen was an only child. He had always been precocious and strong-willed, but Jan had mothered him with boundless pride and affection. Along with Tony, Stephen had been a central part of Jan's longtime adult identity as a devoted wife and mother. Coincidental to Tony's abrupt illness, Stephen's sudden but welcome marriage also marked some fundamental realignments in the way Jan defined herself in the economy of her family and mushrooming professional roles. By marrying Teri, Jan says she didn't have to be so concerned about Stephen's well-being: "The role of mother didn't demand so much anymore." Stephen's marriage "allowed me to give my undivided attention to Tony while he was recuperating." Jan had always been concerned about "Tony's satisfaction and happiness. I was always concerned about what he could eat, and that he was healthy. Tony's cancer increased my concern about his health." Following Tony's recuperation and Stephen's marriage, however, while still a committed wife and mother, the actual amount of time and energy Jan spent in forwarding her future professional career increasingly dwarfed the equivalent expenditures of time and attention she spent in maintaining her domestic roles.

In hindsight, Jan sees that working at a different institution than Tony enabled her to develop an academic identity apart from his. At IUPUI, Jan says she "felt freer to be myself," in defining her new academic status and cultivating her own collegial relationships. In particular, she "was less concerned about how Tony would react" to her newly emerging departmental and university duties. Jan candidly admits that, at the time, she and Tony experienced emerging disagreements over women's roles in academia, with Tony's "courtly male chauvinism" being a significant part of the problem. Major changes were taking place both in society and in the academy, where roles for women were swiftly changing. Older male faculty members, like Tony, as well as academic administrators, resisted many of these changes.

Administrators at IUPUI were not exempt from this resistance to increasing roles of women, including Tony Sherrill, Jan's department chair in religious studies. Like Tony, Sherrill had southern roots, having been born and raised in North Carolina. And also like Tony, he had what Jan describes as "old-fashioned, southern ideas about women." Perhaps not surprisingly, the two men hit it off and got along very well together. Thus, Jan says there were "two Tonys" in her life: "one at home and one at school." Both men thought Jan was a notable exception to their prejudicial notions concerning women academics, while simultaneously considering most women in academia to be a problem. According to Jan, "Neither one had much use for lady professors." Jan consequently felt that she was dealing with the same ambivalence about her rightful roles at the university as well as at home. The contradiction of "both Tonys" expressing pride in her academic accomplishments (especially her teaching) while disparaging the emerging status of women in academia was an ongoing source of irritation for Jan at this stage of her professional development. For both Jan and Tony, there was a need in their marriage to clarify Jan's role at home and the university as more than just a wife and classroom teacher.

According to Jan, there were limits to what Tony thought the increasing roles of women in academia should be. He clearly considered *teaching* to be an appropriate woman's occupation, and Jan says he was always interested in and "very prideful of my classroom teaching." After all, both his and Jan's mothers were public school teachers, and for years he had encouraged Jan to do the same. He, however, was not yet on board with the idea that active women scholars should be taking the lead in their professional fields, or, especially, that women should play leading roles in academic administration and decision-making. Nevertheless, Jan's career was rapidly heading in this direction, which did create some obvious strains. These were somewhat eased by Jan and Tony working in different institutions.

At this stage of her life, Jan's unswerving pursuit of academic success often contributed to misperceptions by others concerning her own traditional view of marriage. For example, Jan regularly met for lunch with a group of IU women professors and female graduate students. The purpose of these luncheons was to informally mentor aspiring young women in the profession. On one occasion, the particular topic of discussion was marriage and long-term relationships. When Jan was queried by the women concerning her long-lasting marriage in the context of a successful academic career, Jan's blunt reply was: "My marriage is more important than my career." According to Jan, "This was not the response the women wanted to hear." All of them knew and liked Tony at the university. In an effort to qualify Jan's pronouncement, several of the women wanted to attribute the longevity of Jan's marriage to a vacuous bromide: "It's just that Tony is such a nice guy," they quipped. Jan, however, demurred at this characterization and repeated that her marriage was more important than her career, implying that she had been (and still was) willing to compromise if not sacrifice *her* professional interests to keep her marriage.

While Jan never sacrificed her professional career for Tony (once it belatedly got under way), over the years she carefully negotiated and managed her marital relationship. Jan frequently subordinated her education to Tony's career aspirations and employment at Utah State and the University of Colorado and, later, always sought his approval of academic and professional appointments that came her way in both Colorado and Indiana. Jan likes to say that she *consulted* with Tony in making mutual decisions that affected their marriage, while always trying to be sensitive to his feelings and personal wishes. At the same time, when push came to shove on occasion, Jan insisted on pursuing her own career interests. Her personal determination in achieving her goals should not be underestimated. When Tony wanted her to drop out of graduate school to have another child, she refused. For Jan, they had one son to raise and that was enough. Likewise, although Tony was never keen about Jan's increasingly dense, organizational ties with the Mormon scholarly community, she pursued them headlong as though Tony was staunchly supportive. It was in spite of wholehearted approval from Tony that Jan became a renowned Mormon Studies scholar, not because of it.

All of this is to say that, like most enduring marriages, Jan and Tony's relationship was sustained with its fair share of peculiar inconsistencies, dissonance, and mutual compromises. What stands out, perhaps, is both of their traditional commitments to marriage as a virtual end in itself. On another occasion, when Jan and Tony were attending a cocktail party in Bloomington, a number of married, professional women talked about taking back their surnames as an emphatic declaration of their individuality and independent status as women. When questioned why she didn't change her name back to Barnett, Jan replied, "Because nobody would know me," and then added, "*We* [both Tony and Jan] are known primarily as the parents of Stephen Shipps," to which Tony nodded his affable assent.

One other example of Jan's outward deference to Tony was her practice of calling him from conference hotels to notify him of her whereabouts in the evening hours. This was particularly the case when male MHA members would assemble in her hotel room (which jokingly became known as the "Shipps's Smoker"[9]) following the closing banquet for late-at-night discussions and collegial camaraderie. While many of the male scholars would be accompanied by their wives at these informal gatherings, Jan was never accompanied by Tony, who resisted attending Mormon history conferences.[10] Her calls home informing Tony in advance of these room gatherings served both to reassure him of her conjugal loyalty and to demonstrate to colleagues her marital bona fides. While Jan had to occasionally cope with male sexual advances in other professional organizations, this was never a problem in the tightly knit, group-oriented meetings of the Mormon History Association. There, her colleagues would respectfully wait for her to make her obligatory call home to Tony before gathering in her room. In the meantime, Jan says

---

9. "Smoker" is an outdated term for brothels where "blue movies" were exhibited around the turn of the twentieth-century.

10. Eventually Tony began attending occasional JWHA meetings with Jan. Jan says he was already acquainted with non-Mormon historian Larry Foster, who taught history at the Georgia Institute of Technology in Atlanta, and developed friendships with some other JWHA members. On the few occasions when Tony accompanied Jan to MHA conferences, however, he would go to a local library to read and do his own work. Among other things, MHA conferences became too large for Tony, who felt more comfortable at the smaller JWHA meetings.

her Mormon colleagues often joked (until actually meeting him in later years) that "Tony was a fictitious character."

Promoting Mormon Scholarship: The "Shippsification" of Mormon Studies

Hand in hand with inevitable tensions and compromises in her marriage, Jan's increasing self-confidence as an established scholar and university academic, independent of her husband's credentials, was set to hold center stage for the remainder of both her and Tony's professional lives. Not only did Jan become one of the central figures in the Mormon intellectual community, she also became an active and influential member of numerous other professional societies in both history and religious studies, where she regularly promoted the importance of Mormon Studies. Years later in his retrospective essay on Jan's importance to Mormon scholarship, Philip Barlow coined the phrase "Shippsification of Mormon Studies" to credit Jan's leading role in promoting the respectability of Mormon Studies as an academic field.[11]

Thus, after accepting appointments to serve on the councils and program committees of the Mormon History Association (1973) and John Whitmer Historical Association (1974), Jan subsequently sat on the advisory board of the National Historical Society (1976), joined the program committee of the Western History Association (1978), became director of the IUPUI Center for American Studies (1978), ascended to the position of president of the Mormon History Association (1980) as both the first woman and first non-Mormon to occupy this position, was invited to serve as a section chair for the American Academy of Religion (1980), became a council member for the Indiana Academy of Religion (1980), and later was elected president of that organization (1983). At the same time, Jan was advancing rapidly in academic ranks at IUPUI, from Assistant Professor in 1973, to Associate Professor in 1976, and to full Professor in 1983—just two years prior to publishing *Mormonism*. In 1985, Jan also became a council member of the American Society for Church History.[12]

In the wider academic world of American history and religious studies, Jan's active involvement in numerous professional organizations made it possible for her to advocate effectively for the importance of Mormon history and Mormon Studies in those organizations' conference repertoires. For example, as a member (and chair) of the program committee of the Western History Association and as a regular presenter at its meetings, Jan frequently admonished the assembled scholars that Western historians had left out the Mormons in their work. In doing this, she articulated her "hole in the dough-

---

11. Philip Barlow, "Jan Shipps and the Mainstreaming of Mormon Studies," 412–26.

12. For a more complete and updated record of Jan's professional affiliations and academic appointments, see the curriculum vitae in the Appendix.

nut" thesis regarding the lack of serious historical study of the Mormons in Western American history: "The history of the American West has been written," she would say, "like a doughnut. Everybody has written *around* the Mormons, leaving a hole in the historical narrative." On one of these occasions the renowned Western historian, Martin Ridge, looked up and replied: "And you're the one who has written about the hole!"[13] Likewise, for a number of years the American Academy of Religion (AAR) was reluctant to include sessions on Mormonism on its annual conference program because it wasn't recognized as a sufficiently important topic. This changed when Jan became an AAR section chair in 1980 and argued successfully (or, as Jan puts it, "stomped her foot") that Mormon sessions be seriously considered for inclusion in AAR conference proceedings.

Moreover, as an officer and program committee chair for both the Mormon History Association and John Whitmer History Association, Jan strongly encouraged the practice of soliciting reputable non-Mormon scholars (such as Mark Leone of Princeton University and Mario DePillis of the University of Massachusetts) to be commentators on conference papers presented by Mormon scholars. Together, Jan and Mormon historians Richard and Claudia Bushman proposed that the MHA sponsor was to become the Tanner Lecture series, featuring well-known, outside speakers to address Mormon conference sessions. Over the years, the lectures would include notable scholars such as historians Gordon Wood (Brown University), Timothy Smith (Johns Hopkins), Martin Marty (University of Chicago), Martin Ridge (Cornel University), and sociologist Rodney Stark (University of Washington).[14] Besides adding professional luster to these meetings, the Tanner Lectures simultaneously exposed outside speakers to the scholarly standards maintained by Mormon historians and provided those in the association with important additional outside perspectives.

Another example of Jan's unique ability and role in bridging Mormon and non-Mormon scholarly circles is her 1975 invitation to "renegade" Mormon historian Fawn Brodie to address an adjunct MHA session at the annual meeting of the Organization of American Historians (OAH) in Boston. By then, Brodie was a faculty member at the University of California, Los Angeles and was famous not only for her controversial and naturalistic biography of Joseph Smith, but, outside of Mormon circles, for her highly regarded biographies of Thaddeus Stevens, Sir Richard Burton, Thomas Jefferson, and later

---

13. Shipps, *Sojourner*, 21.

14. Tanner Lecture speakers and the full texts of their MHA lectures from 1980 through 1999 can be found in Dean L. May and Reid L. Neilson, eds., with Richard Lyman Bushman, Jan Shipps, and Thomas G. Alexander, *The Mormon History Association's Tanner Lectures: The First Twenty Years*.

Richard Nixon.[15] Brodie's appearance drew a large audience of OAH conferees, as well as MHA members. Jan's task was to introduce her to the gathering. To appreciative laughter and applause, Jan began by saying, "The first time I 'met' Fawn Brodie, she was locked up," and then went on to recount how, as a student doing research, she had "liberated Brodie" from the Logan Public Library (and also later on a trip at the University of Virginia Library) where Brodie's *No Man Knows My History: The Life of Joseph Smith* and (in the UV Library) *Thomas Jefferson: An Intimate History* were kept behind the circulation desks, because they were thought to be too scandalous for display in the open stacks. Later at the conference, Brodie attended a MHA-sponsored luncheon at which University of Utah historian Dean May gave the keynote address. Brodie was impressed and wrote to Jan later to say "how pleased she was to have come, and how fascinated she was with Dean's paper, and how astonished she was at what the Mormon History Association was doing . . . that we were talking at such a high level."[16]

Jan enjoyed getting personally acquainted with Brodie, who she described as being "pretty charming, pretty smart." Brodie appreciated Jan's acquaintance as well, and characterized Jan's introduction of her at the OAH conference as "the best one she had ever had." Jan's invitation of Brodie was made possible through the auspices of Alfred Bush, a Princeton historian and colleague of Jan's, who was also a Mormon and a long-time friend and colleague of Brodie. After the presentation, Brodie remarked to Bush: "She [Jan] is just as interested in all of this [Joseph Smith and Mormonism] as we are." Thereafter, the two women engaged in a brief correspondence.[17]

Center for American Studies

As a new research university situated in a major urban center of the American heartland, IUPUI was anxious to advance its national standing and reputation as a serious research institution and not just as a good teaching school. Lilly Endowment, Inc., headquartered in Indianapolis, had (and con-

---

15. See Fawn McKay Brodie, *No Man Knows My History: The Life of Joseph Smith*; *Thaddeus Stevens: Scourge of the South*; *The Devil Drives: A Life of Sir Richard Burton*; *Thomas Jefferson: An Intimate History*; and *Richard Nixon: The Shaping of His Character*.

16. Shipps, Oral History, 31.

17. Jan had written to Brodie years earlier while a graduate student at Colorado, inquiring if Brodie could share any of the research materials used in writing her Joseph Smith book. The disappointing reply was, "No, sorry, I've thrown all my notes away." Jan does not know exactly what has become of her correspondence with Brodie. We are hopeful that it will turn up in her voluminous paper files once they are sorted through, catalogued, and archived at Utah State University. (In Chapter 8 we compare and contrast Jan's background and scholarly work with Brodie, and also with Juanita Brooks.)

tinues to have) a vested commitment to funding mainstream religious studies programs and Christian education in America. When Lilly offered financial support to the IUPUI College of Liberal Arts to institute a religious studies program, the college dean, Joseph Taylor, jumped at the proposal and began recruiting faculty who were well-known scholars, such as Anthony Sherrill and Ted Mullen, as well as junior faculty, including Jan, whom Taylor correctly intuited had the potential to become active researchers.

From the newly funded religious studies program came the idea of instituting a "Center for American Studies," whose primary purpose would be to sustain a conversation among academics about the role of religion in American life and not just serve as an outlet for a mélange of separate papers written for publication in esoteric journals. Robert Lynn (Lilly's senior vice president, who was also both a religious scholar and student of Richard and Reinhold Niebuhr) strongly supported the idea. In the second year of its existence (1978), Jan was invited to be the director of the center and, in collaboration with Tony Sherrill, established a plan for it to sponsor three conferences annually. These would not be conventional academic conferences with concurrent sessions and numerous papers. Instead, the conferences would be somewhat similar to Jan's own pedagogical style, with each conference focusing on a particular topic subsumed under the general theme of contemporary religion in America and then devoting the entire conference to its in-depth discussion. A major speaker (such as Martin Marty of the University of Chicago Divinity School or Yale University historian Jon Butler) would be invited to give an address Thursday evening. The next morning attendees would engage in group discussions of the speaker's paper. A second speaker's paper would then be pre-circulated prior to its presentation and discussion Friday night. The manifest intention of these meetings was to promote extensive conversations among influential academics on topics relevant to religion in American life, which they could then share and disseminate through their teaching and writing at their own institutions.[18]

Initially, Jan and Sherrill only expected to draw a dozen or so participants, but the center-sponsored conferences quickly began attracting groups of thirty-five to fifty scholars who came from all over the country. As director of the center, Jan immediately began inviting Mormon colleagues to attend as well, particularly Tom Alexander and Val Avery, who came three times a year for every conference. Other Mormon scholars who participated over the years

---

18. In 1989, the Center for American Studies became The Center for the Study of Religion and American Culture, whose mission is to "explore the connection between religion and other aspects of American culture. We are a research and public outreach institute that supports the ongoing scholarly discussion of the nature, terms, and dynamic of religion in America." See RAAC IUPUI, "About."

included Richard and Claudia Bushman, both of whom gave major papers that were discussed at the center. Mormon participation at these conferences soon became part of the legitimation of Mormon Studies in the larger scholarly world of religious and American studies.

University of Illinois Press

As the newly installed president of the Mormon History Association, Jan was fortuitous to meet with Liz Dulaney, senior editor at the University of Illinois Press, at the 1980 MHA Conference in Canandaigua, New York, inaugurating a long and mutually beneficial friendship. In a recounting of her experiences with Jan years later, Dulaney elaborated on their initial encounter:

> My first encounter with Jan Shipps was (probably to the surprise of no one who knows her) over the telephone. The University of Illinois Press was at that time looking for an adviser for a book manuscript about Mormon patriarch Heber C. Kimball, and Jan had been suggested to me by a historian at the University, Mary Lee Spence, who said without hesitation, "Call Jan Shipps; she knows everything about Mormons.". . . Shortly thereafter, Stanley Kimball, the author of the Heber Kimball biography—which we did subsequently publish—suggested that the Press might be interested in attending a meeting of the young Mormon History Association, which in 1980 was meeting in Canandaigua, New York, and for the first time was mounting a book exhibit, whose president that year, as luck would have it, was Jan Shipps! The Press at that time had published two notable books on Mormon topics: *Nauvoo: Kingdom on the Mississippi* by Bob Flanders in 1965, and *The Carthage Conspiracy* by Dallin Oaks and Marvin Hill in 1975. I added to that small pile John Unruh's prizewinning *The Plains Across*, and several other western history titles, and off I went to Canandaigua—and a subsequent long-lasting association with Mormon history and the Person Who Knows Everything About Mormons. . . . I came away from Canandaigua totally impressed by all I had experienced and everyone I had met. Energized by discussions with Jan, I forged ahead, determined to work toward expanding our small list in Mormon history, which with Jan's help, advice, and encouragement, I proceeded to do.[19]

Dulaney subsequently promoted Mormon Studies manuscripts at UI Press, providing an outlet for an impressive string of key scholarly works. The timing was serendipitous, as a few years later the LDS Church History Department would be essentially shut down, ending Leonard Arrington's projected large-scale and long-term Mormon history project. The many competent scholars involved with the project were in need of a new venue to publish their research, and UI Press filled the void, soon becoming the premier publisher of scholarly books on Mormonism up to the time of Dulaney's retirement in 2007. In the years that UI Press was prolific in Mormon

---

19. Liz Dulaney, "Jan Shipps."

Studies, Dulaney invariably asked Jan to read and comment on virtually every Mormon-related manuscript submitted to the press. According to Dulaney,

> Jan's first book, *Mormonism: The Story of New Religious Tradition*, was published by the University of Illinois Press in 1985, followed by a trickle and then a stream of other titles in Mormon history.... When I retired in 1998 (and again in 2008) Illinois had published well over 100 titles in Mormon history, making the topic, in the process, a respectable publication venture for the rest of the publishing community, who have subsequently taken up the torch.[20]

These examples, of course, are merely illustrative of Jan's catalytic influence in helping to legitimate the study of Mormon history as an important topic in the fields of American history and religious studies.

Publication of *Mormonism: The Story of a New Religious Tradition*, 1985

Once Jan acquired tenure at IUPUI, and as she continued solidifying her active involvement in both Mormon and non-Mormon organizations, she continued to produce a significant amount of scholarly work in the forms of conference presentations and journal articles. Unquestionably, however, the most celebrated achievement of Jan's career was the publication of her first book, *Mormonism: The Story of a New Religious Tradition*, five years after she became president of the Mormon History Association in 1980. Well before this time, Jan was not only known to Mormon historians and other academics in the Mormon intellectual community, she had also become increasingly visible to LDS Church leaders, the press, and other people interested in the contemporary affairs of the Church of Jesus Christ of Latter-day Saints. As a non-Mormon whose professional work and scholarly credibility were obviously respected by Mormon scholars, the press in particular began turning to Jan as an expert source to comment on news stories involving the Church's beliefs, organizational history, and contemporary programs. During this time she also developed a working relationship with Jerry Cahill, Director of Press Relations and Public Communications for the Church.

Press Relations and Contacts with LDS Ecclesiastical Officials

Jan's initial interest in Mormon history for her PhD dissertation was not on Mormon origins per se, but on the development and transformation of Mormonism after it became established in the Utah Territory. Thus, her particular interest had been in later nineteenth-century to early twentieth-century Mormonism, both before and after the practice of polygamy was ended. Now, with increasing press interest in the rapidly growing Church of

---

20. Dulaney.

Jesus Christ of Latter-day Saints both internationally and at home, Jan felt the need to understand and stay abreast of current Mormon events.

Through Cahill, Jan was invited to have lunch with key LDS general authorities, some of whom she met for the first time, including Gordon B. Hinckley in an interview meeting arranged by Cahill.[21] At the time, Hinckley was first counselor to the aging presidents Ezra Taft Benson and Howard W. Hunter and was recognized public spokesman for the Church during their tenures before becoming president and prophet himself in 1995. Hinckley had a background in public relations and was open to talking to Jan about Mormon history. At the time, Jan was working on an IUPUI project on religion and urbanism in the United States, and she asked Hinckley questions about how modern Mormonism was doing in urban areas like Southern California. Hinckley perceived that rather than being focused on criticizing the LDS religion, Jan was instead interested in understanding and explaining growth and change in the modern Church. Over the years, Jan became good friends with Hinckley, and later, when he became president of the LDS Church, she was able to conduct a two-hour private interview with him.[22]

Jan's personal impressions of Hinckley and other LDS general authorities she has met and talked with over the years are that they seem much the same as the leaders of other religious organizations (Methodist, Baptist, Catholic, Jewish) that she has come to know: "They're no different than ecclesiastical leaders of other major denominations; they seem sincere, not unscrupulous or manipulative. They're committed to promoting what they believe is best for their church as an institution."

After publication of her book, Jan's expert credibility was solidified. The press was particularly interested in the issue of the Mormon priesthood's ex-

---

21. Through her Mormon scholarship, Jan already knew Henry B. Eyring when he was president of Ricks College and later when he was Commissioner of Church Education, prior to his becoming an apostle and ultimately a counselor in the LDS First Presidency. Likewise, she became acquainted with Dallin Oaks when he was president of Brigham Young University prior to his ascension in the LDS hierarchy as an apostle and, like Eyring, a member of the First Presidency. While he was BYU president, Jan first met Oaks at a gathering at the home of BYU historian James Allen. When introduced, Oaks referred to Jan (whom he'd never met before) as the "Mormon watcher," immediately indicating his academic cognizance of Jan's respected status in the Mormon scholarly community.

22. The tape recording of the interview resides in Jan's personal archives that have been bequeathed to Utah State University under the aegis of future biographer, Philip Barlow, former Leonard J. Arrington Chair in Mormon History and Culture at Utah State University.

clusion of black males and later in the Mark Hoffman forgeries and murders.[23] Jan was contacted for her views both by the press and by Cahill on these, as well as numerous other Mormon-related news stories. Being an outsider gave Jan credibility with the press as an unbiased expert on Mormonism, and her integrity as a scholar uninterested in trafficking embarrassing exposes of the Church gave her credibility with Cahill and with leading LDS authorities. Given these broadly shared perceptions of her impartiality, Jan was able to act as an effective liaison between the secular press and the LDS Church. Further, as Jan herself has observed,

> When news stories about the Saints need to be set in context for the general public, reporters hunt up "outside-insiders," as well as "inside-outsiders" [like Jan]. This may help to explain why the national media seems to find the opinions and explanations of persons like Sterling McMurrin or the late Fawn Brodie of greater interest than the opinions and explanations of LDS ecclesiastical authorities.[24]

Finding a Publisher

It was in the professional context of Jan's growing stature as an insider-outsider authority in Mormon Studies that the Indiana University Press approached her about writing a book on *twentieth-century* Mormonism. Jan was pleased by the press's implicit confidence in her ability to compose an original scholarly treatise on the subject and commenced to write. But uncharacteristically for Jan, her writing eventually began to bog down: "I realized I was writing a different *kind* of book in the *footnotes*" than the one IU Press had solicited. In telling the story of the twentieth-century church, she discovered that she felt more and more compelled to explain first the story of early Mormonism, without which the contemporary church would not make adequate sense to serious readers outside of the faith. At an arranged lunch

---

23. For academic sources on the torturous history of race and LDS priesthood eligibility, see Lester E. Bush Jr. and Armand Mauss, *Neither White Nor Black: Mormon Scholars Confront the Race Issue in a Universal Church*, and Newell G. Bringhurst, *Saints, Slaves, and Blacks: The Changing Place of Black People Within Mormonism*, and Russell M. Stevenson, *For the Cause of Righteousness: A Global History of Blacks and Mormonism, 1830–2013*. In 1978, the LDS Church dropped its priesthood ban for males of African ancestry but waited until 2014 to officially repudiate the folklore and pseudo theological justifications that previously had been used to defend its discriminatory racial practices. The latter acknowledgement can be found in a the LDS Church's Gospel Topic Essay entitled "Race and the Priesthood." On the Hoffman forgery/murder case, see Linda Sillitoe and Allen Dale Roberts, *Salamander: The Story of the Mormon Forgery Murders*, and Richard E. Turley, *Victims: The LDS Church and the Mark Hofmann Case*.

24. Jan Shipps, "An 'Inside-Outsider' in Zion," 153.

with her editor, Jan informed him she wanted to change the focus of the book from the twentieth century to Mormon origins. His response to this was a definitive "No thanks"; he only wanted a book on modern Mormonism. He didn't even care to see what Jan had drafted.

Jan was nevertheless determined to continue writing the book she intuited needed to come out. Comments, suggestions, and support from LDS scholar-friends Klaus Hansen ("Of course, this must be published, even though I'm arguing with you on every page") and Richard Bushman (with whom Jan had thirty- to forty-minute phone conversations twice a week while working to complete her manuscript) were particularly helpful and encouraging. The hard work of actually writing the book had to be sandwiched in between her teaching and committee duties at IUPUI and domestic obligations at home. Jan arranged her schedule so that she would only have to drive to Indianapolis every other day (one hundred miles round-trip), staying overnight on the days she had classes and scheduled meetings. With uninterrupted time during her stays in Indianapolis, a good deal of the book was written in the middle of the night. Jan further utilized the long commute to compose sentences in her head and occasionally pull off the road to write them down. When she finally felt she had a solid draft in hand, Jan contacted Liz Dulaney at the University of Illinois Press and offered them her manuscript.[25]

Roger Clark, a former friend at the University of Colorado who had joined UI Press, had been, along with Dulaney, very interested in seeing Jan's draft. The manuscript was subsequently sent out for critical review—resulting in highly positive reviews by Bushman (who had discussed the project through extensive conversations with Jan), religious studies scholar Martin Marty, and RLDS scholar Paul Edwards. Review comments from both Bushman and Edwards were published as publicity plugs on the dust jacket of the first printing. Bushman wrote, "This may be the most brilliant book ever written on Mormonism, in the sense of shedding new light on virtually every aspect of Mormon history and in offering a perspective that both Mormons and others can accept." Bushman also credited Jan for vivifying "Mormon Studies," not just doing Mormon history. In Edwards's view, "*Mormonism* is historically valid, insightful, and provides a kind of 'past-prophetic' understanding. . . . It is not beyond what I expected Shipps to do, but I for one am always a little amazed when people live up to their full potential."

Mormonism: The Story of a New Religious Tradition was published in 1985 to glowing reviews from both LDS and non-LDS reviewers. According to

---

25. Coincidentally, Dulaney's father at the time was Dean of Library Science at the University of Michigan, where Tony had received his master's degree in library science in the late 1950s while the Shipps were living in Detroit.

Jan, IU Press regretted turning down her suggested change of focus, and the editor wrote her a one-sentence letter after Illinois published her book, saying, "It hurts, it really hurts." In years to follow, the University of Illinois Press, with the continued editorial support of Liz Dulany, strengthened its standing as a leading academic press committed to providing an outlet for serious scholarship in Mormon history and Mormon Studies.

Scholarly Approach to Writing about Early Mormon History

In spite of Jan's subtitle, "The Story of a New Religious Tradition," the story she tells is not a conventionally detailed or comprehensive narrative of Mormon history and the organization of The Church of Jesus Christ of Latter-day Saints. Jan's approach is to instead understand the rise of nineteenth-century Mormonism using comparative, analytical, and theoretical religious studies methods. While the seven chapters of her book can all be read as separate essays, combined they sustain a coherent thesis about the relatively rare emergence and organizational transformation of a new religious tradition in the context of nineteenth-century American history and religious culture.

Jan's central thematic argument requires that we not only consider early Mormonism in the context of American religious history, but that we also see it in broader historical comparison to the rapid rise of Christianity as a new religious tradition from its initial incarnation as a Jewish sect. By new religious tradition, Jan means explicitly that the theological beliefs and associated religious symbols, rituals, and religiously mandated practices diverge so much from the parent religious tradition that they burst the bounds of the old and must be grasped as something fundamentally new and distinctive. In her words,

> But as Christianity developed, as Greeks and Jews were together 'in Christ' brought beneath the covenant that God had made with Abraham, it gradually became clear that the way espoused by the apostles included important elements that were not part of Israel's tradition. Without fully and consciously realizing that they were doing so, the followers of Jesus established a new religious tradition.[26]

In the case of the Mormons, Jan argues that their peculiar history in America

> is in many respects analogous to the history of those early Christians who thought at first they had found the only proper way to be Jews. Despite the surprising similarity between some of the modern cultural manifestations of Mormonism and American evangelical Protestantism, Mormonism started to grow away from traditional Christianity almost immediately upon coming into existence. It began as a movement that understood itself as Christian, but as 'the new dispensation of the fullness of times' commenced with the publication of the Book of Mormon, the 'restoration of the Aaronic priesthood,' and the recognition of Joseph Smith as prophet, these nineteenth-century Latter-day Saints

---

26. Jan Shipps, *Mormonism: The Story of a New Religious Tradition*, ix.

Jan with a copy of *Mormonism: The Story of a New Religious Tradition*, circa. 1985.

(as they came to be called) embarked on a path that led to developments that now distinguish their tradition from the Christian tradition as surely as early Christianity was distinguished from its Hebraic context.[27]

Thus, the insights about the emergence and subsequent development of Mormonism that Jan produced began with an *analogy* to early Christianity.[28] Analogies are heuristic devices that stimulate possible solutions to unresolved problems or debated questions. The debated questions about Mormonism are: What kind of religion is it? Is it Christian or non-Christian? How and why did it emerge and spread so rapidly when and where it did in nineteenth-century America? How did it not only survive furious resistance as a perceived Christian heresy, but ultimately flourish to become a rapidly expanding international religion in the twentieth-century? And in the process of doing this, what kind of religion did it consequently become for its adherents both at home and abroad? These are the kinds of questions that concern Jan's analysis of Mormonism and not merely a descriptive, chronological account of its history and most prominent leaders.

Traditionally there have been two primary ways to write religious history: eschatologically or naturalistically. The eschatological approach is predicated on the belief that religion is inspired by God, that religious history is guided by God's purposes, and that the duty of historians is to describe the events and major personalities of that history as expressions of the ultimate realization of God's will. Historians who write from this perspective to vindicate or promulgate their particular faith tradition's religious claims may be regarded as apologists or defenders of the faith. In contrast, the naturalistic approach is predicated on the belief that religion is a human product, that all history—including religious history—is socially constructed by human beings, and that the duty of historians is to describe and explain the events and major personalities of that history in human terms—as the record of human actors seeking ultimate meaning and justification for their lives while pursuing their economic, political, and cultural interests. Historians who espouse this perspective may be regarded as humanists or, in some cases, as critics of the implausibility of supernatural religious traditions.

Eschatological history is fundamentally theistic and, in the Christian tradition, may also be called "salvation history." Human salvation from death through compliance with God's will is the ultimate goal of Christian

---

27. Shipps, *Mormonism*, ix–x.
28. As Jan notes, "In everyday life Mormons have no need for theoretical models or sophisticated conceptual frameworks to understand Mormonism. . . . But unless suitable analogies are found to enable *non-Mormons* to make sense of the Restoration Movements, avoiding misconceptions and misunderstandings is almost impossible." See Shipps, "Inside Outsider," 158; emphasis added.

salvation history. In contrast, naturalistic history is not theistic. This is not to say, however, that it is necessarily atheistic either. Properly understood, naturalistic history is *agnostic* with regard to the intervention of God or other supernatural forces in the unfolding of human events. Whether God exists or not—or actually guides human destiny through the events of history to ultimate salvation—is a moot point from the naturalistic perspective; it is simply not subject to empirical proof. At the same time, the explanatory principles of psychology, economics, political science, sociology, and anthropology are considered to provide sufficient grounds for understanding human events, including the events of religious history.

The agnostic orientation of naturalistic history actually makes possible a third way to think about writing religious history. Religious believers trained in the naturalistic methods of contemporary academia may come to believe that the rigorous application of these methods and a judicious analysis of their results will, in the end, be consistent with a faith-based understanding of their religious tradition. This third approach to religious history was characteristic of the New Mormon History movement Jan encountered when she resumed her active involvement in the Mormon History Association. Advocates of this approach wanted to professionalize the study of Mormon history as a legitimate field of study in the larger context of American history; they wanted to "bracket," or set aside, Mormonism's ultimate truth claims while employing naturalistic methods of historical study to produce credible and academic accounts of the Mormon past and to win respect from academic historians who were not members of the LDS faith. Two of the most notable Mormon historians advocating this approach at the time of Jan's book were Leonard Arrington and Richard Bushman.

Scholarly Reviews and Family/Peer Reactions

Both Bushman and Arrington published scholarly biographies of Mormonism's major prophetic leaders, Joseph Smith and Brigham Young, respectively, that were reviewed simultaneously with Jan's book in 1985 in *The New York Review of Books* and *The New York Times Book Review*. These two reviews were arguably the most prominent and widely publicized critical assessments of all three books. Both reviews were respectful of the scholarship displayed by the authors, but they were especially positive in assessing Jan's work in comparison to Bushman and Arrington.

In the *New York Review of Books*, David Brion Davis of Yale University expresses admiration for Bushman's and Arrington's attempts to address non-Mormon skepticism of the objective validity of the scholarly work produced by Mormon historians, but he also spotlights their personal dilemma in attempting to reconcile a professional history approach to Mormonism while endeavoring to maintain a subtext in their writing that was ultimately consistent with the eschatological narrative of the LDS faith. Without an implicit underlying apologetic agenda or loyalty to LDS truth claims, Davis concludes that *Mormonism* was substantially more persuasive to non-Mormon readers and the professional history community while, paradoxically, providing Mormon readers with an account reconcilable with their own interpretation of their religious history. Davis writes:

> Bushman himself is quoted as saying that Shipps's short collection of essays "may be the most brilliant book ever written on Mormonism," a judgment I am inclined to share even though the essays are somewhat repetitive and lacking in overall coherence. Mormon intellectuals long ago adopted Shipps as an "insider/outsider" and "den mother" of historians, in part because of her political tact and in part because her efforts to fit Mormonism within a comparative religious scheme confirm Mormon claims to be a chosen, unique people.[29]

In the *New York Times Book Review*, Cornell professor Lawrence Moore followed up on this latter point by fastening attention to the issue of Mormon exceptionalism as a new religious movement in America. He perceived that all three writers challenged contemporary American historiography by offering "renewed versions of the case for Mormon exceptionalism." Moreover, Moore shared Davis's judgment that, as a non-Mormon, Jan made a more persuasive case for the consideration of professional historians than did Bushman or Arrington. In his opinion, Jan's "most enviable achievement" was finding a way "to understand the Mormons that truly will please both believers and nonbelievers":

> Like Mr. Bushman and Mr. Arrington, Mrs. Shipps takes Mormons' perceptions of themselves at face value. However, since she is interested not in documenting what actually happened on the Hill Cumorah but in exploring the consequences of what Mormons came to *believe* about themselves, the procedure works very well for her. In an analysis of how Mormons created their own sense of distinctiveness, it simply does not matter whether the Book of Mormon was an ordinary 19th-century book or the translation of an ancient document. In the best chapter of the book, "History as Text," Mrs. Shipps rereads the 19th-century history of the Mormons not as a series of sequential events but as a gradual recapitulation, appropriation and finally radical transformation of the Judaic-Christian tradition.... Mrs. Shipps' case for Mormon exceptionalism furnishes an original perspective on Mormon history, and that's no mean achievement. She recognizes, as do Mr. Bushman and Mr. Arrington, that the story of Mormonism cannot be told solely in terms of its similarity to other stories.[30]

These two reviews, along with a dozen others in scholarly journals, confirmed Jan's reputation as a major authority on Mormon history, as well as

---

29. David Brion Davis, "Secrets of the Mormons."
30. R. Lawrence Moore, "Prophets in Their Own Country"; emphasis added.

Mormonism's place in the broader reach of American history. They also sustained her long-held position that Mormonism is an important case study in religious studies for understanding the transformation of a new religious movement into a major religious tradition that transcends the boundaries of its host society.

By the time Jan published *Mormonism: The Story of a New Religious Tradition*, Tony had become thoroughly accommodated, if not overly enthusiastic, to Jan's intense commitment to professional organizations aligned with Western American history, religious studies, and especially Mormon history and Mormon Studies. He had always shown an interest in Jan's teaching but was mainly indifferent toward her scholarly work in Mormon history. Because of this disinterest, Tony did not fully grasp the value of her scholarship until the publication of *Mormonism*. Jan says that Tony "was stunned" by the scholarly reviews and acclaim it received and that "it took Tony a long time to realize my work was original." Jan had never given Tony any of her manuscripts to read (and is unsure if he has ever read the published book), so when laudatory reviews of her book began to accumulate, it was "the first time he realized I was doing something important." Stephen, who at the time was a member of the Cleveland Orchestra, was likewise relatively oblivious to the significance of Jan's scholarship. He may have been somewhat more appreciative than Tony, however, of her rising stature in the field. Stephen was impressed by the fact that his mother had numerous speaking engagements and, from time to time, was quoted in the *New York Times* and other newspapers.

Uncharacteristically, Tony copied and shared reviews of Jan's book with all the staff at the IU Library and commenced bragging her up. "He was so proud," Jan recalls. "This was a wonderful thing to me." It should be no surprise that Jan dedicated her book to Tony, but she did so in a subtle, almost veiled manner by simply inscribing "For A. W. S." on the dedication page. Few people outside of Jan and Tony's immediate family and closest circle of friends would know that these initials stood for Anthony Wimberly Shipps, Tony's full birth name.

Upon reading *Mormonism*'s many acclamatory reviews, Jan's IUPUI colleagues were also taken aback by its impact and praise—especially among members of the religious studies faculty who, heretofore, hadn't considered Mormon Studies to be an especially important field of study. The IU historians in Bloomington were likewise surprised by the critical reception of the book. They too had been mostly dismissive of Jan's preoccupation with the study of Mormonism as a marginal topic of study. Tony's colleagues in the IU English Department, with whom he and Jan regularly socialized, were similarly surprised and belatedly admiring of Jan's scholarly achievement.

Praise for *Mormonism: The Story of a New Religious Tradition*

"Shipps' research is thorough, her logic compelling, her literary expression quietly forceful, and her reflections illuminating."
— Martin E. Marty, School of Divinity, University of Chicago

"Shipps' work is an excellent piece of interpretive analysis."
— David Martin, *Times Literary Supplement*

"Without a doubt, Shipps has emerged as the most knowledgeable non-Mormon scholar in the field of Mormon studies."
—Thomas Alexander, *Dialogue: A Journal of Mormon Thought*

"A stunning tour de force."
—Klaus Hansen, *Journal of Mormon History*

"A highly sophisticated, scholarly analysis of cultural and religious origins and development. . . . Shipps is not only a leading authority on Mormonism but a cultural historian of a very high order."
—Sterling M. McMurrin, *Essays and Monographs in Colorado History*

"Shipps supplements historical method with a phenomenology that emphasizes the continuities between Mormon experience and patterns of religious activity that long antedated the nineteenth century. The methodological issues are complex. Because Shipps explores them with insight and judgment her book should receive careful attention from historians of religion in America."
—E. Brooks Holifield, *Indiana Magazine of History*

"Required reading for anyone interested in understanding Mormonism."
— S.C. Pearson, *Choice*

"In Mormonism, Jan Shipps combines the impressive skills of a distinguished historian, thorough researcher, and lucid writer with a quality rare among those who observe and write about the Church of Jesus Christ of Latter-day Saints: she understands us."
—Jerry P. Cahill, public communications department, Church of Jesus Christ of Latter-day Saints.

Although highly regarded for years by the Mormon intellectual community, delayed acknowledgement of her stature as a major scholar by Tony and her Indiana colleagues was sweet vindication for Jan. She had spent much of her adult life in Tony's academic shadow, subordinating the prospects of her own career to the upward trajectory of his. Arguably displaying inordinate sensitivity toward Tony's feelings (but perhaps also nursing prideful resentment for his lack of attention to her work over the years), Jan says, "it was important that I never made a lot about my success at home." Tony's published reference answers in both *Oxford Notes and Queries* and the *New York Times* were deemed just as important in the Shipps household as Jan's growing, impressive body of scholarly work. Tony was still researching, writing, and publishing "Answers to Queries" for the *New York Times* when *Mormonism* was published, and he had long been well-known as "the Quotation Sleuth." Ever committed to sustaining her marriage, Jan began encouraging Tony to write a book about his work, believing that it was important as a boost to his self-esteem: "It was very important for Tony to have a book too." Through Liz Dulaney, Tony eventually published a book in 1990 by the University of Illinois Press entitled *The Quote Sleuth: A Manual for the Tracer of Lost Quotations*.[31]

Hofmann Forgeries, the McLellin Papers, and Mitt Romney[32]

By 1985, Jan had gained the esteem of both Mormon and non-Mormon scholars, as well as her Indiana colleagues. And at long last, her scholar-husband Tony and musician-son Stephen fully realized the stature she had achieved in the world of academic scholarship. For this reason we take 1985 to be an arbitrary but convenient stopping point in our biographical sketch of Jan Shipps's social and intellectual development. Through her career Jan effectively cultivated the mutual trust of LDS and RLDS historians, enabling her to play a significant role in mediating the two factions' efforts to cultivate collegial relationships and benefit more completely from one another's research on topics of shared interest. Likewise, her dense organizational ties in both Mormon and non-Mormon professional associations and her own

---

31. Anthony W. Shipps, *The Quote Sleuth: A Manual for the Tracer of Lost Quotations*.

32. For a much more detailed discussion of matters we briefly summarize in this section, readers should consult Shipps's Oral History interview. Topics covered in that interview include the following: the rapid growth and increasing professionalization of the Mormon History Association during Jan's leadership tenure; the origin and establishment of the annual Tanner Lecture series; renewed rifts and tensions between LDS and RLDS scholars; the LDS Public Commination Department's media relations concerns and Jan's increasing status as an unbiased authority on Mormon topics of interest to the press; the Hoffman document swindles and murder trial; and Jan's own assessment of the organizational structure and arguments she put forth in *Mormonism*.

widely-respected scholarship allowed her to play an important bridging role in promoting Mormon scholarship to non-Mormons and vice versa. As a result, Jan would frequently find herself either commenting on or mediating between contending parties when Mormon topics hit the national news.

The Hofmann Case

Jan's coincidental though possibly influential meeting with Mark Hofmann in 1974 (when he was a student at Utah State University) gained retrospective importance a decade later when Hofmann, now a respected documents dealer, claimed to possess what would come to be known as the Salamander Letter. The Salamander Letter purported to be a letter written by early Mormon convert and Book of Mormon financier Martin Harris. The letter contradicts the LDS Church's traditional narrative of the Book of Mormon and describes Joseph Smith's discovery of the "Gold Bible" through the aid of an "old spirit" that is fantastically transfigured from a white salamander. Hofmann cynically hoped Church authorities would pay handsomely for the document in order to keep it hidden from public view. A deal was never reached, however, and Hofmann finally sold the letter to document collector Steven Christensen for $40,000. Christiansen wanted it authenticated and then donated to the Church. In the spring of 1984, Jan acquired a photocopy of the Salamander Letter from a staff librarian at the Bloomington Library, a native Salt Laker who, apparently, was one of Hofmann's document contacts. This was unknown to Hofmann, who thought he had a list of everyone who possessed a copy. Because it was consistent with what she knew about the magical elements of religion in nineteenth-century frontier America, Jan thought at the time the Salamander Letter might very well be legitimate. Meanwhile, Hofmann had told *Sunstone* editor Peggy Fletcher that he would discuss the Salamander Letter at the 1984 Sunstone Symposium in Salt Lake City, but subsequently backed out, leaving Fletcher in the lurch. Needing to put together a substitute opening session for the symposium, Fletcher prevailed upon Jan, Richard Bushman, and Valeen Tippetts Avery (co-author with Linda King Newell of *Mormon Enigma: Emma Hale Smith*) to talk on how their historical research affected their understanding of Joseph Smith. In her talk, Jan referred to the Salamander Letter as an example of the role magic often plays in the formation of new religions in certain cultural environments. In this respect, Jan said Joseph Smith was typical of founders of new religions and that the Salamander Letter demonstrated the magical elements of early Mormonism. John Dart of the *Los Angeles Times* was in the audience and afterward asked Jan for a copy of her talk, so Jan gave him her handwritten notes. Dart then wrote a lengthy article for the *Times* about the

Salamander Letter and its implications for Mormonism's "idealized portrait" of Joseph Smith.[33]

Hofmann, who didn't want the Salamander Letter publicized, was upset by the story. He approached Jan in the LDS Church Library the day after Dart's article was published and insisted on knowing how she had acquired a copy of the document. Jan refused to reveal her source, saying only that "I have friends you don't know about." Hofmann came to Jan at the library the next day and persisted in asking to meet with her. Jan acquiesced to have lunch, where Hofmann peppered her with additional questions about her access to the letter. Jan demurred answering directly, saying only that "It was not in Utah. I read it in the library of a Big Ten university." A little over a year later, under mounting financial pressure due to his convoluted forgery dealings,[34] Hofmann delivered two deadly pipe bomb packages in Salt Lake City—one Steven Christensen and another to Christensen's former business associate, J. Gary Sheets—in an attempt to misdirect a police investigation. Christensen and Sheets's wife, Kathy Sheets, were killed by separate explosive devices. Hofmann accidentally injured himself in the detonation of a third bomb, leading to his arrest, prosecution, and conviction.

The McLellin Diaries

Prior to his murderous acts, Hofmann, in an attempt to solve his growing financial debt, claimed potential access to a set of rare documents which he referred to as the "McLellin collection"—writings by early LDS leader William E. McLellin, who left the LDS Church in its first decade over disagreements with Joseph Smith and other leaders. As with the Salamander Letter, Hofmann hoped that by claiming the collection had potentially embarrassing content for the Church it could be sold for a large sum of money.

---

33. John Dart, "Mormons Ponder 1830 Letter Altering Idealized Image of Joseph Smith."

34. Hofmann was arrested in January 1986 and charged on twenty-seven counts, including first-degree murder, delivering a bomb, constructing or possessing a bomb, theft by deception, and communication fraud. In January 1987, Hofmann pleaded guilty to two counts of second-degree murder, one count of theft by deception for forging the Salamander Letter, and one count of fraud for the phony sale of the "McLellin collection." Hofmann agreed to confess his forgeries in court, in return for which prosecutors dropped additional charges against him. He was sentenced to five years to life in prison. But in 1988, appalled by his own callous recital of his crimes before them, the Utah Board of Pardons determined he would serve the remainder of his life in prison, without prospect of parole. See Turley, *Victims*. For a review essay on the books about Hoffmann, accompanied by a chronology and bibliography of other sources, see David J. Whittaker, "The Hofmann Maze: A Book Review Essay with a Chronology and Bibliography of the Hofmann Case," 67–124.

This time, however, Hofmann was in over his head and unable to forge the necessary documents, leading to the crimes he committed to protect himself.

Following the tragic Hofmann episode, LDS leaders were informed by the LDS Church Historical Department that they, in fact, had the McLellin diaries. Before announcing this to the press, Church officials wanted to know precisely what was in the diaries. They consulted Richard Bushman, who in turn advised them to contact Jan, who by this time was both trusted by LDS Church historians and the press. In 1991, Jan was contacted by Richard Turley, Managing Director of the Church Historical Department, who frankly told her that the Church not only wanted someone who was historically competent to both assess, edit, and annotate the diaries, but also someone who could credibly assure national media reporters that the Church was being honest in publishing an un-expurgated rendition of the complete set of diary entries. Jan agreed to review the diaries for their contents and was sent a photostat copy to read, which her IUPUI department secretary converted into a typescript document.

It turned out that there were two sets of McLellin diaries. The first consisted of his early diary entries as a convert to Mormonism and devout exponent of the faith, which were very positive and not critical of the Church or its leadership. The second set was written after McLellin became disillusioned, had left the Church, and was negative and critical of its leaders, especially Joseph Smith. When Jan began reading McLellin's early diary entries to Tony, he told her it reminded him of the New Testament; it was reminiscent of Paul and the other disciples of Jesus, full of missionary conviction and zeal to testify and win converts. Comparing early Mormons like McLellin to the first Christians reinforced Jan's belief that Mormonism, like primitive Christianity, was the beginning of a new religious tradition. Jan saw the historical importance of these documents and received permission to edit the diaries and publish a scholarly edition. She was not interested, however, in the second set of McLellin diaries, which would not be edited and published until 2008.[35]

Brigham Young University law professor John Welch was keenly interested in the McLellin diaries and, in 1992, learned that Jan had obtained copies. As the editor of *BYU Studies* and founder and president of the Foundation for Ancient Research and Mormon Studies (FARMS), Welch apparently believed he was a more appropriate person to edit and publish these historic manuscripts. According to Jan, Welch flew to Indianapolis, phoned her, and said, "I am calling on behalf of the general authorities." He pointed out that the Church *owned* the papers and claimed authorization to work on them. Although it was not clear to Jan what authorization Welch actually had (perhaps, Jan mused, he had in fact persuaded Church officials to include him

---

35. Stan Larson and Samuel J. Passey, eds. *The William E. McLellin Papers 1854–1880.*

on the project), Jan had by now realized that editing the diaries would take a tremendous amount of her time, and Welch had graduate assistants to do footnote checking and other necessary clerical tasks. So she agreed to collaborate with Welch but informed him that she had already talked with Liz Dulaney at the University of Illinois Press about publishing the diaries.

Illinois Press subsequently worked with *BYU Studies* to cover the expenses of publishing *The Journals of William E. McLellin, 1831–1836*.[36] Jan says that she and Welch "got along pretty well" working on the manuscript, but that, in her opinion, he had a sizeable ego and "wanted to take a lot of the credit." She negotiated a written, signed agreement with Welch, stipulating that her name be listed as first co-editor, and that she had the right to edit his students' footnotes before publication. Jan says she had learned her lesson about authorial credit in academic publishing when she worked at the Kinsey Institute and was never credited for her work on *Homosexuality: An Annotated Bibliography*. In the end, Jan says LDS Church authorities were "quite pleased" with the published and annotated edition of the McLellin diaries, and so was she.

Mitt Romney's Presidential Campaign

Another more recent Mormon-based story was, of course, the 2008 and 2012 campaigns of Mitt Romney for president of the United States, during what the press dubbed as the "Mormon Moment"—a prolonged news event that generated numerous calls from the press for Jan's observations and commentary. This included two articles written for Trinity College's biannual *Religion in the News* series, entitled "Romney and the Mormon Moment" in 2007 and "The Saints Come Marching In" in 2012.[37] In between the Hofmann and Romney stories, there were a great number of other Mormon-related events that have drawn press interest and commentary from Jan over the years, including the 2002 Winter Olympic Games staged in Salt Lake City and the more recent Ordain Women movement that seeks priesthood ordination for LDS women.[38] A more complete and thorough biography of Jan Shipps's life would find many more biographical facts and pertinent events to include for consideration and assessment than we have offered here. We trust, however, that our abbreviated sketch of Jan's academic history ad-

---

36. Jan Shipps and John W. Welch, eds, *The Journals of William E. McLellin, 1831–1836*.

37. For Shipps's articles on Mormonism for Trinity College's biannual *Religion in the News* series, see her listing in Religion in the News, "Contributors Archive."

38. For Shipps's comments in response to the excommunication of Ordain Women executive board officer Kate Kelly, see Brady McCombs, "Mormon Church Excommunicates Women's Group Founder."

equately demonstrates her impact on the emergence of Mormon Studies as a recognized field of professional investigation. Jan, of course, was not the only important scholar who promoted the study of Mormon theology, history, and culture as legitimate topics of scholarly inquiry. Undoubtedly, however, she was among the most effective and persuasive ones who did so, not only through her overlapping organizational affiliations but, importantly, through the authority of her own writing.

Assessing the trajectory of Jan's academic history, we again observe that she regularly seemed to be in the right place at the right time to forward her career. Thus, for example, Jan's determined quest for a tenure-track position coincided with IUPUI's plans to establish a research-oriented religious studies program. Shortly after she was hired to teach both history and religious studies, the university received financial support from the Lilly Endowment to launch the American Studies Center, which helped to thrust Jan into the national limelight. Good fortune or "luck," however, does not suffice as explanations for Jan's success and influence. Jan had the imagination and drive that many of her peers lacked. She was highly collegial and good at gravitating to and working effectively with other people of true ability. She was neither intimidated nor unduly egocentric when working with such people, which in academia often become obstacles to productive collaboration. Others who are provided similar opportunities to shine fail to capitalize, whereas Jan took full advantage of the chances that came her way. In addition to her research skills, Jan is a pragmatically action-oriented person who is organizationally effective at using institutions to get things done. These are among the personal qualities that we examine at greater length in the following chapter.

CHAPTER 6

Major Intellectual Influences and Turning Point Events

Statistical generalizations can be made about the stages and corresponding chances of people's occupational careers over time.[1] Individuals' personal ambitions and career aspirations are always mediated by existing opportunities and mobility channels which, in turn, are structured by institutions of social class, education, and the relative prevalence of discriminatory ethnic, racial, and gender norms. Predictably, people's access to educational options and other career opportunities that enhance or hamper human mobility are correlated with the ascribed statuses they inherit at birth.[2] If, however, we shift attention from the statistical analysis of career outcomes within groups and populations to the biographies of particular individuals, we must be prepared to see a substantial range of individual differences and statistically rare achievement outcomes.

Internal and External Contingencies in the Development of an Individual's Career

Some individuals with inherited opportunities and easy access to vital mobility channels may squander their advantages and experience lackluster careers. Others who lack inherited advantages may, nonetheless, push ambitiously forward and achieve noteworthy careers in spite of their initial

---

1. An overview of theories and research in the study of occupational mobility is provided by Donald J. Treiman, "Occupational Mobility." For recent statistical studies of occupational mobility in the United States, see Katja Dlouhy and Torsten Biemann, "Path Dependence in Occupational Careers: Understanding Occupational Mobility Development Throughout Individuals' Careers," 86–97, and Chris Robinson, "Occupational Mobility, Occupation Distance, and Specific Human Capital," 513–51. Analysis focusing on *women's* mobility prospects over the life course is provided by Shirley Dex, *Women's Occupational Mobility: A Lifetime Perspective*.

2. For a sampling of research on the relationship between educational and career opportunities based on ascribed versus achieved status characteristics, see François Nielsen, "Achievement and Ascription in Educational Attainment: Genetic and Environmental Influences on Adolescent Schooling," 193–216; Bridget Smith Pieschel, "The History of Mississippi University for Women"; Gijsbert Stoet and David C. Geary, "The Gender-Equality Paradox in Science, Technology, Engineering, and Mathematics Education," 581; and Tony Tam and Jin Jiang, "The Making of Higher Education Inequality: How Do Mechanisms and Pathways Depend on Competition?" 807–16.

handicaps. Biography is necessarily an idiographic enterprise that stresses the unique traits and life experiences of particular individuals. While every person's life constitutes a biography, relatively few people's lives or occupational careers are of sufficient importance to others to warrant composing a written narrative for public contemplation. It is those people's lives that have had a discernable impact on the communities in which they live and work that typically become the subject matter of written biographies. Of particular biographical interest are those individuals who not only have impacted their communities but have done so by overcoming personal or institutional obstacles in pursuit of their careers that make them statistical anomalies.

Jan Shipps's working-class origins as a girl growing up Methodist in the American South during the Great Depression were not biographical facts especially conducive to becoming a renowned Mormon Studies scholar later in life. What is particularly surprising in the development of her academic career, however, is not so much her class origins or gender, but the fact that she is not a member of the Church of Jesus Christ of Latter-day Saints and knew virtually nothing about the Mormons until moving to Utah as a young mother and recommencing her undergraduate education at the age of thirty. At that stage of her life, nobody, including Jan herself, could possibly have predicted that she would eventually become the first woman and non-Mormon president of the Mormon History Association and, subsequently, publish a book praised as being perhaps "the most brilliant book ever written on Mormonism."

Focusing attention on the biographical details of a particular person's career does not, of course, mean we can ignore the shaping and mediating influence of existing cultural and social institutions. The latter always represent the crucial context in which even statistically unusual individuals must construct and live their lives. Therefore, before proceeding we think it would be useful to introduce some framing concepts for understanding the ultimate direction in which Jan Shipp's academic career emerged and developed.

Our approach emphasizes that the unfolding of an individual's career is always a social process that allows for a substantial degree of human agency in responding to turning point events and contingency factors in its evolutionary development. Turning points are significant moments in life in which a person has the chance to move in a new or different direction, which is typically done through either acting on or abdicating conscious choices. Turning points themselves are shaped by various contingencies. *Internal contingencies* are factors connected to the capabilities of individuals: their talents, native intelligence, and moral character, especially including individual differences in cognitive complexity, motivation, and achievement orientation. *External contingencies* are factors connected to the relative influence of other persons or social circumstances that impinge on the lives of individuals: their social networks, primary and secondary group relationships, and the opportunity structures and mobility channels afforded by institutions and historical events. To adequately explain an individual's relative success (or failure) in pursuing different careers requires that we assess both the internal and external contingency factors that shaped the turning point stages of their development.[3]

It should also be understood that, in many ways, internal and external contingencies are *mutually* contingent: An individual's talents, intelligence, and moral character are shaped by their social networks, and primary and secondary group relations, as well as the opportunity structure and mobility channels of their society. Conversely, group norms, cultural values, and the structure of existing institutions can be impacted and modified by the thinking and actions of influential individuals (who, in turn, become prominent candidates for biographical consideration).

In what follows we identify (1) what we consider to be Jan Shipps's primary personal capabilities that have been activated as internal contingencies at various turning point moments in her life, and (2) the people and events that have operated as key external contingencies in the unlikely development of her academic career as a Mormon Studies scholar.

Primary Personal Capabilities
Conducive to a Successful Academic Career

All human beings develop complex personalities and individual capabilities that set them apart from others. But the study of individual differences also allows us to identify key characteristics that, to a greater or lesser degree, are shared in common by different types of individuals in human populations.[4] What are the primary personal capabilities conducive to a successful academic career? The personal capabilities we have chosen for characterizing Jan's career include intelligence, curiosity and tolerance, ambition and determination, a capacity for abstract thinking and comparative imagination, and collegiality and networking aptitudes. On the written page, these all appear as highly positive traits. We introduce them not simply as paeans to Jan Shipps, but for their explanatory utility in understanding the trajectory of

---

3. We have extrapolated from Turner and Killian's "contingency theory" (involving both internal and external contingencies) in the developmental careers of social movements and applied it to the biographical analysis of an individual's career development. See Ralph H. Turner and Lewis M. Killian, *Collective Behavior*, 241–61.

4. While always acknowledging individual differences, personality theories in psychology seek to identify and explain the key biological, social, and cultural variables that produce different types of personality. For a comprehensive review and assessment of different theories of human personality, see Oliver P. John, Richard W. Robins, and Lawrence A. Pervin, *Handbook of Personality: Theory and Research*.

her academic career. Furthermore, we do not claim that our designated set of capabilities constitute either a necessary or sufficient set of qualities for different kinds of success in academia; nor do we claim that it is an inclusive list of Jan's personal traits and characteristics. Presumably there are less stellar traits and personal quirks that also are part of Jan's personality that we have not included in our intellectual portrait. But we would argue that the qualities we identify here clearly represent some of the most important ones for understanding Jan's ultimate success as an academic and Mormon Studies scholar.

Intelligence

Any assessment of people who have pursued highly successful academic careers should include recognition of individual differences in intelligence. While the several different kinds of intelligence identified in human beings are all influenced by sociocultural factors in the developmental process of growing up, a quantifiably unknown degree of individual intelligence is genetically inherited.[5] Though unmeasured, this is what we may call innate or native intelligence. Genetically inherited intelligence may also be thought of as *potential* intelligence that awaits the operation of various external contingencies in the social world for its development and full realization.

---

5. Following the publication of Richard J. Herrnstein and Charles Murray's controversial book *The Bell Curve: Intelligence and Class Structure in American Life*, concerning the genetic basis of intelligence, the American Psychological Association formed a task force to survey the scientific literature on human intelligence. The results of the task board's survey were published as an article entitled, "Intelligence: Knowns and Unknowns," 77–101. The article concluded that intelligence is the product of both genetic and environmental variables, but that their relative weights vary a good deal and are still largely unknown. According to the task force, "Like every trait, intelligence is the joint product of genetic and environmental variables. Gene action always involves a (biochemical or social) environment; environments always act via structures to which genes have contributed. Given a trait on which individuals vary, however, one can ask what fraction of that variation is associated with differences in their genotypes (this is the heritability of the trait) as well as what fraction is associated with differences in environmental experience. So defined, heritability can and does vary from one population to another. In the case of IQ, [it] is markedly lower for children (about .45) than for adults (about .75). This means that as children grow up, differences in test scores tend increasingly to reflect differences in genotype and in individual life experience rather than differences among the families in which they were raised. The factors underlying that shift—and more generally the pathways by which genes make their undoubted contributions to individual differences in intelligence—are largely unknown. Moreover, the environmental contributions to those differences are almost equally mysterious. We know that both biological and social aspects of the environment are important for intelligence, but we are a long way from understanding how they exert their effects."

While we have little more than anecdotes to go by, we can infer that both of Jan's parents were intelligent. Jan's mother, Thalia Jenkins Bell Barnett, had a college degree (so did her sisters)—a statistically rare achievement for women in 1920s America, especially in the southern regions of the Old South. Thalia was also a reader—a schoolteacher who actively participated in a women's book club and strongly encouraged Jan's reading interests. While her father, William McKinley Barnett, did not have a college education, Jan describes him as "even smarter" than her mother and that he "could do anything." William's intelligence revealed itself primarily in his practical skills and entrepreneurial confidence. He was especially capable of finding creative ways to earn a living in support of his family during times of economic hardship—despite his own contributions to family instability through his drinking and gambling inclinations.

Further circumstantial evidence of Jan's inherited, native intelligence comes from the fact that her siblings were also bright and talented. Both of her brothers were good students in school, went on to get college degrees, and had musical ability. Jan's sister Sue, however, who suffered from undiagnosed dyslexia, was not very successful in academic subjects at school. But her creative talent in art and dance were apparent from an early age, and her popularity with peers was strengthened by a certain kind of self-confidence, leadership ability, and moral courage that she expressed in voicing opposition to injustice and discrimination as the two sisters matured.

Jan herself showed early signs of native intelligence as a child. She "learned her letters" and began reading before she started school. Because of her advanced scholastic aptitude, Jan was promoted a grade in school and subsequently graduated from high school at the age of fifteen, excelling in virtually every subject she studied. She was an avid reader from early age and frequented the public library for books to read and take home with her. She had an aptitude for music and began piano lessons at the age of five. Jan practiced diligently throughout her childhood and teen years, including private lessons at the Birmingham School of Music. By the time she was twelve, she played piano for the local Methodist Church and received constant recognition from both adults and her peers for what they perceived as her precocious musical ability.

Finally, as Jan herself admits, one of the self-insights that sustained her confidence for the future during uncertain times in adolescence and young adulthood was simply this: "I always knew I was smart." Jan's native intelligence and musical talent were, of course, strongly reinforced by parental example and encouragement, as well as the support of her "rich Aunt Sue," while she was growing up in Hueytown. But it is also fair to infer that Jan was genetically favored with her share of innate talent and intelligence that provided her with a considerable amount of potential ability for development and future realization.

Curiosity and Tolerance

One of the attributes of intelligence is curiosity. Curiosity pushes thought beyond traditional prejudices, justificatory platitudes, complacency, and the constraints of risk aversion. To be curious is to be motivated to expand one's knowledge, to seek a more comprehensive understanding, and to be able to explain things that don't make sense. We assume curiosity is a universal human characteristic, but it is also one that shows a wide range of development. Some individuals are far more curious than others. For some, knowledge is largely a utilitarian matter, and their curiosity does not extend much beyond securing a niche within the taken-for-granted social worlds in which they live. For others, however, increasing their knowledge and capacity to explain their experience has intrinsic value. To what extent curiosity is learned and conditioned or genetically inherited is, like intelligence itself, a debatable question.

We assume that individuals who are drawn to academic careers also display a range of curiosity in how and what they think about. But, on average, we would guess that academics are more motivated by curiosity in their work than most people in other occupations. The intrinsic value of greater knowledge and explanatory modes of thinking is routinely celebrated in mathematics, science, the arts and humanities, and the social and behavioral sciences.

It is in the humanities and social and behavioral sciences that, in conjunction with curiosity, human tolerance becomes a critical attribute. The subject matter of these disciplines entertains all things human—a staggeringly diverse assortment of beliefs, values, normative practices, and of people who look and talk in ways that are radically different from one's immediate family and neighbors. Individuals who lack genuine curiosity about people and cultural traditions that differ from their own are poor candidates for pursuing professional careers in fields that take humanity as their subject matter. Tolerance of personal and cultural differences is a requisite capacity for genuine curiosity about other people, and, reciprocally, genuine curiosity about other people is essential to the development of human tolerance.

As previously noted, what perhaps is the most unforeseen development of Jan's academic career was—as a lifelong Methodist—her rapid gravitation as a scholar to the study of Mormon history. Granted, when she recommenced her undergraduate studies for a bachelor's degree at Utah State, she was fortuitously influenced by Mormon historian Everett Cooley's historiography class, in which he required students to do primary research on a Mormon topic. But her sudden academic interest in Mormonism did not simply sprout from nowhere. There were dozens of other students who took Cooley's class—all of them Mormons—but none who were anywhere near as intent as Jan was in researching her topic on the history of the Logan temple. The truth is, prior to taking Cooley's class, Jan had already become highly curious about local Mormon culture in Logan and especially about the widely divergent views of faithful Latter-day Saints and "Jack Mormons," with whom Jan and Tony associated. By way of contrast, Tony was not the least interested in the peculiar religion of the Latter-day Saints and was certainly not curious to learn more about it. Before her schooling in the value-free methods of historical research, Jan was *already* intensely curious about their new surroundings and the people who lived there. She wanted to understand them, not judge them. She had already cultivated a healthy mixture of curiosity and tolerance in her intellectual outlook on life—an orientation essential to the academic trades of history and social science. Where did this come from?

Here we need to recall Jan's experience growing up in Hueytown during the Great Depression and Second World War: the social gospel principles to which she was exposed at the Methodist Church, her parents' own take on religion as an organization more important for helping others than inculcating doctrinal dogmas, her close attachment to a black caregiver at a young age, early associations with black children as friends and playmates, and her admired older sister's rejection of racial segregation norms in the Jim Crow South.

We should also recall Jan's impactful experience of leaving the small-town South as a young married woman to make a new life with Tony in the alien northern environments of urban Chicago and Detroit. Adrift from her family and cultural moorings, Jan clung to Tony, but she also commenced to read extensively about the history of the South and the Civil War to make sense of her own cultural background. She read about Jewish history in America to gain greater appreciation for the group cohesion necessary to survive as a people when cast out as a despised ethnic minority. The fiction she devoured was about people struggling to adjust their lives to new social and cultural settings in which they had arrived as outsiders. And in both Chicago and Detroit, Jan enthusiastically took on the role of mothering troubled city girls, cultivating in the process a respect for clinical methods of counseling in preference to doctrinaire moral lecturing with its implicit conviction of moral superiority.

All of these maturing experiences, in combination with her intelligence and capacity for learning, augmented Jan's native curiosity and the cultivation of a tolerant outlook toward people of divergent backgrounds, especially those facing institutional disadvantages and historical discrimination. As a mature mother and young adult returning to school, Jan had already concluded that she was more interested in learning about people living their lives than she had ever been about her former music major. When she coincidentally encountered Mormons and their history on the campus of Utah State University, she was already primed to learn as much about them as she could. And her initial studies of Mormon history and culture deepened her interest in learning yet more, stimulating her curiosity to explain and make greater sense of the Mormon past.

Ambition and Determination

Like socially inherited advantages, native intelligence and curiosity alone do not guarantee occupational success in life. Practically speaking, without applied discipline and the desire to develop one's gifts, native talent or intelligence amounts to very little. Intelligence must be complemented by other personal attributes, especially the qualities of ambition and determination that coincidentally are predicated in the competitive mobility systems of American culture. While often sublimated to teamwork roles in pursuit of shared goals with significant others, Jan's underlying competitive orientation also stands out in many of her most important partner relationships. We see this in her relationships with her older sister growing up in Hueytown, with male student peers at Utah State and the University of Colorado, with her academic colleagues at IUPUI and in the Mormon History Association (again, mostly males), and, perhaps most decisively, with her husband, Tony.

In the context of social settings that are normatively structured for competition, competitors are viewed positively as ambitious, achievement-oriented individuals. True competitors are undaunted by the demanding work and struggle implicit for success in a competitive culture; they are motivated by challenges to their efforts and excel when confronted by the standards set by other achievement-oriented individuals. Unrelenting determination to achieve socially defined goals of success, despite obstacles obstructing their path, is a key attribute of successful, achievement-oriented people in competitive social systems.[6]

Capitalizing on her native intelligence and musical aptitude, Jan was considerably motivated to excel in school to compensate for her perceived shortcomings in physical looks and athleticism compared to these dominant qualities of her sister, Sue. Likewise, Jan's musical talents became instrumental in creating a social niche for her to share in her sister's popularity with their school peers. Later, as a married woman and mother, Jan became highly motivated to quickly succeed in college in order to both meet Tony's achievement standards and acquire a teaching credential so she could contribute to the family's financial well-being. In the process of reigniting her dormant college education, she discovered she could outperform younger students, including and especially male history majors at Utah State University.

---

6. See David C. McClelland, *The Achievement Motive, Talent and Society: New Perspectives in the Identification of Talent*, and *The Achieving Society*. McClelland's pioneering studies of the connection between achievement motivation and the normative structure and cultural values of the larger society remain highly influential.

Reinforced by her undergraduate success, Jan's confidence and academic ambition accelerated as a graduate student at the University of Colorado. While juggling her traditional marital commitment to support Tony and mother their son, she again pursued a fast-track course, pushing herself to complete all her coursework requirements—in competition for top grades with mostly male students—while writing both a master's thesis and doctoral dissertation in a concentrated span of just four years. Jan's capacity for focused self-discipline in pursuing academic success in her coursework was matched by her determination to master subject areas related to her scholarly interests through self-initiated reading and personal study outside the boundaries of a formal curriculum. This was especially the case in Jan's absorption of the vast literature on Mormon history and her later foray into the more theoretical field of religious studies. Along the way, Jan's proclivity for rapid self-teaching through personal initiative was also evident in her acquisition of quantitative methods skills as a research grant director at the Kinsey Institute for Sex Research.

The most prominent defining characteristic of Jan's relationship with both her Mormon history associates and IUPUI colleagues was collegiality, but embedded in these relationships was a shared commitment to ambitious standards of scholarly achievement that promoted both admiration for, and invidious comparisons between, the most accomplished scholars in their fields. Jan was obviously flattered by the attention and recognition she received from her mostly male colleagues. She also was obviously proud of being a woman scholar who could hold her own with the men who dominated her fields of study, and she was highly motivated to meet and even surpass their expectations of academic excellence.

Finally, the expanding achievement motivation that fueled Jan's belated emergence as a scholar placed her in implicit competition with Tony's academic status and accomplishments, which he had toiled his entire adulthood to achieve. This unspoken competition for academic achievement and recognition by scholarly peers increasingly became part of Jan and Tony's changing marital role-dynamics, during which process Jan eventually far surpassed Tony's lifetime achievements.

All of this, of course, illustrates the underlying character traits of ambition and determination to succeed that gave impetus and direction to Jan's native intelligence and curiosity. These traits, in conjunction with others discussed below, functioned as internal contingency factors at critical turning point moments in the emergence and development of her academic career.

Abstract Thinking and Comparative Imagination

Even among academic scholars there are substantial differences in modes of thinking and approaches to intellectual work. In science, for example, a stereotypical distinction is commonly made between researchers and theorists. In the social sciences, researchers are viewed as scholars committed to designing and carrying out the empirical investigation of discrete human problems, with a primary emphasis on the methodological rigor and factual accuracy of their studies. Social theorists, on the other hand, are typically viewed as scholars whose primary concern is to propound abstract concepts for generalizing the connections between related facets of human experience and explaining the general causes and consequences of these connections.

In *The Sociological Imagination*, C. Wright Mills famously criticized what he perceived as two debilitating trends in contemporary social science—namely, "abstracted empiricism" and "grand theory."[7] In Mills's view, the practitioners of abstracted empiricism carried out research without theoretical guidance for making larger sense of history and society, while the grand theorists' constructs were so abstract that they were irrelevant to the understanding or solution of contemporary human problems. Taken to extremes, these two tendencies lead in opposite directions, producing a discipline of facts without theories, or one with theories without facts. Mills called for a robust integration of factual research and theoretical analysis, wherein discrete studies of individuals may be made meaningful in the larger context of history and contemporary institutions. For Mills, the sociological imagination was the *quality of mind* necessary "to grasp history and biography and the relations of the two within society. . . . It is the capacity to shift from one perspective to another . . . to range from the most impersonal and remote transformations to the most intimate features of the human self—and to see the relations between the two."[8] The task and the promise of the sociological imagination, according to Mills, were to avoid narrow, scholarly compartmentalization while addressing three essential sets of questions inherent to its subject matter: "What is the structure of this particular society as a whole? Where does this society stand in human history [and] what are the mechanics by which it is changing? What varieties of men and women now prevail in this society and in this period [and] what varieties are coming to prevail?"[9]

While Jan was not trained in sociology, with only a modicum of imagination, we can specify "Mormonism" in lieu of Mill's "this particular society" in his above statement, and particularize "American history" in place of his generic reference to "human history." Doing this we consequently may appreciate the extent to which Jan's major work, *Mormonism: The Story of a New Religious Tradition*, conforms as a case study to Mill's dictums concern-

---

7. C. Wright Mills, *The Sociological Imagination*.
8. Mills, 5, 7.
9. Mills, 7.

ing the exercise of the sociological imagination. Thus, we should ask: What is the structure of Mormonism as a whole? Where does Mormonism stand in American history, and what are the mechanics by which it is changing? What varieties of men and women *now* prevail in Mormon society in this period, and what varieties are *coming* to prevail? Jan's work is not a definitive answer to any of these questions, but she does address them, and she does so with imaginative intelligence and the intellectual capacity to sustain theoretical comparisons between the rise of primitive Christianity—in the context of Roman-ruled Judaism—and Mormonism's emergence in Protestant America—in the early flux of its democratic experiment with republican government and industrial capitalism.

When we asked Jan what elements of her education and intellectual growth she thought contributed most to her ability to think conceptually and analytically about historical topics, she was unable to provide us with a confident answer. She simply pointed out that as a child she had "good pitch musically, and I thought everybody else did too." She didn't recognize it as a relatively rare talent. She suggests this is analogous to the assumption that everyone thinks conceptually and analytically in pursuit of factual explanations, whereas this mode of thinking may mostly be true only of certain kinds of academic scholars, let alone of most other people. Jan says she didn't realize her analytical ability was much different than her friends and colleagues until she started getting scholarly feedback regarding her work. As Jan puts it, she "discovered" her ability for conceptual analysis only after she returned to school; it was a dormant talent she didn't know she had until she was an adult and began engaging the literature in her newly discovered field of study, with a critical eye toward applying what she read to making comparative sense of questions that arose in her own research on the Mormons.

In retrospect, and by way of comparison, Jan describes Tony as academically careful and exact but not analytical like her. For all his fastidious scholarship, Tony never did any theoretical analysis. Likewise, she says her musician son Stephen's mode of thinking is more like Tony's than hers. Both possess acute memories, but neither is disposed to interpretive, theoretical thinking.

In a closely related vein, we asked Jan about her writing skills, which, of course, she relies on to communicate her analysis of historical topics. She says, "It could have been just a gift," but agrees that her writing was significantly impacted by extensive reading, much of which was ingested over the years before returning to school. When she became a graduate student at the University of Colorado, her thesis advisor, Hal Bridges, asked: "Where did you learn to write?" Jan again said she didn't really know. Likewise, when asked the same question by Mormon historian Leonard Arrington, she replied, "I learned to read." Naively at the time, it never had occurred to Jan that writing well was a relatively rare skill. As with her analytical capabilities, she assumed all educated people could write and simply took her own writing ability for granted. Later, as a junior faculty member, Jan says she "learned so much about writing" from her IUPUI colleague, Tony Sherrill. Sherrill, who had training in both religion and English literature, would carefully read her manuscripts and critique her prose for clarity and precision, enabling Jan—who was ever eager to improve her abilities in exchange for the recognition of significant others—to become an even better writer.

To us, Jan described writing "as a creative process": "When one is writing, there are points in time when words come through inspiration." By this she means that, in her experience, ideas and the language for expressing them emerge more or less spontaneously. But like Tony, Jan is also a perfectionist in her work. "I rewrite every page twenty times, paragraph by paragraph, before moving on," constantly editing and polishing as she goes. She has a basic thesis in mind but doesn't work from a detailed outline that she labors over before writing, and she doesn't dash off a rough draft of the whole manuscript before going back to rewrite. Thus, sentence by sentence, constructing intelligible *paragraphs* seems to be Jan's basic unit of composition: "I write a paragraph and rewrite it until I can live with it," before moving on to write the next paragraph. Paragraph by paragraph her composition emerges. This approach to writing is based on a certain kind of confidence: it is the confidence that one has something to say and will be able to say it, but exactly what that will be, is not determined until it appears on the page. Once a specific idea or aspect of the larger thesis is articulated in a coherent paragraph, it leads logically or stylistically to the next unit of thought in the composition.

Thus, for Jan, writing about history is a creative process that emerges through sustained, concentrated thought on a topic, about which one already has acquired a good deal of factual knowledge and, supported by confident language ability, one then pursues the ultimate goal of connecting these facts in a credible explanation of their causes and consequences within the existing culture and institutional structure of a changing society.

Collegiality and Networking

While we have emphasized Jan's ability to think comparatively and conceptually about Mormonism's emergence and developmental history, it is more than just the substance of her scholarly writing that has been influential. It is the quality of her work *combined* with her ability to function collegially in academic organizations that has made her an important figure in the closely related fields of Mormon history and Mormon Studies. Through Jan's cultivation of close friendships within both the Mormon History Association and the John Whitmer Historical Association, she not only made friends in both communities but, as a non-Mormon woman, was able to bridge their divisions and mediate some of their antagonisms through encouragement of cooperative enterprises. Her persistent efforts through active involvement in multiple scholarly organizations to legitimize Mormon Studies and the importance of Mormon history in the context of American history paid substantial dividends to the growing recognition of these subject fields. Likewise, her seriousness of purpose, combined with eager collegiality, resulted in close and mutually supportive ties with her religious studies colleagues at IUPUI. According to Jan, her collaborative interaction with IUPUI faculty had an even greater impact on her thinking and writing about religious topics than did her Latter-day Saint and Community of Christ associations. And it was not only her accumulating credentials as an objective, non-Mormon expert on issues pertaining to Mormon history and the contemporary LDS Church that gained her the confidence of the news media as a trustworthy source—they also went to Jan because of her accessibility and congenial openness to their queries.

As an academic woman, Jan is not aloof, imperious, or contentious. She actively seeks academic comradeship and thrives on collegial debate and discussion. Her energetic organizational involvement and leadership in scholarly associations have been a hallmark of her academic career. Jan's level of professional organizational involvement may be profitably contrasted with the scholarly careers of Fawn Brodie and Juanita Brooks (which we will attempt in the next chapter).

Social Networks and Influential Others

To restate our basic thesis: Individual's occupational careers emerge as a result of the interaction between their personal capabilities and social circumstances (which, more abstractly, we refer to as internal and external contingencies) in the context of a series of turning point events over the course of their lives. Up to now we have identified what we consider to be among the most important personal capabilities that Jan has demonstrated in forwarding the development of her academic career. We now turn to a consideration of people who occupied key positions in her primary and secondary social networks—including significant family members, mentors, and colleagues in academic settings—who exercised major influences on her thinking, values, and career aspirations.

Significant Family Members

Among the Barnetts, both of Jan's parents, her older sister Sue, and her "rich Aunt Sue," all stand out as influential figures in her childhood and adolescence. Perhaps it's a cliché to say that one's parents are critical to the early formation of one's attitudes and expectations, but it's not always the case that children grow up admiring their parents and retrospectively appreciating or understanding their limitations after they themselves become adults. Lifelong resentment or repudiation of one or both parents is far from uncommon in families that have been permanently divided by abusive relationships, divorce, authority conflicts, sibling rivalries, or disagreements over fundamental lifestyle decisions.

In Jan's case, even though her father's drinking and gambling eventually became a disruptive element in the Barnett's efforts to cope with the economic hardships of the Great Depression, Jan and her siblings maintained a shared commitment to one another and to both of their parents. The Barnett family's collective sense of themselves as a cohesive primary group, through thick and thin, stands in contrast to Tony's experience growing up in foster care as a result of his parents' bitter divorce and the ambivalent feelings he harbored as an adult toward both of them.[10]

While Jan became much closer to her mother, Thalia, it's also clear that she admired her father, William, as a child and virtually idolized his practical skills and jack-of-all trades competence in providing for his family. As an adult, Jan still remembers her father as a handsome, "charismatic," and self-confident man who naturally seemed to be in charge—an adult who knew what to do when troubles threatened his family. Even when Jan, at a later age, became aware of William's alcoholism, she did not renounce her childhood respect for her father's authority. His periodic binges were disenchanting trials for Jan's stoical mother to endure, but he was never verbally or physically abusive to her or the children. He was, as Jan puts it, a functioning alcoholic. His rugged individualism (which inspired categorical rejection of any sort of government aid during the Great Depression) and his inculcated racist beliefs were softened by what Jan perceived as his compassion for others and practical kindness to people in need—including people of color. He was far from being puritanical or pious, but he both preached and modeled for his children his belief in the virtues of hard work and personal achievement—without making excuses for one's failures—and the imperative of rendering generosity toward acquaintances and strangers alike.

These are all attitudes we see in Jan's repertoire of character traits, and they are attitudes that were also taught and reinforced by her mother. Thalia and William were in accord on many things, including how to rear their children to respect adult authority, take initiative and accept personal respon-

---

10. Jan takes some credit for bringing Tony and his mother closer together by continually encouraging him to visit her and vice versa. It was Tony's mother's visit to Bloomington in 1980 that coincided with Jan's renewed involvement in the local Methodist Church. As for Tony, in spite of his feelings of abandonment in childhood, he shared interests and had much more in common with his mother (a love of libraries, books, and English literature) than with his father.

sibility for their actions, strive for achievement and success, and be thoughtful and considerate of others. These attributed traits may again sound like an uncritical recitation of Sunday school virtues, but it is not inaccurate to say that Jan took them to heart growing up, and that her parents should be given credit for the values they attempted to instill in their children.

It was Thalia who encouraged Jan to read and strongly reinforced her early academic success. Likewise, it was Thalia who detected and promoted Jan's precocious talent for playing piano, which in turn accustomed Jan to long hours of practice and personal discipline. In experiencing so much early realization of a talent that was richly rewarded with adult praise, Jan learned the lesson that, whatever one's innate talents might be, high achievement required sustained, dedicated effort. At the same time, Thalia insisted that she resist feelings of superiority because of her talent, intelligence, and higher social status relative to the poor, rural families she taught and worked with during the Great Depression. Ancillary lessons learned by Jan as a consequence of the personal modesty emphasized by her mother arguably included empathy for others different than oneself and, consequently, an inclination to take greater interest in the lives of other people. These social attitudes, in conjunction with both of her parents' lack of religious dogmatism and forbearance of Jan's and her siblings' casual association with black children growing up on the mountain in Hueytown, likely contributed to Jan's adult capability for tolerance and curiosity as a student of human history.

Not to be overlooked in its imprinting influence was the sheer fact of Thalia's own working career as a capable and self-sufficient woman. Her college education, her work for the Works Progress Administration during the Depression, and her lifelong career as a public school teacher were all taken-for-granted aspects of Jan's growing up. Jan's model of womanhood was an educated working mother who was not inferior to men in intelligence or talent, and who confidently assumed leadership roles in her church and among other women in the community. Jan always assumed she would follow in her mother's footsteps and go to college. Although she dropped out of school to be a wife and mother, there was scarcely a time as an adult that Jan didn't work. When she resumed her college education in later life, her goal was always connected to obtaining a degree in order to pursue a professional career, first as a public school teacher like her mother, and ultimately as a college professor.

As an academic, Jan has never been shy about accepting leadership positions. Like Thalia, she has proactively engaged with peers to advance her career in organizational settings rather than moving, like some, to the social margins of academia to function as an independent scholar.[11] In contrast, while Jan's father was gregarious and popular with friends, he was also highly individualistic and entrepreneurial, confident in his personal abilities rather than resorting to work in organizations to realize occupational goals. Compared to her father, both Jan and Thalia were far better at cultivating collaborative, collegial relations as an essential part of their working lives.

Describing the influence of Jan's mother on Jan's thinking and sense of purpose, we should not neglect to make mention of the similar influence of Jan's Aunt Sue on her early impression of smart, educated women in her life. Aunt Sue was also college educated and had a teaching degree. She had "married well" and didn't have to worry about making a living the way Thalia did. But she also was not a subservient woman and took an active interest in her nieces' growth and development, paying for their extracurricular lessons, buying clothes for special occasions, and adding an important adult voice of praise and encouragement for their successes in school and elsewhere. Aunt Sue modeled sophistication and self-confidence and was proof of the possibility of rising in the world from relatively humble beginnings.

While Jan sustained a basic loyalty to both her parents and her two younger brothers, undoubtedly the single most significant family member for Jan growing up was her sister Sue. A year older but occupying the same grade in school from their elementary years forward, Sue was Jan's earliest role model. At the same time, however, she also was a competitor for their parents' approval as well as for acceptance among their neighborhood friends and peers at school. Unlike most siblings who, though close in age, cultivate different friendship groups and social activities, Jan and Sue Barnett did virtually everything together. They cared for and supported each other and, quite apparently, negotiated a tacit understanding of their complementary role-identities.

---

11. For the first two decades of her writing career, Fawn Brodie was an independent scholar before accepting a faculty position at UCLA in 1967, while Juanita Brooks was an independent scholar over the entire course of her publishing career. Today, the label "independent scholar" conveys an ambiguous connotation. In "Stop Calling Me 'Independent Scholar,'" for *The Chronicle of Higher Education*, Megan Kate Nelson explains: "The term [independent scholar] usually describes a person with a Ph.D. who does not have an academic affiliation but who still participates in academe—by going to conferences or publishing books with academic presses, for instance. It does not matter whether this person is unaffiliated by choice or because of the terrible job market. 'Independent' is inherently referential; you are independent of something. While 'scholar' refers to a specialist in a branch of study, the combination 'independent scholar' is a status simultaneously defined by academe and separate from it. It both claims and marginalizes unaffiliated scholars." See Megan Kate Nelson, "Stop Calling Me 'Independent Scholar.'"

Attractive and practical like their father, Sue took the lead socially and won kudos for her athleticism and art ability. Channeling her mother's aptitudes and aspirations, Jan was "the brain" and scholastic achiever who wowed everyone with her exceptional piano-playing talent. Sue was considered a beauty and had lots of boyfriends. In comparison, Jan saw herself as homely and sought the compensatory approval of adults rather than the flirtatious attention of boys. These were Jan and Sue's sisterhood identities, by which they were known to their friends and adults alike. They undoubtedly also experienced some mutual jealousies and petty annoyances with one another, but Jan and Sue typically integrated their contrasting strengths to function as a team—the Barnett girls—for establishing their Hueytown standing and reputations.

What developmental traits did Jan acquire from her close relationship with her sister in childhood and adolescence? At a minimum, we can surmise that she learned how to simultaneously cooperate and compete in primary relationships with significant others. Maintaining this kind of balancing act over time is not easy. The end goal is to maximize the shared rewards of cooperation while also pushing one's own self-interest. The trick is to not undermine the former by overdoing the latter (which many highly competitive people are prone to do). Effectively combining long-term cooperation with competitive self-interest in primary relationships requires patience and more than occasional willingness to put someone else's interests ahead of one's own. But self-sacrifice runs against the grain of competitive self-interest and ultimately must be compensated by other rewards. For Jan, the compensatory rewards of her marriage with Tony Shipps, hand in hand with her childhood apprenticeship of learning to engage in cooperative competition with her sister Sue, served her well in negotiating the tensions of managing both a marriage and a professional career. Being skilled as a competitive-cooperator also worked to Jan's advantage as she vigorously advanced her academic career through collegial collaboration with her IUPUI colleagues and in the various professional associations in which she participated.

As Jan transitioned from adolescence to adulthood, Tony Shipps, clearly and decisively, supplanted Sue as the most influential person in her life. Tony was Jan's first serious suitor. He was smart, better educated than Jan, older, and had plans for higher education that would enable them to grasp the fresh opportunities for mobility arising in post-war America. To top things off, Tony thought Jan was beautiful. Jan was smitten. She couldn't believe her fabulous good luck. As a teenage bride she became immediately devoted to supporting and advancing Tony's career aspirations. She also quickly learned about Tony's insecurities: his mistrust of the authenticity of intimate relationships, his need for regular reassurances that Jan's priority commitment was to him and not to her family—a need Jan determined faithfully to fulfill.

Jan and Tony, circa 1988–90.

It's fair to say that meeting and marrying Tony Shipps was the single most critical turning point event in Jan's life. Had she not married Tony, the odds are virtually zero that she would ever have lived amongst Mormons in Utah or acquired an undergraduate degree in history at Utah State University, both of which gave her the impetus for making Mormon history the focus of her PhD studies at the University of Colorado. Without Tony in her life, Jan would never have become the author of *Mormonism: The Story of a New Religious Tradition*, and we would not be writing this book to comprehend her intellectual biography.

Having acknowledged this, it is also true to say that Jan profited tremendously in other ways intellectually as a consequence of her devoted marriage to Tony Shipps. He provided Jan with her first true model of academic discipline, of what it meant to be a scholar, and of demanding rigorous adherence to the standards of scholarly inquiry. Jan proactively offered her research and editing assistance to Tony in his work as a graduate student and later as an academic librarian, and Tony gladly employed her help. Moreover, Tony's love of books coincided with and reinforced Jan's own and stimulated her already acquired habit of self-education through persistent, self-directed reading, which was to become so typical of her intellectual expansion as both a student and professional academic.

The fact that Tony never shared Jan's boundless enthusiasm for learning about the Mormons is retrospectively irrelevant. To a greater or lesser degree, he tolerated what appeared to be her eccentric interest in Mormon Studies and, ultimately, rendered his acquiescent support. As a budding scholar, to Jan this meant everything. At the same time, parallel to Jan's own acquiescence to most of Tony's wishes, we should also recall her underlying and determined persistence in pursuing important personal goals. Along with her capacity for effective teamwork in competitive settings, these are vital internal factors for understanding both the endurance of her marriage and success in her professional career.

Mentors and Colleagues

By the time she became a scholar, Jan's essential character traits had already been well formed in her primary group relationships with family members and subsequently were reinforced through her marriage to Tony. The later influences of mentors and colleagues had little to do with shaping her personal qualities but were of critical importance in both narrowing her eclectic intellectual interests and expanding her appreciation of the varieties of conceptual approaches and methodologies for producing genuine scholarship.

Chief among Jan's mentors was Everett Cooley, who happened to be filling in for Leonard Arrington (who was on sabbatical) during Jan's one year as an undergraduate student at Utah State University. Cooley guided Jan into the world of Mormon history and did so in such a way that Jan was captivated by the experience of conducting actual historical research through finding and examining documents that were pertinent to answering questions about a community's past. Cooley was also the first to awaken a self-realizing glimpse of her promise as a research scholar. He challenged her, pushed her, and embodied the same commitment to scrupulous scholarship that Tony exhibited as a quotation sleuth in the study of early English literature. Himself a Latter-day Saint, Cooley's academic integrity in documenting and interpreting Mormon history topics greatly impressed Jan. In contrast to the insular piety of her Cache Valley neighbors and corresponding cynicism of Tony's Jack-Mormon associates in the USU library and English department, Cooley demonstrated how serious historical study should address the questions her own curiosity had prompted about Mormon society. Not only this, but recognizing and nourishing Jan's potential, he encouraged her to stay in contact with him after she and Tony departed for Colorado, and he became her *de facto* thesis and dissertation advisor when she chose to specialize in Mormon history as a graduate student. Virtually everything Jan learned and wrote about Mormon history as a graduate student at the University of Colorado was guided by and bore the imprint of Everett Cooley.

Though much less directly involved with her early development as a history major than was Cooley, Leonard Arrington also became a significant mentor to Jan. It was through Arrington's classic study *Great Basin Kingdom:*

An Economic History of the Latter-day Saints, 1830–1900, which examined Mormonism's nineteenth-century transition from religious communitarianism to integration with the national corporate economy, that Jan was first exposed to a professional, scholarly treatment of the Mormon past. However, it wasn't until she was a graduate student at Colorado doing archival research in Salt Lake City for her dissertation that Jan first became acquainted with Arrington. He immediately showed highly supportive interest in her work as a non-Mormon scholar and encouraged her early participation in the Mormon History Association and other like-minded gatherings (such as meetings of the Utah State Historical Society). When Jan commenced active affiliation with the Association a decade later, Arrington warmly welcomed her into active involvement and mentored her rapidly expanding connections within the Mormon intellectual community. Arrington was the same age as Everett Cooley (twelve years senior to Jan), and both were like supportive older brothers facilitating a pathway for a bright, younger sister to follow in their footsteps. As acknowledged authorities in Mormon scholarship, Jan cherished from both men their prescient appreciation of her potential and their generous guidance of her early efforts to establish a reputation among Mormon historians.

While Cooley and Arrington had a much stronger impact on Jan's career than her graduate advisors at the University of Colorado, we should not discount the influence of Lee Scamehorn and especially Hal Bridges, whose academic and personal interest in mysticism left a permanent mark on Jan's later interpretation of early Mormonism's visionary beginnings. Perhaps Scamehorn's biggest contribution to Jan's career was his willingness to work with her to expedite the accelerated completion of her PhD in the context of faculty turmoil at Colorado, and particularly his willingness to accede to Everett Cooley's unofficial role in overseeing the research and writing of Jan's dissertation—something that many proudly egocentric academicians are loath to do. Bridges, on the other hand, had a genuine impact on Jan's thinking about religion. A serious scholar, but also a mystic, Bridges took a genuine interest in Mormonism founder Joseph Smith's prophetic claims and accomplishments, and he did not denigrate Jan's preoccupation with Mormon history. Rather than dismissing out of hand the claims of religious visionaries, he imparted to Jan the importance of comprehending what she likes to call the "religious dimension" for making sense of new religions and their leaders.

If promising students succeed in building successful academic careers for themselves, then former mentors may also become colleagues. This was certainly the case for Jan with respect to Everett Cooley and Leonard Arrington. At the same time, of course, junior scholars must also cultivate professional connections with other peers in their fields of study with whom they both cooperate and compete. Among Jan's most important peers were Doug Alder, Klaus Hansen, and Paul Edwards. There were many other colleagues who were influential in the development of her career, such as Thomas Alexander and Richard Bushman, but Jan was probably closest to the former three. Of them, it was arguably Paul Edwards who had the greatest influence on Jan's thinking about Mormon history.

Paul Edwards was a lifelong member of the RLDS Church, now known as the Community of Christ. A few years younger than Jan, he was trained both in history and philosophy and maintained an active interest in theological issues.[12] He served for Jan as an intellectual counterweight to the LDS narrative of the restoration that she had been exposed to by her mentors and most of the people she had known as Mormons in Logan and in the Mormon History Association. In turn, Edwards was an admirer of philosopher and University of Utah professor, Sterling McMurrin—a lifelong Latter-day Saint with deep family roots in the Utah Mormon community.[13] McMurrin was considered a heretic by some orthodox Church leaders for his frank agnosticism and public criticism of LDS Church policies. But Edwards was deeply impressed by McMurrin's philosophical erudition, particularly as encapsulated in the *Theological Foundations of the Mormon Religion*, McMurrin's best-known work,[14] and he engaged Jan in challenging debates about the kinds of theo-

---

12. Edwards earned a doctorate from St. Andrews University in Scotland and subsequently was employed as a professor of philosophy and history at Graceland College (now a university)—the seat of higher learning for the RLDS Church/Community of Christ—where he served when he and Shipps became collegial friends. In later years, he also was elected to serve as president of both the John Whitmer Historical Association and the Mormon History Association.

13. McMurrin, the grandson of Joseph W. McMurrin—a member of the LDS First Quorum of the Seventy—obtained his PhD in philosophy from the University of Southern California, and also did postdoctoral studies at Columbia, Princeton, and Union Theological Seminary. He was professor of philosophy at the University of Utah for thirty-two years and retired in 1978 as the dean of the university's graduate school. In 1961, he was appointed by President John F. Kennedy to serve as US Commissioner of Education. For reflections on McMurrin's work, see Kathleen Flake, "The LDS Intellectual Tradition: A Study on Three Lives." See also L. Jackson Newell, "Remembering Sterling McMurrin," 10–11.

14. Sterling M. McMurrin, *The Theological Foundations of the Mormon Religion*. In the early 1950s, LDS Apostles Joseph Fielding Smith and Harold B. Lee believed McMurrin should be excommunicated for his heretical writing and speaking. President David O. McKay, however, disagreed and said he would testify in McMurrin's behalf. This effectively derailed the movement to have McMurrin expelled from the church. This episode is recounted in Gregory A. Prince, *David O. McKay and the Rise of Modern Mormonism*.

logical issues McMurrin addressed. Jan was drawn to theoretical analysis—which had not been emphasized in her own historical training—and came to value highly her stimulating talks with Edwards. As for McMurrin's work, which she read at Edward's urging, Jan concluded that it was "written by somebody who knew something besides Mormonism"; it provided a valuable comparative context within the Christian theological tradition for assessing what was distinctive about LDS beliefs.[15] Evidently, this kind of comparative analysis, stimulated by discussions with Paul Edwards, began modifying how Jan thought about Mormon history. Concomitantly, however, Jan says that having to develop and teach religious studies classes, along with intense interactions with her religious studies colleagues at IUPUI, had even greater impact on her thinking about comparative religion than McMurrin's book, or discussions with Paul Edwards. It is to these influences that we now turn.

Before accepting a tenure-track position at IUPUI in 1973, Jan had taught only American history classes and never anything about religion per se. Her joint position in history and religious studies forced her to commence a rapid, self-study review of texts and the literature in religious studies. While some of this literature overlapped with what she already had learned from her study of the Mormons (for example, Thomas O'Dea's classical sociological

---

15. In an interview with Jackson Newell, McMurrin observed, "In order to appreciate the real strengths in Mormon theology, as well as its weaknesses, a person has to have some kind of comprehension, it seems to me, of the history of religion and theology and know a good deal about what has been going on in the world in those areas, in order to compare the Mormon theology with others. You mentioned a book of mine, *The Theological Foundations of the Mormon Religion*. That was written originally as lectures given at the University of Utah. Then the university press wanted to publish it as a book. Then one of my colleagues, Sidney Engleman, who no doubt, some of you would have known, a non-Mormon, a highly cultivated Mormon watcher, very critical of Mormonism in a sophisticated way said to me when he read the book, 'You know, you have made Mormonism look a lot better than it really is.' I said, 'That is exactly what I intended to do. The other writers make it look worse than it is.' I mean that quite seriously. Mormon theology has strengths that virtually all, not all, but virtually all of the writers in the church seem to have been unaware of." See Sterling M. McMurrin, "Jack Newell Interviews Sterling McMurrin." Jan reports she didn't know much about theology prior to encountering McMurrin, and that subsequently she read *Theological Foundations* "twenty to thirty times"; it became something of a model for her later at IUPUI in presenting an analytical theological approach to her religious studies classes. It also no doubt had some bearing on development of her own big picture understanding of the theological underpinnings of Mormonism, even though she came to think that McMurrin didn't really understand day-to-day, lived Mormonism from the perspective of ordinary Mormons.

work, simply entitled *The Mormons*),[16] most of it was entirely new and emphasized a more conceptual, theoretical approach than what her training in historiography had provided her. More than this, her IUPUI religious studies colleagues were all productive scholars who expected Jan to join them in their monthly, seminar-style discussion sessions and to be conversant in the religious studies literature.

Anthony (Tony) Sherrill, her religious studies department chair, combined expertise in both religion and English literature. Jan's writing had always been one of her strengths, but Sherrill's probing critiques of her writing went beyond standard copyediting for enhanced accuracy: they called attention to her basic suppositions and obliged her to think more imaginatively about what she was saying. Her department colleague, Ted Mullen, not only gave her manuscripts a careful reading, he also engaged her in extensive conversations about comparative religion in general and the historical dynamics between ancient Judaism and the rise of Christianity in particular. The influence of Mullen's expertise in Jewish and Christian hermeneutics on Jan's thinking was both supplemented and reinforced by the biblical scholarship of her Methodist pastor, the Reverend Ross Marrs, who also engaged Jan in lengthy discussions about her research interests in the Mormons. To these three colleagues, Jan attributes a fundamental change in how she conceptualized Mormon origins. It's conceivable that without their influence, Jan may have proceeded to write the book that the Indiana University Press originally had solicited—a straightforward study of twentieth-century Mormonism—rather than the theoretically imaginative one she increasingly felt compelled to write on Mormonism's nineteenth-century emergence and transformation as a new religious tradition.

Turning Point Events

Thus far we have identified and described what we consider to be Jan's primary capabilities pertinent to understanding her intellectual development and the most important individuals in her life who contributed significantly to the formation and exercise of these capabilities. To this we now add a recitation of key turning point events that set her path in directions that we can see clearly in retrospect, but, without which, we are entitled to surmise that her life and work would have been very different than what they eventually became. In doing this, we of course run the risk of substantial redundancy in our narrative, but our conceptual framework for comprehending the ways in which Jan's academic career emerged and developed impels us to examine the interplay of all the relevant factors involved in this process.

---

16. Thomas O'Dea, *The Mormons*.

To reiterate the basic aspects of our approach, we offer a social process model of development for explaining the course of Jan's career as an academic scholar of Mormonism. We submit that occupational careers are the result of both internal and external contingencies that mutually affect one another. The idea of contingencies includes the supposition that human outcomes are not uniform and perfectly predictable, that they are contingent on a combination of factors—including human agency and "turning point events"—which, for individual cases, are typically unknown in advance. Furthermore, the working out of these contingencies occurs within already established normative frameworks and institutional structures that both limit and enhance individual possibilities. Internal contingencies are significant personal capabilities; external contingencies refer to persons who have been influential in shaping an individual's personal capabilities, as well as to turning point events in one's developmental history.

It should be kept in mind that the normative order and institutional structures that silently frame our analysis of Jan's metamorphosis (from small town, Methodist schoolgirl growing up in the American South during the Great Depression and wartime, to acclaimed scholar of Mormon Studies at a large urban university in the American Midwest) include the following: cultural values of individualism and competition; religious liberty and democratic government; romantic love and freedom of choice in selecting one's marital partner; belief in social mobility—in meritorious progress and personal success through hard work and diligence; access to formal education and occupational training; and, in the aftermath of economic depression and World War II, renewed optimism about the efficacy of democratic government, the prospects of progressive advancement of material wellbeing, the human benefits of science and technology, and the growing national need for higher education and professional development. These idealized assumptions of American society circa the mid-twentieth century, when Jan and Tony Shipps were seeking their futures, were also offset, of course, by both *de jure* and *de facto* racial discrimination, subordination of women's prerogatives to the authority of men, intolerance of non-Christian faiths, and uneradicated poverty and social class inequities. Added to this in the present century, we witness growing, not declining, economic inequality and a corresponding decline in shared optimism about the efficacy of democratic government, public education, and the universal beneficence of science and technology for increasing the quality of human life. This negative, retrospective side of the American picture does not vitiate, however, the world that enveloped Jan's coming of age and advancement toward her profession in mid-twentieth-century academia.

In what follows, we must again be selective in our analysis. People make uncounted decisions over the course of a lifetime that affect their careers. To understand occupational careers, we must focus on those occasions in which people are faced with life-changing choices, and when their decisions in these occasions produce decisive consequences for their future lives. In identifying what we consider to be the most important turning points in Jan's life and academic career, we focus on a select handful of events, without which it is highly improbable that she would have achieved fame as an authority on Mormon history and the religion of the Latter-day Saints. While we may have slighted various important aspects of her experience, major turning point events in Jan Shipps's life and academic career certainly include the ones we have listed below.

1. *Marriage to Tony Shipps.* In a sense, Jan's life prior to Tony was all prelude, a time when she was acquiring many of the personal attributes that would make her ultimately successful as a scholar. Without Tony, we have no idea where Jo Ann Barnett would have ended up in life. It's conceivable that she might have married another academic scholar who would end up taking her to Utah. Or it's also conceivable that without a complicit marital partner, Jan might have pursued an academic career anyway, entirely on her own, that somehow could have led to her preoccupation with Mormon history. The likelihood of either of these conjectures, however, is exceedingly slim.

2. *Move to Logan, Utah.* Jan was married to Tony for eleven years and lived with him in Georgia, Alabama, Chicago, and Detroit before ever learning anything about the Mormons and their peculiar religion. As with all of their moves, it was primarily *Tony's* decision, based on *his* career priorities, which took them to Logan, Utah and, subsequently, to Boulder, Colorado. As his wife, Jan eagerly supported these moves. She could have chosen to make a fuss about being uprooted by them, but she didn't. Her commitment to Tony and their marriage superseded any personal preferences she might have had. Jan's willingness to dutifully accept Tony's career decisions, and the half dozen geographical moves they consequently undertook, constituted a series of turning point events that coincidentally were critically conducive to the development of Jan's own career. It was, however, the fateful decision to move to Utah that precipitated all of Jan's subsequent contacts with academic mentors, influential colleagues, and the world of Mormon scholarship.

3. *Decision to Switch Academic Major from Music to History.* Before we pass on from the far-reaching consequences of the Shipps's move from Detroit to Logan, Utah, we must also include Jan's very practical but also critical decision to resume her undergraduate education at Utah State University and to switch her major from music to history. While Jan was perfectly in agreement with making these changes, we again see Tony's directing influence in

the early years of their marriage. While Jan had always liked reading history, switching from music (which Jan already concluded was not her professional destiny) to history as an academic major was, first and foremost, the quickest ticket to a teaching certificate so that Jan could contribute to the Shipps's family income, which is what both Jan and Tony felt she needed to do. Had she not concurred in this decision, Jan would have continued finding the Mormon community in Logan strangely interesting and, perhaps, continued to have read books about them on her own. But there would have been no historiography class, no career-shaping mentorship by Everett Cooley, and no realization that history was a career choice that would allow her to blossom as an innovative researcher and writer.

4. *Decision to Continue as a Graduate and PhD Student at the University of Colorado.* Moving to Colorado for the sake of Tony's career, the central concern for Jan's contribution to the marriage continued to be finding a teaching job. Stymied by her lack of a recognized teaching certificate to teach in Colorado schools, the quickest route to gaining one was to acquire an expedited master's degree in history at the University of Colorado. The true turning point, however, arrived a year later when Jan was offered a graduate fellowship and modest stipend for continuing at Colorado as a PhD student. When Jan accepted this offer, the die was cast. It meant she was abandoning her objective of making an income as a public school teacher. It meant she now realized her potential for academic scholarship in higher education, even if it also meant several more years of scraping by financially. And it meant—possibly for the first time—that she put her career wishes ahead of Tony's, who initially asked her to drop out of school in order to have and raise more children. Because of Jan's decision to continue her graduate education, we not only see her steady movement from that point forward toward becoming a specialist in Mormon history, we also see the beginnings of a subtle shift in the dynamics of her marriage to Tony Shipps.

5. *Move to Bloomington, Indiana.* When Tony made another career move to accept a position as library specialist in English literature at Indiana University, we see a temporary reversion in the Shipps's marriage to Jan's subordination of her own interests in support of Tony. While Jan had not been able to secure a full-time academic appointment in the Boulder area after obtaining her PhD, she at least had her foot in the door as an adjunct and part-time instructor at the University of Colorado's Denver Center. By accompanying Tony to Bloomington with their growing son, Stephen (who would require increasing parental involvement to nurture his emerging talents), Jan's employment opportunities in higher education were effectively squashed. Increasingly

frustrated as a meaningful career track appeared to have vanished, she turned to encourage Stephen's musical exploits and development by throwing herself into refurbishing her own musical skills to accompany his recital performances. With no job prospects of teaching history in Bloomington, however, Jan finally resorted to obtaining employment at Indiana University's famous Kinsey Institute. Her work at the Institute proved to be occasionally interesting and challenging, as she took initiative to become actively involved in the management and implementation of Kinsey research grants for conducting research in human sexuality. It wasn't, however, what she had aspired to do, or was trained for, and she came to feel thwarted and defeated. Jan and Tony's early years together in Bloomington were an abyss for Jan's career. In retrospect, however, it was also a fallow period in which her work at the Kinsey Institute paid important dividends in the eventual revitalization of her scholarly interests. Moreover, while she was treading water in Bloomington, events were beginning to transpire to the north in Indianapolis that would soon present Jan with one of the most significant turning event opportunities of her professional life.

6. Reconnection with the Mormon History Association. Without an academic job, and with her spirits lower than they had ever been before, Jan benefitted hugely from a decision Tony came to make when he realized how unhappy Jan was in Bloomington. He encouraged her to attend a Mormon history conference that was scheduled to take place on the campus of Southern Illinois University in Edwardsville, Illinois. Jan had been out of touch with Mormon colleagues for several years and was no longer engaged in doing research in Mormon history. Would she have attended this conference without Tony's blessing? In an interview with us, Jan said no, that Tony's encouragement was critical. Had Tony been indifferent or openly hostile to the idea of Jan attending a Mormon conference—of her driving over three hours on her own to get there and spend the night—Jan would not have gone, and she would not have reconnected with the Mormon scholarly community. Of course, there might have been other opportunities for her to do so, but this was the one she eagerly seized, at a moment of near despair, and it rejuvenated her. Several more years were to transpire before she obtained a full-time teaching position at IUPUI, but the Edwardsville conference was a turning point in creating for Jan a genuine sense of belonging among LDS scholars and revitalizing her interest in doing research in Mormon history.

7. Researching and Presenting "From Satyr to Saint" to the Organization of American Historians. It was one thing for Jan to experience a renewed sense of camaraderie with members of the Mormon scholarly community, but, in fact, she had done no original research in Mormon Studies since completing her dissertation at Colorado. This scholarly lethargy was dispelled when she received an unexpected invitation from Emory professor Bell Wiley to present a paper in Chicago at the annual meeting of the OAH. It was this invitation that prompted Jan to capitalize on the statistical methods she had learned at the Kinsey Institute to do a content analysis of periodical literature on the Mormons, resulting in her paper, "From Satyr to Saint: American Attitudes Toward the Mormons, 1860–1960," which she presented to an appreciative overflow session of the OAH Chicago conference. Jan's apparent blockbuster performance at this conference made a positive impression on many of the discipline's most prominent scholars who were in attendance, and it led directly to her receiving a tenure-track offer from Indiana University-Purdue University Indiana.

8. *Tenure-Track Hire at Indiana University-Purdue University Indianapolis, with a Joint Appointment in History and Religious Studies.* Jan had been teaching history classes at IUPUI for several years as a part-time adjunct. Her quantitatively based "Satyr to Saint" presentation in Chicago was a turning point: Suddenly Jan Shipps was in demand, and the dean of IUPUI College of Liberal Arts wanted to bring her on board before she was lured away by a competing university. More specifically, Dean Joseph Taylor wanted to recruit Jan to join the college's newly created program of religious studies. To secure Jan for this program, he was willing to grant her a somewhat unusual joint appointment in history and religious studies. Jan was initially dubious. She knew she was untrained and inexperienced in teaching religious studies, and that it would take extra effort on her part to get up to speed. But she also saw some appealing advantages: she already liked and was impressed by some of the faculty members at IUPUI; it was a relatively new school on a mission to encourage and financially support cutting-edge scholarship; and it was close enough to Bloomington for her to commute, yet distant enough from Indiana University for her to develop her own academic career apart from Tony's. Her decision to join the religious studies faculty at IUPUI was a significant turning point. Her engagement with the religious studies literature and collegial discussions with IUPUI colleagues led her to alter the way she thought about religion in general and Mormon history in particular. Achieving tenure in religious studies at IUPUI also put Jan in the right place at the right time to assume directorship of the newly instituted Center for American Studies, which in turn amplified her national standing in the cognate disciplines of American history and religious studies. And, not inconsequentially, accepting IUPUI's offer of a joint appointment in history and religious studies signaled another shift away from her marital dependence on Tony.

9. *Solicitation by Indiana University Press to Write a Book on Twentieth-Century Mormonism*. By the mid-1970s, the Church of Jesus Christ of Latter-day Saints was becoming more and more visible on the radar screens of scholars and journalists, as well as to politicians and the ecclesiastical authorities of other denominations (especially those who were losing members to aggressive LDS missionary efforts). Jan's very active involvement with the Mormon History Association as an outsider-insider and her growing reputation among academic historians led the editor of Indiana University Press to approach her to consider writing a book on modern Mormonism, in its twentieth-century guise, as a growing, bureaucratically regulated church that exercised considerable political influence and economic clout alongside its apparent spiritual appeals to many people worldwide. While Jan was interested in and thought herself capable of writing such a book, it's not the book she ended up producing. Chances are good that, for a number of plausible reasons, Jan eventually would have written a book on Mormon beginnings, but the point is that it was IU Press's invitation that stimulated her to get started. And once started, the book she wrote, *Mormonism: The Story of a New Religious Tradition*, became her most important work, establishing her reputation among Mormon and non-Mormon scholars alike and paving the way for even greater involvement in scholarly organizations and continued scholarship into the twenty-first century.

Summing Up and Looking Ahead

We trust our analysis in this and previous chapters provides an adequate exposition of how Jan Shipps became an acclaimed Mormon Studies authority and expert on Mormon history. Among other things, we have considered Jan's intelligence, curiosity, tolerance, ambition and determination, capacity for abstract thinking and comparative imagination, along with her collegiality and networking skills, to be key personal capabilities central to her academic success. We also have recognized and discussed the pivotal influence of significant family members, mentors, and colleagues in the unfolding of her career. Finally, in the context of twentieth-century American society, we have identified major turning point events in Jan's life in which we observe the mutual activation of her personal attributes and the roles of influential others in the emergence and progression of her career as a celebrated student of Mormon history. When life-altering events and turning point opportunities materialized, it was not merely a matter of being in the right place at the right time: Jo Ann Barnett, subsequently Jan Shipps, was groomed, she was ready, she was the right person to make something of the chances her life afforded.

In the following chapter we return to a more careful examination of the heuristic assertion we made in the preface: that Jan Shipps's *Mormonism: Story of a New Religious Tradition* is one of the three most consequential books ever written about Mormons, our other two candidates being Fawn Brodie's *No Man Knows My History* and Juanita Brooks's *The Mountain Meadows Massacre*. We intend to summarize the scholarly backgrounds of these three women in order to see what they share in common, as well as understand what makes their work distinctive and important.

CHAPTER 7

Career Comparisons with Fawn Brodie and Juanita Brooks

Our larger point for singling out Jan Shipps's *Mormonism: The Story of a New Religious Tradition*, along with Fawn Brodie's *No Man Knows My History* and Juanita Brooks's *The Mountain Meadows Massacre*, is not, of course, to argue that these three books are indisputably the most important or impactful that have ever been written about Mormons and their history. As we stated in the Preface, many truly important books have been written about the Mormon past, and others could justifiably be nominated in place of our selections. If readers have their definite favorites, let them say what they are and give their reasons. In the meantime, however, it is also incumbent upon us to amplify the rationale for our selections.

We trust that we already have said enough about Jan's book to justify our focus on her work. It was published at a time when the rapidly growing Church of Jesus Christ of Latter-day Saints and its religiously conservative way of life were beginning to attract widespread interest by non-Mormon scholars and the national media. Neither polemical nor apologetic, Jan's naturalistic analysis won the respect of historians and religious scholars both inside and outside the Mormon intellectual community. Her core thesis concerning the transformation of early Mormonism—from a populist form of Christian primitivism into a new religious tradition—transcended conventional historical narrative. In making this argument, Jan's analogous, comparative framework—vis-à-vis the rise of global Christianity from a tiny Jewish sect—compelled scholars to broaden their American context for describing Mormonism's distinctive history to analyzing the historically rare conditions under which religious dissent movements may become new religious traditions. *Mormonism* pointed toward the value of nomothetic theorizing as a way to understand Mormonism's institutional and cultural development, rather than simply aggregating greater ideographic detail to the historical record.

In the cases of Fawn and Juanita, we see very different approaches which, methodologically speaking, conform more closely to the principles of conventional historiography. At the same time, there are significant polemical or critical components to both of their books which are altogether lacking in Jan's work. Nonetheless, by our criteria (i.e., their consequential impact on the Mormon intellectual community), both Fawn's debunking biography of Joseph Smith and

Juanita's unsparingly forthright and critical analysis of the nineteenth-century Mountain Meadows Massacre merit careful attention for their subsequent importance in influencing the writing of Mormon history. In what follows, we first summarize and comment on critical reaction to Fawn's and Juanita's books. We then compare their intellectual backgrounds with that of Jan's. Finally, we consider the extent to which contemporaneous gender biases in both academia and society at large affected the work of all three—how they were able, nonetheless, to accomplish what they did—and, consequently, we assess their feminist legacies to current women scholars of Mormon history and culture.

Fawn Brodie and *No Man Knows My History*

No Man Knows My History: The Life of Joseph Smith was published by Alfred A. Knopf in 1945. Fawn Brodie was thirty years old and, at the time, did not have an academic appointment. She was also the niece of David O. McKay, second counselor in the LDS First Presidency, who, six years later, succeeded to the office of President and Prophet of the Church of Jesus Christ of Latter-day Saints. Fawn's own father, Thomas E. McKay, was also an LDS ecclesiastical authority of high rank.[1] These biographical facts are of major importance given that Fawn's book was indignantly denounced by the *Church News* section of the LDS Church-owned *Deseret News* as "a composite of all anti-Mormon books that have gone before."[2] Fawn was branded as a heretic whose religious betrayal shocked and hugely embarrassed the McKay family and the church in which she had been raised. She was formally excommunicated as a member of the LDS Church in 1946, one year after the publication of *No Man Knows My History*.

Fawn's literary style and penetrating, interrogatory approach to the life of the Mormon prophet were almost universally acknowledged. However, her primary motivation for writing the biography was to produce an authoritative exposé of early Mormonism as a religious hoax, a judgement she had arrived at as an adult in spite of her devout Mormon upbringing. Mobilizing her access to and assimilation of documentary sources through her family connections as a McKay, Fawn portrayed Joseph Smith as a talented storyteller and fabricator who parlayed his father's occupation as a treasure hunter into a tale of divinely delivered gold plates as the basis for writing a religious novel (published as The Book of Mormon) to make money for bolstering his impoverished family's financial circumstances.[3] Credulous family members

---

1. Thomas E. McKay occupied the position of Assistant to the Quorum of the Twelve Apostles from 1941 until the time of his death in 1958.
2. Quoted in Newell G. Bringhurst, *Fawn McKay Brodie: A Biographer's Life*, 110.
3. Treasure hunting supported by a "magic worldview" was a common aspect of the folk traditions of early nineteenth-century New England and upstate New

and neighbors attributed prophetic gifts to young Joseph, who proactively responded to their queries for supernatural guidance and longings to be part of a divinely commissioned church. According to Fawn's analysis, Smith's natural charisma and creative organizing skills increasingly led him to believe in the actual authenticity of his prophetic calling, even though he knew there never had been any gold plates and that the Book of Mormon was the work of his own imagination. In Fawn's portraiture, Joseph Smith emerges in the final analysis as a highly creative and even self-deluded imposter.

Fawn was excommunicated from the LDS Church not long after the *Church News*'s condemnatory editorial on the grounds of apostasy for publishing views that were "contrary to the beliefs, doctrines, and teachings of the Church."[4] Well-known Mormon scholars, such as Hugh Nibley, a professor of classics, religion, and ancient languages at Brigham Young University (BYU), assailed Fawn's book for shoddy scholarship and academic dishonesty. Nibley's witty, *ad hominem* rejoinder—entitled "No Ma'am, That's Not History"—satisfied the faithful that Fawn had been thoroughly discredited by competent authority.[5] For years, her biography of the Mormon prophet was virtually indexed by the LDS Church as proscribed reading for worthy Latter-day Saints.

Most non-Mormon scholars, however, were highly impressed by Fawn's work. To them she was an intelligent, eloquent writer, who appeared to have mastered the relevant documentary materials in support of her thesis. The fact that her biography was not merely an impartial exposition but also an

---

York, traditions in which Joseph Smith and his family were actively involved. See D. Michael Quinn, *Early Mormonism and the Magic World View*.

4. Bringhurst, *Brodie*, 112. Prior to Brodie's biography of Joseph Smith, the LDS Church mainly ignored books deemed by authorities to be anti-Mormon propaganda and were not anxious to excommunicate members for their writings, especially if they were inactive Mormons. But Fawn was not, of course, merely an inactive Mormon. She was the daughter of an Assistant to the Quorum of the Twelve Apostles and the niece of the presumptive next president of the LDS Church. These facts, as they became increasingly known to the reading public, were intolerable to Church authorities. As Bringhurst summarizes, "Latter-day spokesmen, official and otherwise, were extremely slow to comment publicly on *No Man Know My History*. Various Mormon publications, most prominently the *Deseret News*, the Salt Lake City-based daily newspaper owned and operated by the Mormon Church, declined to review, or even acknowledge the book's existence for months after its release. In the meantime, Brodie's biography was being noted and/or reviewed in dozens of newspapers and periodicals across the United States. . . . Eventually, 'The biography could no longer be ignored. In addition to extensive media publicity, the book was enjoying brisk sales. . . . Mormon spokesmen finally [in 1946, a year after the book's publication] opened their attack'" (p. 107–8).

5. Hugh Nibley, *No, Ma'am, That's Not History*.

exposé did not trouble them very much, since it was largely consistent with their own beliefs about the Mormon religion. It was regarded by outside observers as the first credible, non-hagiographic analysis of Mormonism's founder. A year before publication, a preliminary draft of Fawn's book was awarded the prestigious Knopf Literary Fellowship, which carried with it a $2,500 stipend.[6] Later, her mentor and respected Mormon historian, Dale Morgan (a non-believer) proclaimed it the "finest job of scholarship yet done in Mormon history . . . a book distinguished in the range and originality of its research, the informed and searching objectivity of its viewpoint, the richness and suppleness of its prose, and its narrative power."[7] For non-Mormon academics, *No Man Knows My History* was for decades the standard, go-to book about Joseph Smith and Mormon beginnings. In 1971 a slightly revised paperback edition was published, which has continued to remain in print.

In short, Fawn's book was perceived by outsiders as a groundbreaking work of scholarship in explicating Mormon origins. This acclaim was galling to faithful Mormons of all stripes, especially to university-trained LDS scholars and historians who were professionally impelled to read the book. Long after it was cursorily dismissed by LDS ecclesiastical authorities and Mormon scholars such as Nibley as merely another specimen of anti-Mormon literature, Mormon apologists have continued to defend their religion's truth claims against Fawn's naturalistic criticisms of Joseph Smith's prophetic authenticity and hence of the divine authority of the LDS Church.[8]

Case in point: sixty years after publication of her book, Richard Bushman, a highly respected Columbia professor of American history (and a believing,

---

6. In narrating Brodie's winning of the award, Bringhurst reports that her application was judged the best of forty-four entries and quotes one of the Knopf judges who described Brodie's manuscript as "a model of intellectual sobriety and lucidity . . . perspicuous, thought through, astringently sane . . . aware of such special interpretations as those supplied by psychoanalysis, economic determinism, religious bigotry, worship and straight debunking, she steers a path that is not so much a mean between these, as simply better than any one of them alone. . . . [It] should satisfy the scholar, impress the layman and absorb both." Bringhurst, *Brodie*, 80.

7. Dale L. Morgan, "A Prophet and His Legend," 7–8.

8. To this day—decades after her death in 1981 and over seventy years after publication of her biography of Joseph Smith—Brodie and her work remain a target of LDS apologetics. Thus, for example, the non-profit website FairMormon (https://www.fairmormon.org), which advertises its mission as providing "faithful answers to criticisms of the LDS Church," currently includes a "FairMormon Analysis" of Brodie's *No Man Knows my History*. The analysis provides "fact-checking" rebuttals to 405 allegedly erroneous claims made by Brodie in her book, as well as links to an assortment of rebuttal articles published in LDS Church outlets in 1968, 1979, 1991, 1996, and 2001.

practicing Latter-day Saint), published *Joseph Smith: Rough Stone Rolling*.⁹ Not coincidentally, Bushman's mammoth tome, like Fawn's, was published by Alfred A. Knopf. Bushman hoped that his biography of Smith would supersede Fawn's as a definitive treatment of the subject but was disappointed by the mixed reviews it received from both academic historians and the Mormon intellectual community. Two years after publication of *Rough Stone Rolling*, Bushman stoically reflected on the book's reception: "We cannot expect a positive reaction to the biography—or to Joseph Smith—from scholars. . . . [A]n epistemological gap yawns between my view of the prophet and that of most academics. Believing Mormons stand on the other side of a gulf separating us from most educated people." He then proceeds to ironically note that "[i]f anything, Mormon reaction is the opposite. While most Latter-day Saint readers enjoy an unvarnished account of his life, others are unsettled by the rough spots." Finally, Bushman reluctantly acknowledges that "Brodie has shaped the view of the Prophet for half a century. Nothing we have written has challenged her domination. I had hoped my book would displace hers, but at best it will only be a contender in the ring, whereas before she reigned unchallenged."¹⁰

As succinctly expressed by Bushman, it is this ongoing, defensive response by Mormon scholars to produce professionally credible histories of the origins of their religion that warrants our designation of Fawn's debunking biography of Joseph Smith as one of the most consequential books in Mormon history.

Juanita Brooks and *The Mountain Meadows Massacre*

In 1950, Stanford University Press published Juanita Brooks's *The Mountain Meadows Massacre*. This was not long after Fawn had published and been excommunicated for writing *No Man Know My History*. Thus, within a span of just five years, two women published groundbreaking books that challenged the LDS Church's largely unblemished and faith promoting, nineteenth-century narrative of divine guidance and prophetic leadership. A long-suppressed dark side of this nineteenth-century history was the horrific Mountain Meadows Massacre.¹¹

---

9. Richard L. Bushman, *Joseph Smith: Rough Stone Rolling*.

10. Bushman, 101–2. Jan herself says comparing Brodie to Bushman is a hard thing to do: "It's hard to keep Fawn Brodie out of your head while you're reading Richard Bushman."

11. In addition to Juanita's pioneering research on the Mountain Meadows Massacre, students of this episode of Mormon-American history should also consult more recent, updated works, especially Will Bagley, *Blood of the Prophets: Brigham Young and the Massacre at Mountain Meadows*; and Ronald W. Walker, Richard E. Turley, and Glen M. Leonard, *Massacre at Mountain Meadows*. Bagley vs. Walker et

In the summer of 1857, a large portion of the United States army commenced a thousand-mile march across the midsection of America to the mountainous region of the Utah Territory to quell what the federal government perceived as the Mormon's defiance of federal courts and to install a new territorial governor in place of Brigham Young.[12] In a state of near hysteria and "war fever" as the army approached, Mormon territorial militia, in cahoots with their Paiute Indian allies, laid siege to the Baker-Fancher party, a wagon train of Arkansas immigrants en route for California at a remote site in Southern Utah called Mountain Meadows. Under the direction of local ecclesiastical leaders, the Mormon assailants determined to leave no credible surviving witnesses to their ruthless attack, and, while under a flag of truce, treacherously murdered all men, women, and children over the age of seven. The few surviving children were distributed to be raised by selected Mormon families living in the area. As the gruesome fate of the Baker-Fancher party emerged, a public outcry arose, demanding that the perpetrators be identified and punished. Initially, LDS Church leaders blamed the Indians and denied any Mormon involvement.

But the magnitude of the crime could not realistically be covered up. Ultimate blame for the massacre began to fall on senior LDS Church authorities in Salt Lake City and, in particular, on Church president Brigham Young. Aggressively pressured by federal prosecutors and the press, Young eventually conceded the participation of some local LDS leaders, who had been indicted for their offenses. Several of the latter, including John D. Lee (a close associate and "adopted son" to Brigham Young), subsequently were excommunicated from the Church.[13] In 1877, twenty years after the ghastly

---

al. are, we should note, deeply divided in their conclusions regarding the complicity of Brigham Young in the massacre. Bagley argues that Young ordered the attack on the Fancher party and is directly responsible for the Massacre. Walker et al. repudiate this thesis and conclude that Young, though guilty of heated rhetoric that inflamed war hysteria in the Utah Territory, was not directly responsible for the massacre that ensued. Brooks, as we state in the text, does not believe that Young ordered the attack but holds him culpable as an "accessory after the fact" for his efforts to obstruct the federal government's investigation of the massacre.

12. For a history of the "Utah War," see William P. MacKinnon, *At Sword's Point, Part 1: A Documentary History of the Utah War to 1858*.

13. For approximately two generations in the nineteenth century (1846–94), Mormons practiced the "law of adoption," in which priesthood holding men were ritually sealed in a father-son relationship to other men in the Church. Thus, Brigham Young was sealed as a son to Joseph Smith in 1846 (two years after Smith's death) and subsequently was sealed as a father to numerous other prominent Mormon leaders, including John D. Lee. For a discussion of nineteenth-century adoption theology and its practice, see Samuel M. Brown, "Early Mormon Adoption Theology and the Mechanics of Salvation," 3–52.

events at Mountain Meadows, John D. Lee—in his own words, "sacrificed" as a scapegoat for the church—was finally convicted and executed for helping lead the massacre.[14] Lee was the only LDS Church member ever punished for orchestrating and participating in the deadly onslaught.

From the point of view of Church authorities, their most important concern was to move on with the religious agenda of building the latter-day Kingdom of God and, in the interest of this higher cause, to maintain official silence about all that had happened at Mountain Meadows. A tacit conspiracy of deliberate obliviousness quickly enveloped Mormon consciousness. By the turn of the new century, ancillary atrocities of the Utah War had mostly been laid to rest. By mid-century—when Juanita published her book—very few Latter-day Saints knew anything about the Mountain Meadows Massacre. Mormon general authorities were righteously dismayed by Juanita's determination to uncover the past, thereby exposing the church's dirty laundry to its critics and uninformed contemporary members.

Unlike Fawn, Juanita was fundamentally a believer in the doctrinal teachings of her church and a practicing Latter-day Saint her entire life. She did not believe, however, that individual ecclesiastical leaders were without fault or above criticism for occasional, injurious decisions they made in exercising their authority, and she was absolutely committed as a historian to the unbiased investigation of historical events, supported by the painstaking assembly of primary source materials. By independently pursuing a factual account of what happened at Mountain Meadows—insistently asking the key historical questions: who participated and why—Juanita knew she was provoking the wrath of conservative Church leaders. Undeterred by the possibility of excommunication, she doggedly insisted on uncovering the truth about Mountain Meadows and holding Church leaders responsible for the dreadful consequences of what took place there.[15] In her account she refused to whitewash

---

14. Lee's life as a stalwart Mormon pioneer and death by execution in 1877 is narrated by Juanita Brooks in *John D. Lee: Zealot, Pioneer Builder, Scapegoat*.

15. Brooks avers, "I do not want to be excommunicated from my church for many reasons, but if that is the price I must pay for intellectual honesty, I will pay it—I hope without bitterness." Levi S. Peterson, *Juanita Brooks: The Life Story of a Courageous Historian of the Mountain Meadows Massacre*, 200. Long before publication of *The Mountain Meadows Massacre* in 1950, Brooks, of course, knew of Brodie's fate at the hands of Church authorities, which put the fate of her own work into question. Peterson reports, "In June of 1946, Juanita informed Morgan of the excommunication of Fawn. Juanita had naively hoped for a less punitive response to Brodie's biography of Joseph Smith. 'Now that it has done its duty on that point,' she sarcastically wrote, 'the Church can feel much more righteous, I imagine.' . . . Inevitably Brodie's excommunication augmented the suspense in which Juanita lived. . . . Dolefully she commented [to

what her Mormon ancestors had done. She explained but did not excuse their motives of retaliation and desperate actions under conditions of war hysteria and unflinchingly portrayed the treachery of the militia's priesthood leadership in promising the immigrants' safe passage from the Indians in exchange for their arms. She also concluded that, though guilty of murderous crimes, John D. Lee had, in fact, been scapegoated by higher LDS Church authorities in Salt Lake City as the only Mormon offender and that President Brigham Young in particular—by obstructing the government's investigation—was an accessory after the fact.[16]

Like Fawn's *No Man Knows My History*, Juanita's book won critical acclaim. But unlike Fawn, her work was never officially condemned by the LDS Church. Juanita never faced excommunication proceedings for her uncompromising portrayal of Mormon guilt at Mountain Meadows. Nevertheless, within the Mormon community, she was typed as a maverick and subjected to both official and unofficial ostracism. Although not excommunicated, Juanita was released from her local position as stake relief society president and informally considered by priesthood leaders to be ineligible for future lay callings in the Church, a steep social cost to pay for an active Latter-day Saint.[17] To liberal Mormon intellectuals, however, Juanita was a scholarly hero. She was perceived by them as a faithful Latter-day Saint who simultaneously insisted on pursuing and reporting the facts about the religious history of her own faith regardless of how flattering or unflattering these might prove to be. Her

---

Morgan], 'I consider it my final bow to the Mormon audience, for I feel sure that as soon as the MMM study is finished I'll be OUT.'" Peterson, 178–79.

16. Arguably, it was Juanita's insistence in holding Brigham Young accountable for attempting to cover up local church leaders' active involvement in a horrendous crime and subsequently scapegoating John D. Lee as the lone Mormon perpetrator that provoked LDS ecclesiastical authorities' greatest indignation in reaction to her book.

17. Among other accounts of religious and cultural estrangement which her book caused, Peterson quotes from a letter Brooks wrote to a friend a year following publication of *The Mountain Meadows Massacre*: "My local people, the bishop and the president of the stake, and all the authorities here never refer to the book—they evade it with delicacy and solicitude that they might show to a mother who has given birth to a monster child." Peterson goes on to surmise that "in her private feelings Juanita was less than amused by the studied silence of local church officials. It seemed to her that they practiced a subtle ostracism, calling upon her and Will [her husband] less often than formerly to serve on committees and to give lessons, prayers and sermons. There were others who ostracized them as well. Certain friends said a curt hello and hurried away or avoided them altogether. A number of relatives expressed strong disapproval. All this Juanita resented more for Will's sake than for her own. She regretted deeply that such a good and guileless man should have to feel to some degree like an outcast." Peterson, *Brooks*, 218-19.

work was a model of how Mormon history could and should be written. Tellingly, in his award-winning biography of Juanita, Levi Peterson (himself a Mormon maverick) chooses the descriptor of "Courageous Historian" for the subtitle of his book.[18]

Appropriately enough, in 1991, Jan wrote both a forew0rd and afterword to the third edition of Juanita's *Mountain Meadows Massacre*. Jan's comments summarize several of the points that we ourselves would make about the enduring importance of Juanita's work. "Rarely in the writing of the history of any controversial or tragic event," Jan writes, "has a single work had such a far-reaching impact as has *Mountain Meadows Massacre*." She went on to say:

> Rarely, too, has any historical monograph stood the test of time so well. First published in 1950 and published in a new edition in 1962, the book went through nine printings in hardback before the editors of the University of Oklahoma Press decided to issue a paperback edition. . . . [T]his has been a pivotal work. . . . [It] set a precedence for future Mormon historians willing to follow the documentary evidence wherever it leads. . . . In her original preface, Brooks started out by making clear that she was and ever had been a loyal and active member of the LDS Church. She realized that "we have tried to blot out the affair from our history," but argued that, "with the old antagonisms gone," she could do her church a service by telling the true story. . . . [I]f the recognition she coveted from LDS Church officials never came in her life time, the fact her work was not officially condemned proved to be an auspicious portent for the future study of Mormon past.[19]

In 1976, at the age of seventy-eight, Juanita received a lifetime achievement award from the Mormon History Association. According to Jan, who by then was a member of the MHA Awards Committee,

> Without any question, this award was also a direct reflection of the collective appreciation of a new generation of Mormon historians just then beginning to understand what implications follow for themselves and their church when all the evidence found in the documentary record of the LDS experience is faced head on.

The inscription on the special citation awarded to Juanita read: "JUANITA BROOKS, for a life of dedication, scholarship, and courage in which she has led the way in an honest and professional study of the Mormon past."[20]

Today, the internet has fundamentally altered the ability of religious organizations like the LDS Church to unilaterally control information about its operations and past history. In an unprecedented effort to maintain its in-

---

18. In his autobiography *A Rascal by Nature, A Christian by Yearning: A Mormon Autobiography*, Peterson recounts his own "vexed and vexing relationship" with the LDS Church and Mormon culture.

19. Jan Shipps, Foreword to *The Mountain Meadows Massacre*, v–ix.

20. See "Mormon History Association Awards for 1976," 84.

stitutional narrative, the LDS Church has begun publishing scholarly essays on heretofore controversial issues concerning certain Church teachings and disputed facets of its history on its own website.[21] This move toward greater transparency, it may be argued, was precipitated in the previous century by a handful of critical books by Mormon authors, especially including Fawn's *No Man Knows My History*, and Juanita's *The Mountain Meadows Massacre*.

Family Backgrounds in Comparative Perspective

The most obvious characteristic Fawn Brodie, Juanita Brooks, and Jan Shipps share is that they are women. It could be argued, of course, that their sex is a sheer coincidence that had little or nothing to do with their groundbreaking books on Mormon history. We will argue to the contrary. A substantial majority of scholars who write about Mormon history are men. This was even more true decades ago when Fawn, Juanita, and Jan published their classic works. Why didn't male Mormon Studies scholars of that era write the kinds of books these three women wrote? Before taking up the question of gender and related feminist issues in researching and writing about Mormon history, we first turn to a consideration of these authors' age and regional differences, family backgrounds, educational antecedents, and academic connections.

Age and Regional Differences

In linking the lives and works of any set of selected authors, we should expect to find certain differences and incongruities no matter how comparable they may be in other important ways. Substantial age differences between in-

---

21. At the LDS Church's official website, one may find a link to "Gospel Topics," which then links to a set of "Gospel Topic Essays" on subjects that LDS authorities have deemed in need of clarification. The preface page to these essays reads: "Recognizing that today so much information about The Church of Jesus Christ of Latter-day Saints can be obtained from questionable and often inaccurate sources, officials of the Church began in 2013 to publish straightforward, in-depth essays on a number of topics. The purpose of these essays, which have been approved by the First Presidency and the Quorum of the Twelve Apostles, has been to gather accurate information from many different sources and publications and place it in the Gospel Topics section of LDS.org, where the material can more easily be accessed and studied by Church members and other interested parties." As of June 1, 2018, officially approved essays were posted on the following topics: "Are Mormons Christian?" "Becoming Like God," "Book of Mormon and DNA Studies," "Book of Mormon Translation," "First Vision Accounts," "Joseph Smith's Teachings about Priesthood, Temple, and Women," "Mother in Heaven," "Peace and Violence among 19th-Century Latter-day Saints," "Plural Marriage in The Church of Jesus Christ of Latter-day Saints," "Race and the Priesthood," and "Translation and Historicity of the Book of Abraham."

dividuals, for example, are typically correlated with transformative events and shifts in historical trends and modes of thinking that alter the consciousness of successive generations over time.[22] Regional cultural differences arguably play an even larger role in shaping distinctive attitudes, talents, and outlooks when individuals are appraised in comparative perspective.

Juanita was born in Bunkerville, Nevada, in 1898 and was thus seventeen years older than Fawn (born in Huntsville, Utah, in 1915) and thirty-one years older than Jan (born in Hueytown, Alabama, in 1929). In turn, Fawn was fourteen years older than Jan. While these differences are not huge, there is enough of a time gap in the ages of these three women to have exposed them to different national preoccupations during their most impressionable years growing up. For example, by age fifteen—even in remote Southern Utah and Nevada—Juanita would have been exposed to the prevailing national confidence and optimism embodied in the reform-oriented ideals of American progressivism, including the drive for women's suffrage and the professionalization of public education.[23] By the time Fawn turned fifteen, the optimism of that era would be smothered by the Great Depression, the nation's most dominating preoccupation of her adolescence. Subsequently, when Jan was fifteen, the country's primary collective concern had shifted from economic depression to patriotic support and sacrifice for American victory in World War II. Whatever impact these assorted national preoccupations may have had in shaping their generational outlooks, the one thing our three authors shared during the different historical eras of their youth was the fact that they were young women growing up in a society that still depreciated the idea of women in higher education and of women competing equally with men in public and professional occupations. The United States was indeed inching toward greater gender equality in both public and private life throughout the first half of the twentieth century, but for these women, the scholarly world to which they all gravitated and aspired was still dominated almost entirely by men.

Everyone must be from somewhere, this being the elementary fact of everyone's starting point in life over which we have no say or control. The most obvious and significant difference between these three women's lives and careers was their chance births and upbringing in very different cultural regions of the United States. Both Juanita and Fawn were born and raised as faithful

---

22. There is a substantial social science literature on age cohort differences in attitudes and values and generational change. For a review, see Martin Kohli, "Generational Change."

23. Mathew Bowman convincingly demonstrates the historical compatibility between the early twentieth-century revision of Mormon theology in conjunction with the rise of progressivism in American politics. See Matthew Bowman, "Eternal Progression: Mormonism and American Progressivism," 53–70.

Latter-day Saints in Mormon Utah. Furthermore, both grew up in what may be described as "Mormon villages"—small, insulated communities in which residents were united in their Mormon faith by strong, reciprocal bonds of sentiment, kinship, and singular religious traditions. Huntsville, Utah, Fawn's hometown, was less removed from city life and the urban influences of Ogden and Salt Lake City than Juanita's hometown of Bunkerville, Nevada—forty-five miles distant from the nearest small town of St. George, Utah. However, as children both women deeply imbibed the cultural and religious parochialism of their Mormon villages. Jan's hometown of Hueytown, Alabama, also provided a relatively small-town environment—but one that was on the outskirts of an industrial, metropolitan area. Moreover, in contrast to the Mormon villages of Juanita and Fawn's childhoods, Hueytown was a community that featured the relatively fraternal interaction of several Christian denominations rather than the domination of a single, religious monolith. Raised in the Methodist Church, Shipp's religious upbringing was one that emphasized practical morality over doctrinal fervor and the eschatological conviction of being God's chosen people in the latter days of human history.

Ethnocentrism is the inevitable product of every cultural region that values its past and competes for standing in the contemporary world. In turn, ethnocentric attitudes of taken-for-granted favor and superiority may be strongly challenged when one leaves one's cultural environs to pursue a future somewhere else in the world. For Jan, the South's recalcitrant conviction of moral and cultural superiority, despite devastating military and political defeat in the previous century, would be persistently confronted as she and her husband Tony migrated north to pursue their educational and occupational careers. For Juanita and Fawn, their childhood identities as guileless Latter-day Saints would also be tested intellectually as their aspirations for higher education pushed them beyond the secure limitations of the Mormon village. Fawn's exposure to the outside world would lead to a painful and irreversible break from her extended family and the traditions of her Mormon upbringing. Less radical and abrupt, Juanita's exposure to outside ways and thinking would temper but not fracture her childhood faith. She would remain a believing Latter-day Saint, deeply embedded in the kinship ties of the Mormon community but also ecclesiastically marginalized by her stubborn insistence on heeding her own counsel in writing unvarnished histories about the Mormon past.

To a greater and lesser degree, Fawn and Juanita distanced themselves sufficiently from the official Mormon faith narrative to become "inside-outsiders," as they wrote perceptively but naturalistically about their chosen Mormon topics. Conversely, as an outsider to Mormon culture and its religious traditions, Jan's challenge and ultimate achievement as a non-Mormon scholar from a culturally alien region of the country was to achieve an insider status among Mormon intellectuals. Unburdened by the constraints of LDS Church membership and corresponding expectations of religious loyalty that complicated reception of Fawn's and Juanita's work, Jan was entirely free to write naturalistically but in a neutral way that did not ultimately challenge, criticize, or threaten Mormonism's fundamental truth claims. As a respected academic historian, it was her refusal to be a religious critic that earned and preserved her "insider" standing within the Mormon scholarly community.

Family Circumstances

At this point in our comparison, more specific details about these women's respective family circumstances—their financial and social standing, personal relationships with parents and siblings, and the assumption of traditional domestic roles in relationship to the men they married and the children they subsequently raised—are in order.[24]

All three women were raised in families with modest economic means. Juanita's parents—Henry Leavitt and Mary Hafen—were of nineteenth-century Mormon pioneer stock, eking out a subsistence living in the desert valleys of southern Nevada and Utah. The home in which she lived throughout most of her childhood was a two-room brick structure over a half cellar built by her father that had no central heat or indoor plumbing. Juanita was a tomboy who readily took to the outdoors, rode her pony bareback, and was proud of her ability to manage her father's horses and cattle. Her parents raised and produced all their own food, as well as other basic household goods such as soap, cotton for weaving, and various household furnishings. They were practical and frugal but cash poor. As a child, Juanita went barefoot in the summer and wore handmade clothes sewed by her mother. In many respects, Juanita's childhood life was little different from that of her pioneer ancestors.

While closer in time and place to modern amenities in their childhoods, the material well-being of both Fawn's and Jan's families was stunted by the Great Depression. Both families struggled financially, especially Fawn's parents. In addition to managing a small family farm, Fawn's father, Thomas E. McKay, received modest incomes from a variety of moonlighting jobs, including a small salary as an elected Utah State senator, and later through his temporary appointment to the Utah State Public Utilities Commission. But he was also deeply in debt and struggled to make payments on the McKay family ancestral house and farm that had been heavily collateralized in failed

---

24. In summarizing relevant facts about Juanita and Fawn for purposes of comparison, we have relied primarily on the published works of Levi Peterson and Newell Bringhurst, their respective biographers. We will cite them in our summaries of Juanita and Fawn only when quoting directly from their work.

business ventures jointly undertaken by Thomas and his siblings.[25] For the most part while growing up, Fawn's family lived in "genteel poverty," and money for extras was always scarce. The family's chronic financial distress was contradicted by the high social and religious status enjoyed by the extended McKay family in Huntsville, Utah—a contradiction that was highly embarrassing to Fawn, who grew up as a sensitive, precocious child.

During the Depression, Jan's family depended on her mother's Works Progress Administration (WPA) and teaching salaries for a modest cash income and on the somewhat less predictable income derived from her father's jack-of-all-trades entrepreneurial skills. Jan's parents were better off than many of their working-class neighbors who had lost employment in Birmingham's nearby factories and mines, and they were able to provide the necessities of life for their children without accepting government assistance. As with Juanita's and Fawn's families, Jan's parents raised food from their own garden and kept a few domesticated animals for milk and eggs. Like Juanita, Jan, as a young girl, also went barefoot in the summer and wore clothes made from feed-sacks sewn together by her mother. At the same time, the relatively commodious house her father built from scrap materials during the Depression (commodious in comparison, at least, to the two-room home built by Juanita's father in Bunkerville) initially lacked indoor plumbing, requiring Jan, like both Juanita and Fawn, to grow accustomed to using an outdoor privy.

None of these authors grew up in affluently privileged families. All were exposed at an early age to the exigencies of economic hardship and struggle to make ends meet, and they were each expected to lend their cooperative contributions to their families' domestic division of labor and efforts to sustain material sufficiency. In conjunction with other motivating factors, we may conjecture that their intensely shared ambitiousness for achievement and success in later life was spurred rather than blunted by a strong work ethic, bestowed on them in part as a result of their families' economic handicaps while growing up. Children from economically strapped families do not, of course, automatically grow up to become adults with a strong work ethic. This must be taught and internalized. In the childhood lives of each of these authors, both parents effectively taught and modeled the virtues of hard work and personal responsibility.

Juanita's and Fawn's parents were strictly observant Mormons and were successful in instilling an achievement-oriented ethic of industriousness and

---

25. Thomas had agreed to be responsible for expenses related to the McKay homestead in return for living on the property with his family. Nevertheless, the "McKay Family Corporation" continued to make management decisions regarding the property, excluding input from Fawn's mother. As she grew older, this arrangement struck Fawn as highhanded and unfair.

personal effort in their children. Even though Fawn struggled ambivalently in her feelings toward her father in later life, whom she regarded as religiously rigid and narrow-minded, she greatly admired his stoical strength of purpose. According to Fawn's biographer, Newell Bringhurst,

> Among Fawn's earliest memories are of her father "doing the work of two men." This was dramatized in his daily routine. He would rise each morning at four to milk the families' twenty-four cows. He then hitched up the buggy, Fawn recalled, "to drive the twelve miles to his job." When he returned home, it was usually after dark. He would light the lantern and walk down to the pasture gate, calling, "Sic, Boss, sic boss," in a strong, even voice that never betrayed his increasing weariness.[26]

Fawn's mother, Fawn Brimhall, was well-educated, artistic, and theologically skeptical, but she nonetheless remained a long-suffering and compliant Mormon mother and housewife. She assumed prime responsibility for organizing and supervising her family's domestic affairs—cooking, washing, mending, cleaning the house, tending the garden, and raising and directing her five children's schooling and household chores—as well as overseeing the farm when her husband was away from home performing his duties for the state utilities commission. She was particularly intent in seeing to it that her children excelled educationally, home-schooling Fawn and her older sister Flora for two years to protect them from exposure to a virulent whooping cough epidemic that plagued the region. She took special pride in Fawn's early precocity in reading and speaking, and persistently encouraged and reinforced her superior scholastic achievements.

Juanita's parents were less well-educated but nonetheless encouraged and supported the education of all their eight children, most of whom went on to attain college degrees. This kind of encouragement was also true of Jan's parents, as well as the McKays, whose children were all groomed to attain a college education. College degrees were, of course, relatively rare achievements in general during the entire time span that encompassed the maturational years of these authors, especially so for females and members of lower socioeconomic households. According to Juanita's biographer, Levi Peterson, "The desire of Henry and Mary [Juanita's parents] for the schooling of their children was intense; education was a bridge to a new world of money, machines, and progress which they themselves were too old to cross."[27] In the meantime, they taught and modeled the discipline of hard work and unstinting personal effort for coping with adverse circumstances.

---

26. Bringhurst, *Brodie*, 16.
27. Peterson, *Brooks*, 69.

Juanita's father, Henry Leavitt, was issued a missionary calling by LDS Church authorities in the first decade of the twentieth-century and dutifully left his young family in Bunkerville to fulfill a proselyting mission in the Midwest. Gone for over two years, his "daughters mourned his absence, and every evening Mary consoled them with her guitar and an inexhaustible repertoire of songs."[28] Though rendered assistance by relatives and her Mormon neighbors,

> Mostly Mary coped by dint of her own labor and foresight. She pruned and irrigated her vineyard, hoed and harvested a large garden, picked cotton on shares, cleaned house for neighbors, and, in the fall of 1903, rented her unfinished second room to the school district for five dollars a month. She was then and later, unrelentingly busy. Every day she planned a project: stitching a quilt, cleaning house, bottling fruit, or drying figs.[29]

Returning from his mission with his religious convictions strongly reinforced that God favors those who strive to make an honest living,

> Henry undertook anew the pursuit of prosperity. With time he acquired wagons and horses, corrals and stackyard, cropland and pasture, and hogs, milk cows, and range cattle. . . . He raised wheat, barley, sorghum, cane, and melons, and Mary continued to raise a large garden and to cultivate her grapes and figs. By this bounty they sustained their increasing family."[30]

As a cash supplement to farming and ranching, he also secured additional work carrying the mail "between Bunkerville and the railroad town of Moapa, a labor he would perform for twelve years. He made the round trip in a buckboard three times a week, departing Bunkerville in the morning, staying overnight in Moapa, and returning to Bunkerville late the next afternoon."[31]

The parents of our three authors projected to their children an attitude of fortitude and forbearance in coping with adversity, accompanied by the axiomatic belief that ambition and unstinting effort would ultimately be rewarded with the realization of one's hopes and goals of personal betterment.

Parental and Sibling Influences

Juanita was very attached to both her parents. She was a tomboy during her childhood years, proudly recalling that the neighbors called her "Hen Levitt's boy" in admiration of her riding prowess and sensitive skills in handling farm animals. On one occasion, nine-year-old Juanita disobeyed her

---

28. Peterson, 7.
29. Peterson, 7.
30. Peterson, 9.
31. Peterson, 11.

father's instructions not to mount his spirited riding horse. The horse bolted with Juanita clinging to its neck and mane.

> At first she panicked. Then came the calming thought that, though she couldn't stop him, she could turn him. She steered him on to an uphill road and stuck to his back until he had run himself to exhaustion. Perhaps Henry was secretly proud; at least he didn't punish his daughter. Long afterward, he and Juanita reminded one another of "how that little bare-headed, bare-footed girl was riding that race horse that thought he was in a national contest of some kind, and just had to win."

Peterson surmises that "[f]rom these and dozens of other incidents, Juanita gathered Henry's voice into her identity, a voice scorning fear, encouraging initiative, approving achievement."[32]

At the same time, as Peterson points out:

> One must not underestimate the compelling model her mother posed for Juanita. Mary had been a constant, affectionate, even querulous and demanding presence. She oversaw garden, larder, and table with a vigorous efficiency. She had no end of wifely projects: a wash to do, soap to manufacture, fruit to dry, a quilt to stitch, walls to whitewash, curtains to starch, straw to replace beneath the rag carpet. Above all, her frequent pregnancies inculcated that ultimate duty of the Mormon housewife Juanita knew she must someday become.[33]

Adding Juanita's research and writing compulsions in later life, this description of her mother would also be a fair description of Juanita herself as an adult woman, strongly attached to her Mormon heritage and devoted to her domestic roles as wife and mother.

Fawn's relation with her parents was much more fraught with ambivalence. Her mother doted on her, and the two became very close. Similar to Jan's mother, Fawn's mother, Fawn Brimhall McKay, projected her unfulfilled artistic and intellectual aspirations on to her namesake daughter, who "was constantly shown off by her proud mother, who would have her recite a poem or give a reading for visitors. According to Fawn, by the age of six, books had become a dominant part of her life: 'I was a bookworm,' Fawn recalled, but 'my parents looked upon my being buried in books with indulgence.'"[34] Both of Fawn's parents "came to believe that if anybody was to excel in the Thomas

---

32. Peterson, 12. About Juanita's childhood growing up in rural Nevada and Southern Utah, Peterson astutely observes: "Perhaps the most important thing she learned from the outdoor circumstances of her childhood was that a girl had as much capacity for a vigorous, adventurous, and enterprising life as a boy. Later, she would extend that lesson, ambitiously entering upon a professional endeavor largely dominated by men." Peterson, 21.

33. Peterson, 22.

34. Bringhurst, *Brodie*, 22.

E. McKay family it would be young Fawn." As Bringhurst observes, "The affection between mother and daughter was especially deep, as evidenced in Fawn's first published work, a poem entitled 'Just a Minute Mother,' which she wrote at age ten, and which appeared in the Mormon Children's periodical, *The Juvenile Instructor*."[35]

But Fawn also became increasingly aware of the divisive religious differences between her parents and her mother's abhorrence of sex, which she saw as an unwelcome wifely duty, solely for the purpose of procreation. Fawn's father was devoutly pious while her mother was a "social Mormon," who outwardly followed her religion's prescriptive norms but inwardly rejected its theological truth claims. Over time, Fawn identified with her mother and her mother's family, the Brimhalls, who were more liberal and tolerant of her youthful inquisitiveness than the pious McKays.[36] Fawn increasingly came to resent the latter for what she perceived as their moralistic hypocrisy. Wholeheartedly religious and perfectionistic as a child, Fawn's feelings of resentment as she matured expanded to especially include her father, whom she respectfully revered, but with whom she never developed a close, affectionate relationship. Growing intellectual and religious disillusionment accompanied her resentments; Fawn's mixed feelings toward her father were a significant source of anguish as she researched and wrote *No Man Knows My History*.[37]

Occupying a kind of middle ground between Juanita's and Fawn's relationships with their parents, Jan was very close to her mother, who also

---

35. Bringhurst, 23.

36. After Thomas E. McKay and his wife Fawn Brimhall returned from presiding over the LDS Swiss-Austrian Mission in 1940, Bringhurst states that Fawn rejoiced that her mother "returned from Europe a thoroughgoing heretic," and goes on to quote Fawn writing to her Uncle Dean Brimhall: "Two years of playing hostess to itinerant apostles, plus some sophisticated literature and the overwhelmingly impressive spectacle of twenty centuries of European art, really shocked her out of that provincialism in which twenty-five years in Huntsville had tried to enshroud her. . . . I didn't think at her age there could come such delightful blossoming of courageous heresy." See Bringhurst, 75.

37. Bringhurst reports that "Brodie was further distracted in May [1944] upon receiving news that her father had suffered a heart attack and was bedridden. She was extremely anxious about his condition, sensing a relationship between it and her own writing and research. She was haunted by the thought that her father might die shortly after her book came out." Writing to her editorial mentor, Dale Morgan, about her concerns, she anguished, "[T]he consequences for my own peace of mind would be simply unbearable. . . . If I didn't have such an affection for my father, who is the soul of kindness, perhaps I wouldn't be so troubled. . . . This whole business complicates an already melancholy personal problem. Sometimes I wish to God I'd never started the book." Bringhurst, 93.

doted on her and promoted her early musical aptitude in much the way that Fawn's mother did in pridefully pushing her daughter's obvious aptitude for language. In fact, all three authors demonstrated early signs of exceptional curiosity and intelligence that were recognized and reinforced by their parents and other adults. It will be remembered that Jan was advanced to the second grade at the age of five and started college at age fifteen. Similarly, Fawn was placed in the third grade at the age of six, graduated from the University of Utah at age eighteen, and completed her master's degree in English literature from the University of Chicago when she was twenty. Juanita largely taught herself how to read as a preschooler and was advanced a year ahead of her age cohort when she started school in the one-room Bunkerville schoolhouse.

Jan's father was periodically absent from home for substantial periods of time and never became as close to her as was her mother. Furthermore, growing awareness of his drinking and gambling as Jan approached adolescence emerged as obvious blemishes on his character. Yet Jan continued to admire her father's practical knowledge and versatile occupational skills and, like her mother, tolerated his shortcomings while never developing the kind of resentful ambivalence that Fawn felt toward her father. Jan maintained amiable connections with both her parents and siblings after becoming an adult, but she also distanced herself from erstwhile parental and family ties to accommodate her husband Tony's acute need for undivided commitment in a way that would have been unthinkable for Juanita.

One observation worth making as we reflect on these variable parental and family relations is that it was Fawn—whose adult relationship to her family was most conflicted—that rejected her inherited religious faith and wrote most polemically as a historian about her subject matter. In comparison, Juanita, whose kinship and family ties remained firmly at the center of her adult life, retained her elemental Mormon faith and religious activity. Jan, whose adult relationship to parents and family was much less intense, drifted away from her childhood religious observance only to reactive her Methodism later in life when her husband Tony began showing some interest in religious matters.

Regarding the importance of their sibling relations growing up, suffice it to say that none of the authors—however doted on they may have been in different ways—grew up as an only child. All had to share the spotlight and earn their parents' attention in competition with multiple brothers and sisters. With two younger brothers and an older sister, Jan's family of six was the smallest nuclear unit of the three. In a slightly larger family of seven, Fawn was second oldest among her siblings of one brother and three other sisters. Finally, Juanita (whose older sister died as a toddler) grew up as the eldest child in a large, traditional Mormon household with four younger sisters and three brothers, comprising a family of ten, whose members somehow managed their daily domestic affairs in highly congested quarters.

Interestingly, all three grew up bonded to a sister very close in age with whom they were virtually inseparable in childhood. Juanita's sister, Charity, was only a year younger. Peterson reports that "Juanita and Charity attached themselves to each other. Because Juanita was small for her age and Charity large for hers, they seemed like twins."[38] Likewise, Fawn's sister Flora, older by two years, was placed by her mother in the same grade of school with Fawn, who had been jumped two grades because of her exceptional scholastic ability. Bringhurst reports that "their mother had a compelling reason for keeping the two sisters in the same grade. She seemingly, almost inadvertently, made her daughters twins, seeking to replicate the circumstances of her own childhood as an identical twin."[39] In Jan's case, her sister Sue was just a year older. Though not treated as twins like Juanita and Fawn had been to their closest sisters, the two progressed all the way through high school in the same grade and were one another's constant companion. Bright and studious, Juanita became a role model for her younger sister Charity, who idolized her and emulated her tomboy tendencies as a child. In contrast, both Fawn's and Jan's older sisters were outdoor types who excelled at sports and other physical activities, while Fawn and Jan achieved parental approbation through their intellectual and artistic accomplishments.

The important thing to discern from these close sister relationships is the diverse ways they helped stimulate and channel the achievement motivations of our three subjects. Juanita embraced the role of big sister and role model who set high standards and watched over her younger siblings. As younger sisters, both Fawn and Jan quickly learned to distinguish themselves by developing talents and excelling in ways that made them stand out in contrast to their older sisters' more practical abilities and predilections.

Marriage, Motherhood, and Husbands

Products of their times and places in early- to-mid-twentieth-century American society, our three authors all married at relatively young ages and anticipated becoming housewives and mothers who would loyally support their husbands' careers. Also, in conformity to the male-dominated norms of their time, all of their husbands were older than they were. Thus, all three women were subject to and shaped by the cultural ideals of female domesticity. At the same time, we should keep in mind that these women also exercised a great deal of personal agency in a world that sought to curtail women's choices. In spite of normative constraints on women's professional advance-

---

38. Peterson, *Brooks*, 6.
39. Bringhurst, *Brodie*, 23.

ment, they—through their independent ambition, intelligence, hard work and resourcefulness—all earned distinction in the heretofore male-dominated fields of history and religious studies.[40]

Oldest in marriage was Juanita, who was twenty-one at the time of her nuptials to Ernest Pulsipher in the St. George Temple. At twenty-seven years of age, Pulsipher was six years older than his bride and, like Juanita's father, was a local farmer and rancher. At age twenty—and on the same day she graduated with a master's degree in English literature—Fawn McKay married Bernard Brodie in a Mormon meetinghouse near the campus of the University of Chicago, where both attended school. Bernard was a twenty-six-year-old PhD student in international relations. He was also a non-observant Jew whose parents had immigrated from Latvia to Chicago in the late nineteenth century. Unbeknownst to her parents, Fawn by now had rejected the exclusive truth claims of her Mormon faith. Her marriage to Bernard Brodie caused a scandalous uproar for both their families. Fawn's parents were stunned that she was determined to marry outside the faith—and to a nonreligious Jew at that—while Bernard's parents were horrified that he had taken a gentile girl for his wife, adamantly refusing to countenance the marriage. At age nineteen, Jan was the youngest to marry. Her marriage to twenty-two-year-old Tony Shipps by a Georgia justice of the peace marked a critical turning point event in her life.

Of the three marriages, Juanita's was the most predictable and conventional in the context of the narrow parameters of her time and place. Her temple marriage to a local returned Mormon missionary was simply the culminating event in a normative pattern of life expected of any young Latter-day Saint woman growing up with extensive kinship ties in a small Mormon community. Their marriage was cut tragically short, however, by Ernest's fatal bout with cancer, leaving her a young widow at the age of twenty-three with an infant son to raise. A single mother for twelve years, Juanita subsequently was courted by and married Will Brooks—a fifty-two-year-old Mormon widower, resident of St. George, Utah, and the county sheriff. Juanita's two marriages to older, local men, who were stalwart in the LDS faith, meant that she would continue to live most of her adult life within a few miles of her birth.

In contrast, Fawn's and Jan marriages would propel them far from their cultural traditions and places of birth. After their Chicago marriage in 1936, Bernard and Fawn Brodie moved their residence a total of five times to differ-

---

40. In spite of cultural and religious constraints, the theme of women's agency in Mormon history and among contemporary Mormon women is discussed at length by various authors in Kate Holbrook and Matthew Bowman, eds., *Women and Mormonism: Historical and Contemporary Perspectives*.

ent cities on the east coast as Bernard pursued his academic and professional career as a systems theorist and military strategist at Princeton, Dartmouth, Yale, the US War College, and the Rand Corporation. They finally settled down in the Los Angeles area in the early 1950s, where Fawn belatedly obtained her own academic position in the history department of the University of California at Los Angeles (UCLA) in 1967. Similarly, Tony and Jan migrated from their family roots in Alabama and Georgia to pursue Tony's academic career in the north. In the process of their several migrations, they also moved a total of five times, living in Chicago, Detroit, Logan, Boulder, and Bloomington before Jan was able to find permanent academic employment at Indiana University-Purdue University Indianapolis (IUPUI) in 1972.

Thus, the upward social mobility of Brodie and Shipps as wives of successful academicians was accompanied by frequent geographical mobility prior to achieving their own academic credentials in middle age. Juanita was also a middle age woman before receiving widespread recognition for her scholarly work. She, however, pursued her career on a different track. Neither of her husbands were sophisticated, highly educated, or worldly men who cast aside their childhood religions as irrational remnants of less enlightened times. And unlike Fawn and Jan, she never occupied a faculty position at a major university. Not surprisingly, as a life-long resident of Southern Utah, Juanita's work remained fixed on locally relevant topics that were pertinent to the history of the West and its early Mormon settlers, many of whom were her ancestors and extended kin. In contrast, through very different marriages and decisive separation from their cultural origins, Fawn was able to compose her bitingly critical book of Mormonism's prophet-founder (and then move on to write other prize-winning biographies), and Jan was able to achieve her celebrated status as a respected outside-interpreter of Mormon culture and its history as a new religion.

Juanita far outdistanced Fawn and Jan in the number of children she mothered. She had a son from her first marriage. When she married Will Brooks she also became mother to his four sons, and together they had a daughter and three more sons—a total of nine children for Juanita to care for. Both Fawn and Jan professed they wanted children but, unlike Juanita, postponed getting pregnant for several years after being married in order to help get their husbands through school by expeditiously finding jobs outside the home. Fawn waited six years to have her first baby boy at the age of twenty-seven, and Jan waited three years before giving birth at the age of twenty-three to her son Stephen. Both women subsequently would suffer miscarriages (Fawn, in fact, miscarried twice). Jan never had any more children after her miscarriage but compensated by "mothering" groups of at-risk girls and delinquent teens in both Chicago and Detroit. Fawn, in turn, eventually had another son and a daughter, for a modest total of three children to care for as a stay-at-home mother and independent researcher.

All three women voiced fulfillment in being mothers, but over time, as they were drawn more and more to their own research and writing aspirations, they also expressed increasing frustration at the incessant disruptions and demands on their time that conscientious childcare requires. According to Bringhurst,

> [Fawn] confessed that "writing came very hard and very slowly. I have to sweat over every line." The task was made more challenging by her responsibilities as a housewife and mother to her young son Richard—or Dickie as he was called during his early years. All of this compelled her to organize her time carefully; from her daily routine she squeezed out four hours for the book [her biography of Joseph Smith] and gave the rest of the time to her baby.[41]

In a letter to her friend and mentor, Dale Morgan, Fawn wrote: "The boy is getting to be more demanding of my attention all the time.... Dickie is pulling at my arm, he demands to be fed. If I could get three consecutive hours of uninterrupted work, I could do wonders—maybe even finish the book."[42] In another letter to Morgan she wistfully yearned for men's freedom from the kinds of distractions and disruptions she experienced as a stay-at-home mom: "I envy you males the continuity in your work. The mere necessity of making a living enforces some kind of continuity."[43] If one is a professional academic, then making a living carries with it the expectation and institutional support for research and writing, luxuries that Fawn didn't have at the time, and neither, as young mothers, did Juanita or Jan. They produced their early scholarly work despite such distraction-free support, not because of it.

Juanita, like Fawn, also carried on a lengthy correspondence with Dale Morgan, complaining regularly about the distractions to her writing occasioned by motherly duties and other domestic commitments. According to Peterson's review of their correspondence, when writing to Morgan "she rarely failed to make some mention of her personal feelings and domestic activities. Often, she mentioned the latter by way of explaining why she was not spending more time at research and writing. In fact, her letters would for years sound a recurring theme of frustration over domestic interruptions."[44]

Thus, for example, while attempting to finish drafting an article on Mormon missionary pioneer, Jacob Hamlin, Juanita wrote Morgan: "If fate is kind, I may get this finished before someone comes to call, or the youngsters storm in from

---

41. Bringhurst, *Brodie*, 83.
42. Bringhurst, 91.
43. Bringhurst, 99.
44. Peterson, *Brooks*, 122.

the show, or my good husband wakes up." She proceeded to explain to Morgan a procedure she had devised for dealing with unexpected callers:

> I long ago hit upon the expedient of keeping my ironing set-up out, with everything ready, so that as soon as there was a knock I could plug in the iron on my way to answer the door. Then it would be easy to say, "Excuse me, please, my iron is burning," or "Come on in, I'm ironing." Then as soon as they left I'd pull out the plug.... The trouble is, I get more ironing and mending done than writing.

Peterson goes on to observe, "Writing was not an adequate reason for slighting a neighbor's visit; housework was."[45] Later, Juanita confessed, "I would like to be able to write, openly and unashamedly, to hire someone to come in and take over much of the routine of my home and set up where I could make a business of writing."[46]

Similarly, Jan had to balance her domestic responsibility and graduate school demands by waiting to do her reading and writing assignments ensconced in the bathroom at night after Tony and their son Stephen had gone to bed, taking Stephen with her to the library and on long trips to Salt Lake City when she was researching her dissertation, and sitting for hours in the family car studying for her PhD exams while waiting for Stephen to finish his violin lessons.

Clearly, a common denominator in the lives of our three authors was marriage and family commitments that subordinated their own scholarly aspirations in support of their husbands' careers. In saying this, we must not overlook how much value and satisfaction they all derived from their investment in domestic roles. Our interviews with Jan make it clear that, whatever frustrations academically she may have had to negotiate to balance her professional aspirations with her family responsibilities, her first loyalty was to Tony and their son Stephen, in whom she continues to take immense pride for their professional accomplishments. Likewise, Peterson records Juanita's spirited defense of conceiving and mothering her many babies as "the finest thing in life," and concludes that "[o]ne can scarcely overemphasize the satisfaction Juanita found in her domestic life"[47]—satisfaction realized, we would add, in spite of the great lengths to which she went in order to preserve a little time and energy for her perpetual research and writing. Similarly, according to Bringhurst, Fawn "extolled the virtues of motherhood as 'enormously fulfilling' and 'wonderfully rewarding,'" while concluding that she enjoyed "the

---

45. Peterson, 134–35.
46. Peterson, 151.
47. Peterson, 112.

'perfect life,' in that she was able to write at home while raising her children, not having to abandon them to nursery schools or babysitters."[48]

Our point, then, is not that these acclaimed women historians were complainingly unhappy with domestic lives that prevented them from realizing their dreams of scholarship and writing. They were not. Rather, our point is that, even though they found fulfillment in marriage and motherhood, their commitment to the latter made it doubly difficult for them to pursue professional careers in ways that were not true for their husbands or other men. As Peterson infers from his comprehensive biographical study of Juanita, "One sees that, despite her undoubted satisfactions as a wife and mother, Juanita constantly desired challenge and creative expression."[49] These mixed feelings of domestic satisfaction and frustrated aspirations for creative expression were perhaps articulated most clearly by Fawn:

> No one expects creative work from them [wives and mothers], as they do from men, and it's taken for granted universally that home, husband and children should have first precedence on a woman's time and interest. . . . [I]ntellectual activity must always take the last ounces of your energy rather than your first. . . . [A] woman who can do everything—husband, home, children, and art—is probably the luckiest person alive. For sheer richness of experience no one does any better. But the penalty is likely to be stomach ulcers or gray hairs at thirty-five.[50]

We are drawn irresistibly to the conclusion that, in their restrictive and demanding roles as mothers and mid-twentieth-century housewives, the scholarly efforts and achievements of Juanita, Fawn, and Jan are especially noteworthy in comparison to the praiseworthy work of male students, authors, and academics with whom they competed for recognition.

One other significant point of marital comparison among our three authors concerns the extent to which their husbands actively supported and even aided their movement into scholarly research and publishing. In this comparison, we see two very supportive husbands (Bernard Brodie and Will Brooks) and one who was considerably less supportive of his wife's scholarly pursuits (Tony Shipps).

Tony Shipps took virtually no interest in Jan's attraction to the study of Mormon history, disparaged "lady professors," never proofread her graduate papers or professional publications, nor, to Jan's knowledge, ever read her acclaimed *Mormonism: The Story of a New Religious Tradition*. Nonetheless, he played a critical turning point role in Jan's career by urging her to attend a Mormon history conference when she had sunk into despair after moving

---

48. Bringhurst, *Brodie*, 118.
49. Peterson, *Brooks*, 114.
50. Bringhurst, *Brodie*, 118.

from Colorado to Indiana to advance Tony's career. We should also remember that, long before Jan went back to school and commenced her graduate studies, it was Tony's meticulous scholarship that provided her with her first exposure to the stringent standards of academic research. Later in life, of course, Tony has cultivated a different attitude toward Jan's scholarly recognition and fame. Today, he expresses enormous husbandly pride in his wife's achievements.

In contrast, Fawn's and Juanita's husbands were at the outset both highly encouraging and actively supportive of their wives' early forays into research and writing. According to Bringhurst, Fawn's early critical pursuit of Mormon Studies was "also driven by her husband Bernard's many questions about her Mormon history, which he found both unique and fascinating."[51] When she commenced in earnest to research the history of Joseph Smith she received significant input from Bernard, "who acted as a sounding board for her ideas and evaluated her written drafts. She praised her husband as immensely helpful in judging her conclusions with a detachment that she herself lacked."[52] Later on, when writing her well-received biography of Civil War abolitionist Thaddeus Stevens, she acknowledged that "Bernard is my severest critic," while simultaneously expressing gratitude for his "stimulation and support."[53] Similarly, when Fawn commenced her study of the English explorer and linguist Richard Burton, she "received significant help from Bernard, on whose editorial skills she had long depended," who gave the manuscript "his characteristic thorough and perceptive scrutiny and criticism."[54] When Fawn was initially turned down for promotion at UCLA, Bernard, who by then also occupied a professorship at UCLA, "was furious at what he perceived as a humiliation of his wife. He talked of confronting those responsible, and he threatened physical violence. 'Whom do I confront and hit?' he thundered to several of his close friends in the political science department."[55]

Though not an educated scholar and accomplished writer like Bernard Brodie, Will Brooks was similarly supportive and helpful. When searching out, collecting, and copying local pioneer diaries for a 1930s WPA project to preserve historical documents, "Juanita's letters frequently recognized Will's contributions to her efforts. He gave her leads and carefully read every diary she acquired. . . . 'Will is even more interested than I,' she wrote. . . . 'He has been influential in securing most of the material I have found.'"[56] On numerous other occasions Will accompanied her to libraries and confer-

---

51. Bringhurst, *Brodie*, 71.
52. Bringhurst, 73.
53. Bringhurst, 151.
54. Bringhurst, 172.
55. Bringhurst, 203.
56. Peterson, *Brooks*, 105.

ences where she had been invited to speak and drove her on research trips to the Huntington Library in Los Angeles. When she was offered access to the Huntington's transcripts of the John D. Lee trials in their possession, Will readily agreed that, "regardless of expense," Juanita should "buy a microfilm in order to make a leisurely study of the transcripts."[57] And it was Will who provided the impetus for settling on a title for Juanita's own autobiography published later as *Quicksand and Cactus*:

> "Will has suggested 'Cactus Bloom,'" she wrote Morgan, "his idea being that with all its spiny hardness, life on the edge of the desert does have some beauty. . . . My father used to hum a little ditty with a line about 'with quicksand in the river bed and cactus on the bank' which seems expressive of the country, so I've been turning over 'Quicksand and Cactus.'"[58]

The kind of abiding personal interest in their wives' professional writing careers demonstrated by Bernard Brodie and Will Brooks was not the case in Jan's marriage to Tony Shipps. To her personal credit, Jan persevered in her ambition to be at the center of scholarly research and writing on Mormon history. To paraphrase an earlier observation, she did so in spite of her husband's lack of enthusiastic interest and support, not because of it. In contradistinction, for Juanita and Fawn, the gender obstacles of motherhood and domesticity norms that delayed the early flourishment of their scholarly careers were alleviated to some extent through the willing interest and support of their husbands.

Educational Preparation, Mentorship Relations, and Professional Academic Affiliations

Juanita Brooks, Fawn Brodie, and Jan Shipps all demonstrated exceptional aptitude for learning from an early age and obtained high marks and recognition for their academic abilities in school. While Fawn's and Jan's public school experiences were arguably more enriched than Juanita's small-school education growing up in the rural isolation of Bunkerville, Nevada, and St. George, Utah, all three women were inveterate readers from early childhood, and, arguably, all gained as much from their extracurricular reading as they did from classroom instruction.

Education

Of the three, Fawn's early, rapid academic advancement was the most noteworthy. She zipped through her undergraduate studies at the University

---

57. Peterson, 145.

58. Juanita Brooks, *Quicksand and Cactus: A Memoir of the Southern Mormon Frontier*; Peterson, *Brooks*, 146.

of Utah while still a teenager and then tarried another year close to home as a nineteen-year-old English instructor at Weber Junior College in Ogden, Utah, before going on to graduate school studies at the University of Chicago. There, she completed her master's degree in English literature at the precociously early age of twenty. However, at that point—largely because of her marriage to Bernard Brodie and consequent undertaking of conventional domestic roles as a supportive wife and mother—she never went on to further her academic career by pursuing a doctorate in history or any other subject.

Like Fawn, Juanita never pursued or obtained a doctoral degree in history. In fact, also like Fawn, her terminal degree was in English literature. In their younger years, both Fawn and Juanita had harbored dreams of writing award-winning fiction before turning to historical studies.[59] Unlike Fawn, however, Juanita's formal college education was much more uninterrupted and much less speedily attained. Graduating from "the old rock church which the town fathers had donated to the use of the high school," Juanita remained in Bunkerville for her first year of college study to enroll in a state-sponsored "normal course" to increase the supply of grade school teachers in Nevada.[60] The following year at the age of twenty she accepted a salaried position teaching grades three through five in nearby Mesquite, Nevada, and subsequently attended one semester of summer school at the University of Utah in Salt Lake City to bolster her teaching credentials. Juanita's marriage

---

59. According to Bringhurst, as an undergraduate English major at the University of Utah, Brodie entertained "fantasies about writing great short stories and fine novels," but was hugely disappointed when her only published work of fiction (for the University of Utah *Pen* magazine) failed to even receive honorable mention in a university student contest, let alone win first place. "Instead, Fawn was informed by one of her English Professors, a Dr. Quivey, that she had no talent for fiction, a criticism to which she reacted with 'ineffable bitterness.'" See Bringhurst, *Brodie*, 53. Talent for fiction or not, it may be argued that it was Brodie's intelligent skills as a college debater (which she shared in common with Juanita Brooks, who also was a college debater) and persuasive essayist that formed the foundations of her later success as an analytical historian and biographer. As for Brooks, her early fantasies of writing artful literature gave way to the realization as an adult that her composition talents lay elsewhere. Thus, in making an invidious comparison between her own writing and that of Maurine Whipple—a Saint George neighbor and prize-winning author of *The Giant Joshua*—Brooks wrote to Dale Morgan: "Boy, how she does write in some places! . . . It makes me feel that I lack the spark somehow, or the touch which distinguishes between just writing and art. I have always said that a quail has its place as well as a canary, but I feel like a quail. Perhaps I should stay with the one thing which I have been able to do—collect materials for others to work into bestselling novels." See Peterson, *Brooks*, 52.

60. Peterson, *Brooks*, 31.

to Ernest Pulsipher in 1919 put a temporary halt to her educational and teaching careers. Widowed with a baby son to care for after little more than a year of marriage, Juanita enrolled for another year of teacher training at the Dixie Normal College in St. George and then accepted a teaching job in the Bunkerville Junior High School. The following year she enrolled for two more years of schooling at BYU in Provo, Utah. Finally, at the mature age of twenty-seven, Juanita graduated from BYU with a Bachelor of Science degree and a major in foods and nutrition.[61] She returned to teach English and debate at Dixie Junior College for three years but then was fortuitously offered a sabbatical leave by the college to pursue a master's degree in English literature. Surprisingly, the school she chose to attend was Columbia University in New York City.[62] This, of course, proved to be one of the critical preparation stages for her scholarly career later in life, but unlike the young Fawn who earned her master's degree by the age of twenty, Juanita was thirty-one years old when she finally obtained hers. Like Fawn, however, she never pursued

---

61. Juanita's choice of an undergraduate major in foods and nutrition, rather than in English or history, may seem odd, but as Peterson notes: "She had often selected courses simply because they coincided with the hours when [her sister] Aura could tend [her five-year-old son] Ernie. Furthermore, BYU was distinctly parochial, its faculty sheltered from national trends by their Mormon piety. Yet it was Juanita's nature to learn eagerly. By accident if not by design, the mix of her courses at BYU had not been bad. She had taken rudimentary courses in economics, chemistry, psychology, botany, and sociology and advanced courses in education, home economics, English, speech, and debate." Peterson, *Brooks*, 68.

62. Given Juanita's strong attachments to family and her Mormon homeland, Columbia University in New York City may have seemed like a surprising choice for graduate training in English literature, but Peterson notes: "In the chapter of her autobiography entitled 'The Outsider,' she wrote of the liberating influence an educated visitor to Bunkerville had upon her in a slightly earlier period of her life. From the back of her pony, the girl Juanita pondered the departed visitor and made up her mind, 'that I would see some of the world beyond the desert, that I would go to college or a university or whatever it was that one went to in order to learn of books, and how to talk like books. I would not wait for life to come to me, I would go out to meet it.' Her fascination with the Outside would accelerate during her high school years. Bright and energetic, she dreamed of challenge and scope somewhere in the world beyond Bunkerville." Directly impactful on Juanita's decision to attend Columbia was her experience several years later as a student in Nevada's yearlong normal course for preparing grade school teachers. There, Peterson reports that Juanita's mentor "was a regal young woman, Miss Mina Connell, fresh from studies in pedagogy at Columbia University. . . . Of cultivated values and firm convictions, she declared that this year of normal schooling would equal that available anywhere in the nation. . . . Unquestionably, Miss Connell was the most impressive representative of the Outside that Juanita had so far encountered." See Peterson, *Brooks*, 31.

her education further in quest of a PhD. Both women were detoured from further educational pursuits to dutifully fulfill their impinging marital and motherhood roles.

As with Juanita's educational path, Jan's pursuit of higher education following high school was interrupted and postponed because of early marriage and motherhood. Both women were mature, non-traditional students when they graduated from college at the ages of twenty-seven and thirty-two, respectively. Unlike both Fawn and Juanita, however, Jan went on to pursue and obtain a PhD. Furthermore, in contrast to the other two authors, both of Jan's undergraduate and graduate degrees were in history.

One other common denominator that should not be overlooked in these authors' educational biographies as professional women is the part that school teaching—one of the few, normatively approved kinds of employment for educated women in the early to mid-twentieth century—played in their respective lives. Fawn was strongly encouraged by her parents to consider teaching as a practical career choice and, in fact, taught English at Weber College in Ogden for a year before going to graduate school in Chicago. After graduation and marriage, she also taught as a part-time journalism instructor at Crane Technical College while working full-time as an assistant librarian at the University of Chicago library to help support Bernard, who was finishing his graduate studies. Jan taught elementary school in Georgia while still a teenager, and later in life went back to college at Utah State and the University of Colorado with the explicit intention of obtaining a teaching degree and license to teach. Juanita was specifically trained to teach in rural schools and spent several years as a young adult teaching both elementary and high school in Nevada and Southern Utah.

Mentors

Once these three women each began in earnest to research significant historical topics, they were all aided by influential mentors at critical junctures in their development as scholars and writers. Jan—both as an undergraduate student at Utah State University and later as a PhD student at the University of Colorado—was crucially guided by Everett Cooley, who first inspired her interest in Mormon historiography, informally directed her thesis and dissertation, and made initially vital connections for her in the Mormon intellectual community. Without Cooley's incidental appearance in Jan's return to college as an adult, it is doubtful she would ever have embarked on a path that led her to being a non-Mormon authority on Mormon history. Of equal importance to the writing and publication of their groundbreaking books in Mormon history, Fawn and Juanita both owed much of their success to highly influential mentoring by yet another Mormon scholar: Dale Morgan.

Dale Morgan was a Utah Mormon by birth. As an adult, however, he drifted away from his inherited faith while retaining an enduring interest in the study of Mormon history.[63] He became an independent researcher and, although not academically trained, was a highly respected scholar of Utah and Western history and an accomplished editor and critic. Morgan became known for his generosity in helping novice scholars by supplying them with relevant historical sources and critical but encouraging feedback to their research and manuscript drafts.[64] As fate would have it, two of the novice scholars he corresponded extensively with about their work were Fawn and Juanita.

The fortuitous fact that Morgan resided close to the Brodies while engaged in government work in Washington, DC, during the Second World War "enabled Morgan rapidly to assume the roles of mentor and critic" of Fawn's early efforts to compose a biography of Joseph Smith.[65] In this capacity, Morgan functioned much like a PhD dissertation advisor—formulating pertinent questions, recommending sources, shaping organizational contents, extensively critiquing chapter drafts, and encouraging her progress. Morgan skillfully tempered his "alarming frankness" concerning weaknesses in Fawn's early manuscript drafts while simultaneously spurring her to greater scholarly ambitiousness by "predicting that her biography had the potential of being 'a landmark in Mormon history.'"[66] In her acknowledgment page when the book was published, Fawn singled Morgan out with special appreciation:

> I have been particularly fortunate in having the friendly assistance of Mr. Dale L. Morgan whose indefatigable scholarship in Mormon history has been an added spur to my own. He not only shared freely with me his superb library and manuscript files, but also went through the manuscript with painstaking care. He has been an exacting historian and a penetrating critic.[67]

---

63. A biographical sketch of Morgan's early years and intellectual development is provided by Richard L. Saunders in "The Strange Mixture of Emotion and Intellect: A Social History of Dale L. Morgan, 1933–42," 39–58.

64. Compiler and editor Richard L. Saunders has published two volumes of Morgan's writings, entitled *Dale Morgan on the Mormons: Collected Works, Part 1, 1939–1951*, and *Part 2, 1949–1970*. Based on Morgan's essays, book reviews, lectures, manuscript drafts, and voluminous personal correspondence over a three-decade span, these two volumes amplify an earlier collection and commentary on Morgan's contributions to Mormon Studies edited and published by John Phillip Walker, ed., *Dale Morgan on Early Mormon History: Correspondence and a New History*. Both of these collections of Morgan's work demonstrate his large, behind-the-scenes influence on the emergence and development of the professional writing of Mormon history.

65. Bringhurst, *Brodie*, 87.

66. Bringhurst, 88.

67. Fawn McKay Brodie, *No Man Knows My History: The Life of Joseph Smith*, xi. Reacting to charges that Brodie deceitfully obtained access to documents secreted

Even earlier than Fawn's association with Morgan in wartime Washington was Juanita's scholarly connection with Morgan through her work collecting pioneer diaries in the late 1930s and early 1940s for the Utah WPA Historical Records Survey, a federal agency over which Morgan was the supervisor. If anything, Morgan's influence in guiding Juanita was even more impactful than his informal tutoring of Fawn. Indeed, the origin of the *idea* for writing about the Mountain Meadows Massacre as a monograph or book, rather than simply as a magazine or journal article, may be attributed to Morgan. Morgan made this suggestion to Juanita in conjunction with his critique of a paper she had delivered on the topic to the Utah Academy in 1940. According to Peterson,

> [Morgan] set forth detailed criteria for "an essential scientific approach" which would include an accurate dating of the Fancher party's progress through Utah, a clarification of the membership of the Fancher party, a determination of its behavior toward Indians and Mormons, and an identification of Mormons responsible for each stage of the developing massacre. . . . [W]hen she would at last boldly commit herself to a study of the massacre, his criteria would provide a systematic and scholarly procedure.[68]

From the inception and laborious writing that followed, to ultimate publication of *The Mountain Meadows Massacre* in 1950, Juanita consulted constantly with Morgan, revising and re-revising her masterpiece in response to his guidance and editorial critiques. Peterson writes,

> Morgan boundlessly admired Juanita's unique amalgamation of agrarian practicality, homey domesticity, and critical reason. Believing her to be a living remnant of the pioneer era, he relied on her expertise on frontier conditions. For her part, Juanita accepted Morgan as her mentor in scholarly and literary matters, finding in their correspondence an intellectual stimulation otherwise absent from her life.[69]

On the acknowledgment page of her book's second edition (first published as a paperback with a foreword by Jan in 1991), Juanita wrote: "Because I felt that I must bear full responsibility for the first edition of this book, I named no one specifically as giving me assistance. Now I wish to make grateful acknowledgement to the following people." The first person she thanked was Dale Morgan, "who supplied material from the National Archives which I would never have secured otherwise; who questioned and argued with me through the mail; who

---

in the LDS Church archives by exploiting her family name, Jan claims that most of Brodie's primary sources were already available in the public domain, and that many of these were suggested or directly provided to her by Dale Morgan from his personal and voluminous Mormonism library.

68. Peterson, *Brooks*, 129.
69. Peterson, 120.

gave me much bibliographical material and directed me in its arrangement; and who was never too busy to pay attention to my problems."[70]

At early, critical stages in their development as historians, all three women depended on the principal guidance of scholarly, male mentors. Why male mentors? The primary reason for this is the same reason that made their scholarly success as women noteworthy: there were very few women mentors in Mormon history circles at the time their respective careers were getting underway. Bringhurst names Utah women writers Vesta Crawford (who also was a friend of Juanita) and Claire Noall as providing Fawn with some relevant historical sources for her research, along with their personal feedback and support for her work. However, neither offered the kind of deep expertise and prolonged assistance as Morgan was able to do. Juanita likewise benefitted over the years from the encouragement and support of other women, but none were able to match Morgan's authoritative credentials and generously shared knowledge of Mormon history and the canons of scholarly writing. In Jan's experience we see much the same dearth of other women mentors or scholarly role models. In our interviews with her, Jan remarks on how the women attending Mormon History Association meetings in its early years were mostly the wives of male historians and not other women scholars. (Today, however, this is very far from being the case, thanks in part to the pioneering work and influence of Juanita, Fawn, and Jan.)

Given the relatively small circle of serious Mormon historians at the time, it was perhaps not entirely by coincidence that Jan's early mentor, Everett Cooley, also cultivated relatively close ties with both Juanita and Fawn. As director of the Utah State Historical Society, Cooley honored Fawn in 1967 as a "fellow" of the society in recognition of her many scholarly contributions, asserting that "the controversial Utah-born author was long overdue in receiving recognition."[71] Upon Fawn's death from cancer in 1981, Cooley, then "director of special collections at the University of Utah and close friend in later years, pointed to the ironic fact that Fawn, while 'Utah's best known and most respected author, remained in her native state a prophet without honor.'"[72] As director of the Utah State Historical Society and editor of the *Utah Historical Quarterly*, Cooley also enjoyed a long professional relationship with Juanita. Beginning in 1960, Juanita was employed for several years as a research associate by the State Historical Society to edit the pioneer diary of Hosea Stout, a prominent Mormon leader during the Utah territorial era. Cooley worked with Juanita to get the diary published (eventually by the University of Utah

---

70. Juanita Brooks, *The Mountain Meadows Massacre*, xxvii.
71. Bringhurst, *Brodie*, 177.
72. Bringhurst, 260.

Press) and also welcomed and promoted her article submissions on Western and Utah history to the *Utah Historical Quarterly*.

One other observation worth noting about the relative dearth of female mentors in times past for serious women scholars interested in the study of Mormon history, Mormon social or cultural studies, and Mormon theology, is the extent to which these three authors' careers intersected with one another. For example, through their lengthy correspondences with Morgan, Fawn and Juanita became admiringly familiar with one another's work. In 1943 Juanita met Fawn personally for the first time in Salt Lake City when the latter was researching documentary sources for her Smith biography. According to Bringhurst,

> In early September Morgan wrote [to Juanita] that Brodie had returned to Washington, where her husband was stationed as a military officer, and had mentioned meeting Juanita in Salt Lake. . . . Encouraged that Brodie had mentioned her name, Juanita wrote a letter [to Brodie] which opened an infrequent yet long lasting and respectful correspondence between the two women."[73]

In writing back to Morgan about her acquaintance with Fawn, Brooks commented on a source she had forwarded to her: "[I]t's just a detail but she might like it. . . . I admire her courage and I will be glad to furnish anything I can."[74] When Fawn's book was published, Juanita—writing again to Morgan—judged it to be "both scholarly and literary," saying that it "established a new and necessary perspective on Joseph Smith." While she didn't think the book would have much impact "on rank and file Mormons, who would simply dismiss it as another anti-Mormon book," she perceptively concluded: "Upon Mormon scholars, however, it would 'have its effect, and in the long run, a very profound effect."[75] Reciprocally, Juanita is mentioned appreciatively by Fawn in her acknowledgement page to *No Man Knows My History* for sharing primary source materials pertinent to her research on Joseph Smith. Later, Peterson reports that following publication of Juanita's book on the Mountain Meadows Massacre, "Fawn Brodie wrote [to Juanita] in a tone close to veneration. 'I can't tell you how much I admire the delicacy, dispassionateness, and understatement with which you have handled a potentially lurid and sensational problem.'"[76]

In addition to the collegial and mutually respectful relationship established between these two budding women scholars, we already have mentioned Jan Shipps's engagement with both of their work as "essential reading"

---

73. Peterson, *Brooks*, 141.
74. Peterson, 141.
75. Peterson, 170.
76. Peterson, 209.

when she commenced her studies in Mormon history and also her later professional encounters with them through the Mormon History Association. For Jan as an outsider to the Mormon tradition, Fawn and Juanita had been from the beginning the most prominent examples of Mormon women scholars whose work was worth emulating in pursuit of her own scholarly career.

Acknowledging the early influence and important impetus that such male mentors as Everett Cooley and Dale Morgan provided Jan, Fawn, and Juanita, we should inquire as to why *these men* did not write the kind of critical, groundbreaking books that their female protégés wrote. Both men had well-established reputations for scholarly integrity and excellence in their work. Morgan especially aspired to write a comprehensive history of Mormonism but never completed it.[77] Instead he authored or edited books and articles on the fur trade and the opening of the American West, as well as numerous other publications on Mormon-related topics that were well-regarded by academic professionals.[78] While writing and reviewing occasional specialized articles on Utah history, Cooley's primary scholarly contributions were made as an effective administrator of the Utah State Historical Society and its archives, as editor of the *Utah Historical Quarterly*, and as director of

---

77. In November 1945, Morgan, writing to Brooks about Brodie's soon-to-be published biography of Joseph Smith, informed her that "when my own opus [a projected history of the Mormons] is finished, one of these years, you are one of the persons I am going to ask to read the manuscript, for the sake of the perspective I'll derive from your mind, which is both rarely independent and essentially sympathetic to the Mormon point of view." See Peterson, *Brooks*, 169. Peterson goes on to note that three years later, in April 1948, Brooks paid Morgan a visit in Salt Lake. "For months her correspondence with Morgan had been infrequent. As he returned to Utah from Washington, determined to begin a three-volume history of the Mormons, Morgan had slowly followed their westward trail across the nation, gathering documents and scouting local landscape." See Peterson, *Brooks*, 190. Clearly this was a project that weighed heavily upon Morgan but one which he found difficulty in concentrating on and completing in competition with his other, wide ranging commitments. In his introduction to *Dale Morgan on Early Mormonism Mormon History: Correspondence and a New History*, editor John Phillip Walker writes: "Until his untimely death in 1971 [at the age of 56], he labored for close to thirty years on what would have been a definitive history of the Church of Jesus Christ of Latter-day Saints. Unfortunately, of a projected three volumes, only the first seven chapters and two appendices were completed." See John Phillip Walker, *Dale Morgan on Early Mormonism Mormon History: Correspondence and a New History*.

78. Morgan's books on the American West published in his lifetime include *The Humboldt: Highroad of the West*; *Jedediah Smith and the Opening of the West*; and *Overland in 1846: Diaries and Letters of the California-Oregon Trail*.

the Western Americana division of the University of Utah Library—but not as an author of big books on the foundations of Mormon history.

As to why Morgan (who so effectively mentored Fawn and Juanita in the craft of writing Mormon history) and Cooley (who did likewise with Jan) never produced transformational histories themselves is an enticing question.[79] For that matter, it may be argued that no other prominent male Mormon historians of their era published books comparable in their critical acuity or intellectual daringness to the ones authored by Fawn, Juanita, and Jan.

Professional Academic Affiliations

In comparing their educational antecedents, Jan obtained a PhD in history, while both Fawn and Juanita ended their formal educational training with master's degrees in English literature. Furthermore, in middle age, Jan went on to attain a tenured position at a research university that financially supported and institutionally rewarded her scholarship prior to her publication of *Mormonism: The Story of a New Religious Tradition*. In contrast, Fawn and Juanita were both homemakers and independent scholars at the time they researched and wrote *No Man Knows My History* and *The Mountain Meadows Massacre*. Later in her career, after her children were grown, Fawn also obtained faculty status at a major research university (UCLA). Juanita, on the other hand, served periodically on the faculty at Dixie State College, teaching English and debate, and also briefly occupied the position of dean of women at that school before marrying for the second time. These educational and professional differences help to explain the different kinds of books that the women authored.

As a university academic, Jan was expected by administrators and colleagues to be professionally active in scholarly associations and to produce

---

79. As already noted, Morgan intended his *magnum opus* to be the definitive history of Mormonism and the Mormon people, but after decades of research, he never was able to assemble a completed manuscript, let alone go through the publishing process to produce a finished work. In his 1986 biographical introduction to *Dale Morgan on Early Mormonism*, editor John P. Walker quotes the reactions of Fawn, Juanita, and Utah-raised novelist Wallace Stenger to news of Morgan's untimely death. Brodie: "He has some great books inside him, and I simply can't bear to think of their not being written. No one but he can do what ought to be done on Mormon history." Brooks: "I have long since ceased trying to figure out the WHY's of the Universe. I can only accept these tragedies with what grace I can muster. The cause of Utah history suffers greatly from his loss." Stegner: "It's a great loss; he was so fine a scholar that almost one's first thought is of the unwritten book—and not only the Mormon one but the fur trade one. And that's heartless, really, because he was also so fine and decent and generous and long-suffering a man that one should think first of the person we've lost, and not of the books."

publishable research. Her joint appointment at IUPUI placed her in a religious studies department consisting of respected male scholars who strongly emphasized the importance of academic research and its publication in reputable scholarly journals. New to religious studies, and as the lone woman in the department, Jan experienced considerable competitive pressure to prove she deserved her appointment and that she could match or surpass her male colleagues. Once on board at IUPUI, Jan quickly became the quintessential academic scholar, one who not only obtained grants to fund major projects but who was also at the center of overlapping collegial networks, and in a position to influence the direction and standards of scholarly organizations in both history and religious studies. With particular regard to her innovative conceptual approach for understanding Mormonism as a new religious tradition, Jan credits her colleagues in religious studies as being more influential than any of her Mormon history mentors or colleagues at that point in her development, as we previously have emphasized.

Given Jan's standing as a university scholar, it's not surprising that *Mormonism: The Story of a New Religious Tradition* is more geared to a scholarly audience than either Juanita's or Fawn's books, both of which have had much wider, popular readerships than Jan's publication. Furthermore, it is her theoretical framework, derived from social science and religious studies literatures, that sets Jan's book apart from other more conventional histories of the Mormon past. It is precisely because of her training and faculty career in both history and religious studies that Jan was able to write the kind of book that she did.

While their scholarship was widely acclaimed, neither Fawn nor Juanita was an academically trained historians. And, though frequently invited to speak at academic gatherings or conferences, neither was centrally involved in the kinds of academic organizations that characterized Jan's professional career. Fawn was invited to join the UCLA faculty but never achieved the kind of professional connections and collegiality that Jan enjoyed at IUPUI. Many of Fawn's male history department colleagues deprecated her English MA credential and did not regard her to be a real historian worthy of tenure. Juanita's spotty faculty and administrative experience was at a small junior college that focused on the practical training and moral education of undergraduate students, not on academic research. Because of her local and regional reputation as an independent researcher of pioneer diaries and manuscripts, Juanita sat on organizational boards devoted to the preservation and writing of Utah and Mormon history, but these were not the same as professional research organizations in academia, with national and international memberships.

The Peculiar Confluence of Gender Obstacles and Academic Norms in the Composition of Landmark Mormon Histories

The upshot of these academic limitations on Juanita Brooks's and Fawn Brodie's scholarly credentials meant that, to some extent, they operated on the margins of academia—especially Juanita—even though their work received widespread attention and renown in scholarly circles. It turns out that, in the history of science and the arts, it's often gifted outsiders to the academy who make breakthrough discoveries or innovative changes to an established discipline. Compared to Jan Shipps, both Fawn and Juanita were less constrained by the institutional norms of academic research that is undertaken in well-established disciplines. Within these disciplines, scholars typically conform their work to the conceptual and methodological parameters of existing paradigms. Over time, existing paradigms in science may weaken because of emerging empirical anomalies, whereas in artistic disciplines, human creative impulses constantly press the boundaries of previous modes of expression. Older scientists or artists schooled in existing paradigms resist changing perspectives and seldom are at the forefront of innovative approaches.[80] Transformative changes typically come from younger practitioners of a discipline, or from gifted individuals—often self-taught—who initially occupy marginal positions in the interstices of society and the academic community.[81]

Though an outsider to the Mormon faith tradition, Jan became a consummate *academic insider*. Though insiders to the Mormon faith tradition, Fawn and Juanita were, to a greater or lesser degree, *academic outsiders*. This latter characterization was especially true when Fawn and Juanita were researching and writing their landmark books in Mormon history. As Latter-day Saints by birth, their critical reinterpretations of key components of the faith's official narrative provoked the ire of ecclesiastical authorities who were committed to supporting faith-promoting histories undertaken by loyal Mormon

---

80. The related ideas of paradigms and paradigm shifts in established fields of study were first laid out in Thomas Kuhn's influential book, *The Structure of Scientific Revolutions*.

81. A Wikipedia article entitled "List of Autodidacts" (https://en.wikipedia.org/wiki/List_of_autodidacts) complies a lengthy list of well-known autodidacts—people who have been partially or wholly self-taught—in the fields of literature (e.g., Herman Melville, Jorge Luis Borges, Ernest Hemingway), playwriting and filmmaking (e.g., George Bernard Shaw, Henry Miller, Orson Welles, Stanley Kubrick), music composition (e.g., Arnold Schoenberg, Heitor Villa-Lobos, Hans Zimmer), architecture (e.g., Frank Lloyd Wright, Luis Barragán, Léon Krier), engineering and invention (e.g., Thomas Alva Edison, the Wright Brothers, Buckminster Fuller), mathematics and science (e.g., Gottfried Wilhelm Leibniz, Srinivasa Ramanujan, Charles Darwin, Michael Faraday), and miscellaneous others (e.g., Frederick Douglass, Booker T. Washington, Malcolm X, Steve Jobs).

scholars. At that time, in fact, Mormon historians were virtually the only scholars genuinely interested in writing histories of the Latter-day Saints, and they did so from a faith perspective that ultimately validated their religion's exclusive truth claims. It was the "New Mormon History" movement of the 1970s and 80s, joined and substantially contributed to by Jan, which finally began to legitimize professional Mormon Studies programs and a naturalistic approach to the study and understanding of Mormon culture and its history.

As pedigreed Latter-day Saints and independent research scholars who wrote critically of the Mormon faith tradition in the 1940s and 50s, both Fawn and Juanita were ostracized by their fellow Latter-day Saints. Fawn, whose debunking biography of Joseph Smith was judged as the ultimate religious defection, incurred excommunication and the infamous brand of heretic. Juanita, who never challenged the ultimate validity of the Mormon faith, was not excommunicated or disfellowshipped but was informally branded as a maverick and lost the trust and support of Mormon officialdom.

So, we have two women insiders to Mormon religion and culture, writing Mormon histories from the institutional margins of the LDS academic community, and one woman outsider to the Mormon tradition writing a history of Mormonism from the institutional centers of overlapping academic communities. Let us engage in some small thought-experiments to clarify the implications of these variable circumstances.

Instead of marginalization, let us imagine that, as DNA Latter-day Saints, Fawn and Juanita had gone through conventional historical training as PhD students at Brigham Young University, the LDS Church's flagship institution of higher education in Provo, Utah. Constrained by the academic norms of mentorship and review of one's dissertation research by an institutionally certified faculty committee, it is extremely doubtful that, as graduate students, either one would have produced the studies that made them famous. Pushing our thought-experiment a little further, it's equally doubtful that had they acquired faculty positions in history at BYU (or any other Church-owned institution), they would have enjoyed the academic liberty—including institutional encouragement, financial assistance and collegial support—to author *No Man Knows My History* or *The Mountain Meadows Massacre*.[82] Even today, two decades into the twenty-first century, issues of academic freedom con-

---

82. As Peterson observes: "For whatever it is worth to Mormondom and the world at large, her [Juanita's] achievements as historian, tragedian, and dissenter derived entirely from her deflection from a conventional academic career. If she had not married Will Brooks, she would in all probability have achieved a PhD and an appointment in a university English department. She would have written books, but they would have been works of literary criticism and would not have been controversial." See Peterson, *Brooks*, 92.

tinue to be significant sources of concern and controversy at LDS Church-owned schools.

The question we ask is: Were these two women somehow better situated to write critical, intellectually daring histories than male Mormon scholars of that era? We would argue that, yes, it was precisely because of their independent status as gifted women researchers and writers that Fawn and Juanita were eventually able to write and publish what they did. When we consider that they were Mormon women at a time when women scholars in academic circles nationally were relatively rare (not to mention in Utah), we are led to an even greater appreciation of their achievements. In response to our question concerning the significance of their gender, we propose the following thesis: Being intellectually curious, independent women in a religious culture dominated by male authority, Fawn and Juanita were less constrained from expressing critical or dissenting views than most of their Mormon male peers. Compared to them, Mormon male academics had to function in greater conformity to the normative strictures of institutional oversight—both in the LDS Church and in church-dominated institutions of higher education; even though knowledgeable and professionally trained, their institutional statuses and inculcated orthodoxy of thought within the Mormon paradigm deterred them from the intellectual boldness displayed in the works of Fawn and Juanita.

As for Jan, we see her resolutely pursuing a standard route, through graduate training and academic ranks, to become a member in esteemed standing of the academic establishment. As a woman who had devoted the first part of her adult life to caring for her husband's career and son's upbringing, Jan also had to struggle against long odds to achieve academic success. Finally winning a faculty appointment at a research university, she was pushed and supported by male academic colleagues to make a name for herself in history and religious studies. Jan wrote and became famous within academic circles for *Mormonism: The Study of a New Religious Tradition*, only after receiving tenure at IUPUI and serving as the first female president of the Mormon History Association. This in contrast to Fawn and Juanita, who had no such institutional backing. As novice scholars researching and writing what would later become acclaimed works of history, they simply relied on their own intellectual passions, encouragement from supportive husbands, and the guidance of Dale Morgan—himself an academic outsider.[83]

---

83. Morgan, who suffered from deafness, studied commercial art at the University of Utah but never pursued graduate studies in history or any other related field of study. He was an inveterate reader who was self-trained in historical methods of primary source retrieval and documentation. See Richard L. Saunders, "Social History of Dale L. Morgan," 39–58.

We thus conclude that the three books we have singled out for consideration as the most consequential in thinking and writing about Mormon history are, in an important sense, products of the peculiar confluence of gender obstacles and academic norms in twentieth-century America. The adjective of peculiar is warranted by conjoining the notion of obstacles with academic norms to explain the composition of these three consummate works of scholarship in the Mormon catalogue. Obstacles, including gender prejudices, convey negative connotations, while academic norms usually connote a positive regard for maintaining exacting standards of scholarly attainment. But under certain conditions, the combination of cultural obstacles and contemporaneous academic norms may lead to unexpected achievements, as indicated by marginalized intellectuals and artists who make stunning innovations to their staid fields of endeavor.

As twentieth-century women, Fawn, Juanita, and Jan all had to struggle with domestic role demands on their scholarship and against gender handicaps in male-dominated fields of study. As a mother with only one child to care for, Jan, through endless tenacity and tactful intelligence, supervened gender obstacles in her pursuit of higher education and academic standing as a tenured professor. It was from this position that she was able to compose a brilliant, scholarly analysis of Mormonism's beginnings and ultimate development as a new religious tradition. Writing to a larger academic audience and not just to Mormon readers, Jan's book conformed to the highest standards of university-sponsored research.

As Mormon mothers with larger families to care for, neither Fawn nor Juanita supervened gender obstacles in the pursuit of higher academic degrees in the field of history. This was especially a handicap for Fawn in her later relationship to the history faculty at UCLA. As intellectually inquisitive and determined Mormon women writing Mormon history, both Fawn and Juanita occupied positions outside the institutions of the male-dominated Mormon academic community. For this reason, as we already have argued, they were much freer to write the kinds of seminal books that their passions pushed them to write.

To summarize: All three women faced gender obstacles in their chosen fields of study, but variation in their religious backgrounds ultimately led them to very different professional careers and attitudes toward their work in relationship to academic norms. As Mormon women, Fawn Brodie and Juanita Brooks wrote books about the Mormon past free from the academic constraints of orthodox Mormon scholarship at LDS institutions of higher learning. A non-Mormon, Jan Shipps pursued graduate education and employment at secular universities and closely conformed her work to the norms of professional advancement in the academy.

Fawn's acerbic biography and Juanitas's detailed and detached rendering of a single event were both exercises in critical historiography based on naturalistic assumptions about their subject matter, qualities rare for LDS-affiliated Mormon scholars of their era. Jan's broader, analytical treatment of Mormonism as a world religion in relationship to Christianity came later when the critical and naturalistic approach to Mormon history, reflected in Fawns's and Juanitas's earlier works, animated the "New Mormon History" movement within LDS scholarship circles. Also, Jan's "outsider" status as a non-Mormon scholar greatly enhanced the credibility and impact of her work for both Mormons and non-Mormons.

Fawns's and Juanita's books stripped away long-standing mythologized curtains from their subjects, thus alarming and antagonizing believing Mormons of that time who were unaccustomed to non-faith-based, critical recitations of their religious history. Nevertheless, they set higher standards for serious Mormon scholars who followed. In contrast, Jan's book, while employing the highest standards of detached scholarship in a later era, gave comforting theoretical support to most informed Mormons' sense of significance in the wider world at the same approximate historical moment when the LDS Church was clearly emerging as an international religion of considerable influence.[84]

Three landmark books: one written by an accomplished non-Mormon academic, the other two by accomplished Mormon non-academics. The authors of all three books were women—women who were generationally and geographically separated, yet whose scholarly careers in writing about Mormon history intriguingly intersected through shared mentors, similar personal qualities of intellectual boldness, and mutual admiration for one another's work.

---

84. The rapid, international growth of the post-World War II LDS Church is reviewed in Robert Gottlieb and Peter Wiley, *America's Saints: The Rise of Mormon Power*; Armand L Mauss, *The Angel and the Beehive: The Mormon Struggle with Assimilation*; Richard Ostling and Joan K. Ostling, *Mormon America: The Power and Promise*; Rodney Stark and Reid L. Nielson, *The Rise of Mormonism*; and Gordon Shepherd and Gary Shepherd, *A Kingdom Transformed: Early Mormonism and the Modern LDS Church*.

CHAPTER 8

Personal Views on Religion and Feminism

Are the religious beliefs of religious scholars pertinent to understanding their scholarship and vice versa? We presume that, to some degree, the answer is yes. What are, in fact, Jan Shipps's own religious views? How were they formed? How and why have they changed over time? How have they affected her academic study of Mormonism, and in what ways, if any, is the reverse also true? It also seems appropriate for us to ask similar questions about the development of Jan's views on the status of Mormon women. As a perceptive student of Latter-day Saint history and Mormon culture—within the context of significant social trends in the larger world—what are her thoughts on contemporary issues of gender equality in the Church of Jesus Christ of Latter-day Saints and the emergence of Mormon feminism as a growing minority movement within modern Mormonism? To what extent are these views implicated in her professional work, or correlated with her standing and influence as an acclaimed woman scholar in a field of study that increasingly has become attractive to other women scholars?

Religious Views

Methodism

Any competent assessment of Jan's views on religion cannot neglect her upbringing as a Methodist. As a child and adolescent Jan was actively involved in the music and youth programs of the Methodist Church. While the Methodism of her youth in Alabama and Georgia was much more closely aligned with biblical literalism than the Methodism of her adult years in Bloomington, Indiana, Jan never imbibed deeply of religious fundamentalism. Even as a young person, she clearly discerned the difference between Baptist hellfire preaching (to which many of her friends were exposed) and a moderate social gospel orientation (much more to her liking) that was emphasized by Hueytown's Methodist preachers.

Retrospectively, the principal explanation for Jan's preference for a social gospel emphasis in religion is the strong reinforcement she got at home from her parents. While uncritically believing in the biblical God of Protestant Christianity, neither of Jan's parents were doctrinally strict in their religious beliefs nor notably pious in their religious comportment. Instead, both strongly emphasized practical morality and compassion for people in need of assistance. For them, and consequently for Jan growing up, religion primarily meant an ethical duty to care for one's neighbor and to be honest and upright in one's dealings with other people. Jan looked up to and respected her parents, even after becoming aware of her father's alcoholism. She was seldom defiant or rebellious, and she absorbed her parents' pragmatic religious ethicalism.

Even though Jan's Methodism was dormant for many years after she married Tony, it remained her religious home and proud family tradition, comparable to the lasting affection and attachment that many Mormon intellectuals feel for their religious heritage as Latter-day Saints. Clearly, Jan's inherited, nondogmatic faith and Methodist upbringing were decidedly important influences that helped shape her curiosity and openness to learning about other religious traditions. At the same time, while Jan was genuinely interested in understanding the historical complexities of different faith traditions and academically drawn to the study of mysticism, she was never an ardent religious seeker looking for something more spiritually compelling than what was offered by the Methodist Church.

Religious Inclusivism

Jan's personal religious beliefs do not reflect a strictly orthodox set of creedal Christian convictions as, for example, put forth in the Apostle's Creed—the affirmation of faith most widely used by the United Methodist Church. According to Jan, "my Methodism has matured," and, concomitantly, she has become more appreciative and accepting of the value of other faith traditions outside of Protestant Christianity. She, in fact, takes a very inclusive view of the legitimacy of different global and historical religions (including Mormonism).

When we pressed her on her religious inclusivism, Jan reverted to describing the "wagon wheel" analogy she used when teaching religious studies classes at IUPUI. In this proposition there is no single, true, or "right" religion. Rather, like spokes radiating from the center of a wheel, Jan believes that all historical religions simultaneously bring their adherents closer to the center—which is the "Divine"—and to each other in the process. Jan believes in universal values (love, caring, compassion, etc.) that unite people of all religious faiths. She postulates that in practicing these values there are different, legitimate paths that lead to God. Becoming closer to God via movement on a particular religious path (or "spoke") to the center of the wheel through the religious exercise of universal values, in Jan's view, ultimately brings people closer to understanding and appreciating others who simultaneously are gravitating to the center via adjacent spokes of different religious traditions.

Jan disclaims being a deist and disagreed with us when we suggested that her wheel analogy was essentially humanistic in its emphasis on the accretion of universal moral values across different faith traditions. She concedes that religion *functions* to unite people, bringing them closer together as they move toward what they perceive to be the sacred or "divine," somewhat analogous to Emile Durkheim's thesis in *The Elementary Forms of the Religious Life*. But unlike Durkheim, Jan believes there really is a "divine center," not just society and its irresistibly powerful institutions that stimulate feelings of transcendent control, reverence, and devotion. She maintains that human meanings and values are not all that there is; that beyond humanly constructed realities there is a transcendent center—"the Divine"—that mysteriously inspires and guides human actors. This, of course, is a statement of ultimate faith that can neither be empirically proven nor disproven. At the same time, it is not an affirmation of conventional Christian fundamentals concerning the biblical creator God, the divinity of Jesus, and the salvific grace of his suffering, resurrection, and atonement for humanity's sins. And it certainly does not promote a messianic second coming to herald final judgment in which ultimate justice is realized through the consignment of immortal souls to heaven or hell.

The Conventicle

In practice, if not doctrinal orthodoxy, Jan's religious life today continues to be anchored in the Methodist Church and especially in the Bloomington First United Methodist "Conventicle," a symposium group that Jan helped found in the early 1980s. In addition to sponsoring guest speakers (often academic scholars who discuss their areas of expertise in relationship to religious topics), Conventicle class members have formed close social bonds and serve as a virtual extended family for both Jan and Tony. Prior to Tony's commitment to membership in the Methodist Church and attendance at the Conventicle, he would cheerfully admonish Jan to "Give them Heaven!" as she left alone for a meeting. Tony became a full-fledged Conventicle participant following his and Jan's 1999 wedding re-enactment ceremony at the church and reception hosted by the Conventicle class to celebrate their fiftieth anniversary. After an adult life of religious indifference, Tony made a formal confession of faith before the congregation. (He had already been baptized a Methodist when he was boy living with foster parents.) Thus, unlike Jan's Mormon associations in the Mormon History Association, she and Tony *share* their Conventicle association as a primary reference group. According to Jan, Conventicle members will be invited to sit with family at both her and Tony's funerals. Very clearly, Jan and Tony's reciprocal devotion to their marriage has been strongly reinforced by their mutual connection to the Methodist Church and Bloomington Conventicle.

Has Jan's reactivated Methodism impacted her study and analysis of Mormonism, or has she kept her Conventicle commitments compartmentalized from her scholarly work? Jan says mainly the latter, that she tries to keep her scholarship separate from her personal religious life as a self-identified Methodist. Although over the years she has brought some Mormon colleagues to participate in the Conventicle forum, there is not much overlap between her Conventicle family and her LDS network ties. Conventicle discussions focus on religious topics, history and doctrinal issues, but, according to Jan, they seldom intersect with specifically Mormon topics. Nevertheless, we will argue that Jan's personal religious beliefs—as well as her active promotion of the Conventicle's agenda of thoughtful religious discussion—are ultimately intertwined with her study and analysis of the Mormon religion.

Prayer and Passing on a Faith Tradition

Perhaps Jan's closest friendship today is with Conventicle co-founder Ed Stephenson. Stephenson is a prominent physicist at Indiana University and, like Jan, was born and raised as a Methodist in Birmingham, Alabama. Consequently, he and Jan have much in common and meet regularly for lunch and conversation during which, among other things, they discuss their similarly inclusive religious principles. Tony also thinks highly of Stephenson and has asked the latter and his wife to be the speakers at his funeral service in the Bloomington Methodist Church. (This is Jan's wish as well.) Jan says this comes as close to an expression of religious feelings by Tony as anything else he has said or done. At the same time, Tony feels he was remiss in his fatherly duties to model any kind of religiousness for their son, Stephen. When we asked Jan to compare Stephen's religiosity with hers and Tony's, she began talking about one of the Conventicle's discussion themes: passing on one's faith tradition to the next generation and how this should be done by scholars like Jan, Tony, and Ed Stephenson.

For her part, Jan says, "While Stephen was in college, he played violin at every church in town" (always accompanied by Jan and Tony to see him perform), but she also says that *she's* sorry that she and Tony didn't do a better job of exposing Stephen to religion at home: "In our minds, when we took Stephen to Sunday School, it was just part of his education, to see religion as an option in the world"—an option that he rejected as a youth. Stephen was preoccupied with music and playing tennis, didn't care for organized religion, and didn't receive a decisive religious direction from either of his parents. As an adult, Stephen began drinking to excess and was troubled by his family's history of alcoholism. (Jan's father, Tony's father, and Jan's brother Bill were all alcoholics.) After decades of his own religious indifference, Stephen subsequently converted to a nondenominational, evangelical mega-church in which he played the violin. Stephen attributes spiritual aid through his church involvement as the reason he was able to give up drinking and, today, is a committed "born again" Christian who gratefully testifies that he has been saved by his faith in Jesus Christ.

What does Jan, a heterodox Methodist, think of this turn of events? "I'm happy they [children] keep a commitment to some religious group" (which, she adds, doesn't have to be the Methodist Church). "To be part of a religious community is a good part of growing up." Jan concludes that the "religious dimension" (a term she often uses) is critical in people's decision to stay or not stay connected to their childhood faith when they grow up. Jan is "grateful for Stephen's turn away from alcohol," even though she doesn't share his orthodox Christian convictions. She reports that Stephen is more concerned about Tony's salvation than hers. When we asked why that was the case, she said because when Stephen was growing up, "Tony didn't believe a thing. Now, he (Stephen) asks me to pray for him." Moreover, Jan told us, "*Tony* also asks me to pray for him," which she regularly does.

What kinds of prayers does Jan offer in Tony's behalf? She addresses Deity as "Heavenly Father" and prays aloud so Tony can hear. According to Jan, "Tony wants Heavenly Father to know that I'm praying for both of us." She says Tony asks her to pray when he learns that someone is grieving, especially when he reads or hears about fire victims. (When Tony was living with his foster parents, their home was destroyed by fire, leaving him with a lifelong fear of fire and its destructiveness). Beyond her prayers for Tony's sake, does Jan engage in personal prayer? Her response is: "Yes, every night but silently, not out loud." She prays mainly for Tony's wellbeing, but also for Stephen, his wife Teri, and her grandchildren, adding, "I worry a lot about refugees and pray for them too."

We should note that Jan's prayers are fairly conventional Christian prayers of petition: She addresses God (as "Heavenly Father"), and her main concern is for the welfare of family and loved ones (especially Tony) and people in need or who are oppressed or treated unjustly. The form and focus of her prayers clearly reflect the human compassion emphasized in her own family history and Methodist upbringing. We should also point out that she does not pray for personal material success or supernatural aid in her writing and scholarly work. In these areas she has confidence in her own abilities. In Jan's personal prayers she is comfortable with a mysteriously vague conception of God as the source of goodness and justice in the universe. This is not the anthropomorphic God of the Old or New Testaments. But Jan—in alignment with her wagon wheel analogy that legitimates the particularities of different faith traditions—is content to follow the customary Protestant form of prayer that she grew up with. When we asked her if she ever prayed to "*Mother* in Heaven," she said, "No. I don't think about God as gendered." The question of Mother God has never been an issue for Jan personally.

Mysticism and the Religious Dimension: Thoughts on Joseph Smith and the Mormon Faith

As a scholar, Jan takes pains to emphasize that she is not a religious seeker. She is committed to the Weberian principle of *verstehen* (the subjective understanding of meaning systems different from one's own beliefs) and historical explanation, and she consciously tries to separate her scholarly passion for Mormon Studies from consideration of religious truth claims. She thinks this sets her apart from most Mormon and "gentile" scholars who study Mormons. She does not see herself as either a critic or defender of the faith. As a historian, she is not interested in apologetics or polemics but only in historical and cultural analysis. At the same time, she does not reject mysticism as a genuine avenue for knowing God.

It is primarily for this reason that Jan also objects to being called a deist. Classical deism posits the existence of God (through the operation of natural law) as the creator or cause of events in the material universe but rejects the idea of divine revelation, miracles, or direct intervention by God in human history. Jan, however, does not rule out the idea of divine revelation and God's guidance in human affairs. As a graduate student at the University of Colorado she was drawn to and influenced by Hal Bridges's study of and personal interest in American mysticism. This focus dovetailed with Jan's own interest in explaining the rise and transformation of nineteenth-century Mormonism and its prophet-founder, Joseph Smith.

Jan's criticism of faithful Mormon biographers of Joseph Smith is that they too often disregard his human shortcomings in order to exalt his heroic standing as God's latter-day prophet. Her criticism of non-Mormon or adversarial biographers is that they dismiss the religious seriousness of Smith and his followers and concentrate on Smith's evident talent as a presumed fabulist and charismatic fraud. Jan, for example, says she has much respect for Fawn Brodie's biography of Joseph Smith, conceding that Brodie raised questions that needed to be addressed and was a great writer. But she also concludes that Brodie, a disillusioned Mormon, "never really understood religious experience" and that she "didn't appreciate the religious dimension of Joseph Smith."

By "religious dimension," which Jan thinks is critical to understanding the emergence of new religions, Jan means belief in an ultimate meaning and purpose of human life congruent with the idea of a providential God who inspires and guides human action. Rather than showing genuine curiosity in an attempt to understand the rise of Mormonism as a religious phenomenon (Jan's perspective), Jan says that Brodie's approach to the biography of Joseph Smith was most essentially that of an exposé, because "she never believed in prophecy." That is to say, Brodie never gave credence to the possibility of genuine, inspired direction by God as channeled through select individuals in different historical times and settings.

In contrast, Jan regards Richard Bushman's more recent biography of Joseph Smith to be a singular work of historical scholarship, but she also believes that it ultimately falls short of its objective to provide a faith-based, yet convincing portrait of the Mormon prophet. Bushman, Jan believes, was so preoccupied with refuting Brodie's many aspersions and literary license, while being overly careful not to compromise the essentials of the Mormon faith narrative, that he failed to offer the kinds of fresh insights necessary for making a humanly convincing analysis of his subject. (In fairness, it must also be said that, in contradistinction to Brodie, Bushman explicitly sought to comprehend Smith's personal religiosity—his "religious dimension"—within the historical and cultural context and prevailing religious world view in which Smith grew up.)

As for herself, Jan believes that Smith was both a genuine prophet and a fraud. "I thought this in 1973 [when she wrote 'The Prophet Puzzle'], and I still do," she told us. When Jan says Smith was a prophet she means she thinks he was a genuinely religious person who came to believe in his prophetic prowess as a gift from God. He wasn't a conscious fraud like the fictitious Elmer Gantry, but he wasn't pious either. He was "a person of his time," Jan says. He was "very human, carnal, not saintly or sanctimonious." His belief in self was shaped and influenced by his religiously doting parents: "If parents think a kid is special, so does the kid." As far as Jan is concerned, "there's not any doubt that Joseph Smith was a religious person from childhood on." Jan doesn't think Smith was an inventive liar, as Brodie argued, who simply made things up as circumstances dictated.

For Jan, the question again is one of religious mysticism. She says she eventually came to think of Smith as not being a mystic in the conventional, classical sense. She sees him as a man of action rather than contemplation. Thus, Jan wants to make a distinction between the mystic and the prophet as theoretical types, each of which claims different kinds of direct experience with God. The classical mystic cannot adequately describe or explain his or her ineffable, mystical experience that, nonetheless, confirms God's indubitable existence. In contrast, the prophet speaks for God as an emissary, persuasively describing and explaining what God wants people to do based on his or her own direct communications with deity. Jan is not a disciple of Joseph Smith. She does not believe with Mormons that their religion reveals the only true way to be Christians and thereby receive God's fullest blessings in the highest heaven, but she does think Mormonism is a genuine religion and that Joseph Smith was an authentic kind of prophet. At the very least, she concludes that Smith was an innovative genius who creatively synthesized new theological ideas by absorbing existing religious cultural elements while drawing upon his own occasional mystical experiences. He did this while also exercising the persuasive, charismatic leadership needed to attract a believing core of followers and then to form, lead, and maintain a complex religious organization.

Prior to our discussion with Jan concerning her take on Joseph Smith's prophetic claims, she had just finished reading Adam Nicolson's *God's Secretaries: The Making of the King James Bible*. Reflecting on the history of the King James Bible, which involved a great deal of argument and debate over the precise wording of its English translation, Jan maintained that this *increased* rather than decreased her confidence in the translation's quality. By extension, she proceeded to comment on Joseph Smith's translating efforts, which he claimed were the result of divine revelation and not human reason. Jan pointed out that the contending Oxford and Cambridge dons of Elizabethan England also claimed divine revelation in their translative deliberations of the King James Bible. To this day, of course, many English-speaking Protestants regard it as the single most authoritative compendium of God's revealed word to humanity, in spite of the very human process of argumentation and debate that produced it. (For its own English-language scriptures, the LDS Church publishes an edition of the King James Bible and uses it almost exclusively for biblical quotations in its various publications and media, while simultaneously recognizing that it is not a perfect translation.)

With regard to the Book of Mormon—Joseph Smith's most famous prophetic work—Jan calls it a "a holy book." By this she means that it has precisely the same holy character for Mormons as other sacred texts have for believers in other religious traditions. For Jan personally, however, the Book of Mormon doesn't have the same literary or religious quality as the Bible. In addition to calling it a holy book, she also refers to the Book of Mormon as "an interesting nineteenth-century book," suggesting that Smith was more of an inspired author than a translator.

In her 1983 interview with Maureen Beecher, Jan describes the impact that Tom Alexander's 1975 MHA presidential address (concerning fourth LDS President Wilford Woodruff's openness to mystical, religious experience) had on her thinking about Mormonism: "It was influential in terms of the way I began to see Mormonism . . . that it was possible not just to talk about what happened, but to talk about how people responded and to really get at the religious dimension . . . the truly religious dimension of Mormonism."[1] At a gathering following the 1975 conference at Alexander's home, Jan spent the entire evening in the kitchen with him talking about applying the concept of mysticism to Mormon history. "Of course it is significant that at this same

---

1. Jan Shipps, Oral History interview by Maureen Ursenbach Beecher, 35.

time I was learning by on-the-job training to teach courses in religious studies (at IUPUI). And so that was very important." The following morning at a testimony meeting that concluded the conference, Jan "bore her testimony" (an LDS elocution referring to a public confession of faith) that if scholars "could find a way to deal with belief and faith and reports of faith, it would not be swimming in muddy water, and that I was finding you could write the religious history of the Mormon people in this way." This realization prefaced Jan's "turn toward the attempt to write the religious history of the Mormon people, which I've been doing ever since. . . . I had not started. I had just come to the conclusion I could do it."[2]

In her 1982 *Dialogue* essay, "An 'Inside-Outsider' in Zion," Jan summarizes how, over time and with much puzzling, she came to the conclusion that Mormonism was not merely another Christian sect or denomination but a new religious tradition—an "original synthesis" of Judaism and Christianity. Thus, Jan regards Mormonism to be *sui generis*, as occupying a unique religious classification of its own. Jan says this insight was a "testimony" to her, that like the "histories of all great faiths, through Mormon history, too, divinity reveals itself to humanity in the lives of the members of a believing community."[3]

Conclusion Regarding Jan Shipps's Religious Views and Her Understanding of Mormonism

Our review of Jan's religious views in general, and her scholarly understanding of the Mormon religion in particular, makes evident the reciprocal influence of these two areas of inquiry over time. Beginning with her native curiosity and relatively nonjudgmental Methodist background, her initial exposure to the Mormons in Cash Valley, Utah, corresponded with an emerging appreciation of her own intellectual potential as a student of history. Subsequently, two factors in her graduate training at the University of Colorado were particularly decisive in the future course of Jan's development as a scholar of Mormonism: (1) Her graduate advisor Hal Bridges's personal attraction to mysticism in the context of American history, and (2) her connection through Everett Cooley with the Mormon scholarly community in Salt Lake City—both of whom she turned to and relied on when none of the Colorado history faculty had any expertise in the history of Mormonism. Bridges's willingness to grant sympathetic interest to Joseph Smith as an American mystic, rather than dismiss him as a fraudulent humbug, lent academic credibility to Jan's own developing interest in Mormon history. It also formed an important element of Jan's later conceptual framework for un-

---

2. Shipps, Oral History, 37.
3. Jan Shipps, "An 'Inside-Outsider' in Zion," 160–61.

derstanding the critical religious dimension of the Mormon movement as it quickly metamorphosed into a new religious tradition.

It was Jan's renewed, collegial attachment to the Mormon History Association that filled the intellectual void in her life after moving to Indiana with Tony. Mormon scholars, who impressed Jan with a combination of their religious sincerity and scholarly rigor, stimulated her dormant interests in religion, contributing in no small measure to what she calls the "maturation" of her own Methodism. Religious maturation for Jan meant broadening her inherited faith to accept the legitimacy of other religions as valid expressions of the human quest for the divine. Once Jan rekindled her active involvement with the Methodist Church in Bloomington, she experienced further stimulation in the maturation of her religious understanding from lengthy discussions with the Reverend Ross Marrs concerning the historical relationship between Judaism and Christianity, as well as from guest speakers at the Conventicle forum class who were invited to present numerous different perspectives on religion. At the same time, she was most strongly influenced in the expansion of her own religious views by her religious studies colleagues at IUPUI and the necessity of absorbing the theoretical literature of religious studies in order to competently teach her IUPUI classes. Reciprocally, Jan applied her enlarged understanding of religion as a fundamental human phenomenon to the analysis of contemporary Mormonism.

In all of this, we see that Jan has not strictly compartmentalized her personal religious beliefs from her scholarly analysis of religion in general or Mormonism in particular. There is a developmental correspondence. As an adult she is neither an atheist nor an agnostic. Neither is she a credal Christian with a vested interest in promoting the superiority of any particular religious faith. She is, however, a religious believer in ultimate ends and ultimate values, predicated on faith in the universal and divine center of human experience. This has made it possible for her to practice her academic trade as a religious scholar less constrained by particularistic religious bias or underlying intent to discredit religious plausibility. Her own growing appreciation of what she calls the religious dimension of human experience was clearly amplified by her scholarly understanding of the role that mysticism and prophecy have played in the historical development of religious traditions. This understanding especially informs her specific view on the emergence and transformation of Mormonism as a Christian restoration movement in nineteenth-century America into one of the more rapidly growing and influential international religions of the twenty-first century. In turn, Jan's willingness to view Mormonism as a valid religious faith that functions spiritually for its adherents as well as any other religion is a logical conclusion from her own expanding beliefs concerning God's inclusiveness. Just as importantly for Jan, this also is an evidentiary conclusion from her decades of collegial contact with scholars and practicing adherents in both the Latter-day Saint and Community of Christ traditions.

The Challenge of Women's Concerns in Twenty-first Century Mormonism

Questions of gender equality have arisen as a major focus of concern for many contemporary religions, especially for conservative faiths like that of the LDS Church, which adhere to a traditional view of divinely assigned differences between the sexes, including gender-based domestic and ecclesiastical roles. When we asked Jan what she considered to be the biggest challenge facing The Church of Jesus Christ of Latter-day Saints in the twenty-first century, she said, "I think it's women," many of whom are happy with the way things are, but "a rising number of younger women want change." Jan specified that she thinks the biggest growing problem for the Church is unattached, single women who are better educated than their mothers, professionally oriented, and outnumber prospective male marital partners in their age cohort. She recounted a conversation she had with LDS Apostle Boyd Packer (now deceased), who also asked Jan what she thought the Church's biggest problem was. When Jan told him "single women," Packer responded, "Don't worry, they'll all find partners in the next life."

Packer's dismissive response to a serious demographic and social problem for the Mormon community suggests that the biggest obstacle to adaptive change in the LDS Church might very well be its ecclesiastical seniority system, in which one's standing in the elite Quorum of the Twelve Apostles is based on length of service in the quorum. Over time this has produced a gerontocracy in which the Church's senior and most powerful authorities are several generations older than young adults who are beginning their families and occupational careers. Senior apostles like Packer become increasingly separated from current trends in society, are often tone-deaf to the changing concerns of young people, and typically are unwilling to sponsor or approve of fundamental adjustments in church policy or practice in response to rapid social changes in the larger society. The corollary central problem for younger, change-oriented women is, of course, Mormonism's all-male priesthood organization—a growing anachronism relative to the functioning of twenty-first-century corporate organizations and government agencies, in which talented women increasingly are assuming leadership roles.

Mormon Women and the LDS Priesthood

Minority discontent among professional Mormon women began surfacing forty years ago when the LDS priesthood hierarchy threw its institutional support behind the reactionary 1970s counter-movement to defeat the Equal Rights Amendment to the US Constitution. Sonia Johnson, a Mormon housewife with a Doctor of Education degree, gained national notoriety when she made critical statements about the all-male priesthood and LDS Church hierarchy while testifying before the United States Senate Judiciary Subcommittee on the Constitution, Civil Rights, and Property Rights. Johnson was an outspoken advocate for passage of the ERA and denounced the LDS Church's opposition to the amendment. In 1979 she was excommunicated for her defiance.[4] Moreover, several years prior to the fight over the ERA, influential female scholars like Laurel Thatcher Ulrich and Claudia Bushman (wife of Richard Bushman) had been encouraging sister Latter-day Saints to reflect on their religious history from a feminine perspective via the publication of an independent women's magazine called *Exponent II* (named after an early LDS women's publication). *Exponent II* both anticipated and gave expression to a renewal of concern over issues of women's equality among educated Mormon women. All of this was happening just as Jan was about to assume office as the first non-Mormon, female president of the Mormon History Association.

Early 1970s feminists, both inside and outside the Mormon intellectual community, exerted pressure on Jan as MHA president to advocate for Sonia Johnson's defiant stand. In her Beecher interview, Jan recalls:

> I got letters from organizations that asked the Association to speak out.... There [was] one particular one that came to me as president of the Mormon History Association, asking me to speak out as president of the Mormon History Association on this point. I wrote back and said I could not do it, because the Association was non-political. It was not a popular decision, from the standpoint of me as a woman holding a position that was perceived from the outside as a position of power in the Mormon world.... I also had two phone calls from people who asked me to speak out or asked me to comment. One was from a news magazine reporter and one was from a regular newspaper reporter. And I refused. In every case they wanted me to comment as president of the Mormon History Association.

Jan adds: "I know there were women in the Association that were unhappy with my decision."

Adding fuel to the fire, Jan wrote an article, "Sonia Johnson, Mormonism, and the Media," for the *Christian Century* shortly after assuming office as MHA president. In her article, Jan characterized Johnson's confrontational tactics as counterproductive to the advancement of women's concerns within the LDS Church. She wrote, "People who felt that Sonia Johnson was

---

4. For Johnson's autobiographical account of her opposition to male priesthood authority and repudiation of her Mormon faith, see Sonia Johnson, *From Housewife to Heretic*.

mistreated saw me as a defender of the faith . . . but I think that probably the most important single action that I took as president was to keep the Association out of politics."⁵

To fully appreciate her decision to keep the Mormon History Association out of politics, we may also surmise that Jan did not want to jeopardize her hard-earned standing as Mormonism's "inside-outsider." But even more important to her, she didn't want to jeopardize the Association's tenuous relationship with the Church at a time when MHA founder Leonard Arrington—who then also occupied the position of Church Historian—and his Mormon history colleagues were under attack from ecclesiastical conservatives for undermining the Church's religious narrative with their "New Mormon History" approach. Jan acknowledges she did not consult the MHA Board regarding her decision to remain neutral concerning the politically charged issue of the Equal Rights Amendment and Johnson's militant opposition to the Church's active efforts to defeat it. She considered it to be her personal responsibility as president of the Association to protect it from charges of political bias. She had no doubt that succumbing to what she saw as political pressure would hurt the Association and set a bad precedent that would undermine its scholarly credibility. In Jan's view at the time,

> The issue was not a historical issue. Now if they [LDS ecclesiastical authorities] had closed the Archives of the Church, that would have been different. I made a great effort and pushed from the standpoint of Jan Shipps, scholar [not as MHA president], to try to keep the Archives open. But if they had closed the Archives, we should as an Association have taken a position, because that would have been our business. But Sonia Johnson wasn't our business.⁶

Years after the ERA debate and Sonia Johnson affair, Jan recounted to us that Harvard scholar (and co-founder of *Exponent II*) Laurel Thatcher Ulrich told her, "LDS general authorities liked me because I didn't take up women's issues or feminist causes in my scholarly work." Jan concedes that "this is mostly true." Until Ulrich and other critics challenged her feminism by saying LDS leaders liked her because she wasn't critical or theologically dangerous, Jan hadn't thought much about women's issues in the Church. These concerns "were not at the top of my agenda; I haven't focused on them in my writing or speaking." Furthermore, while Jan follows the academic work of contemporary female Mormon Studies scholars (such as Ulrich, Claudia Bushman, Marie Cornwall, Kathryn Daynes, Kathleen Flake, and

---

5. Quotes regarding the contested issue of support for Sonia Johnson's defiance of LDS priesthood authority are taken from Shipps, Oral History, 51–52. Also, see Jan Shipps, "Sonia Johnson, Mormonism, and the Media," 5–6.

6. Shipps, Oral History, 52.

Andrea Radke-Moss) and has praised their work in interviews with us, she has not developed close connections with Mormon feminists and is not at all acquainted with younger Mormon women who are active in the Ordain Women movement.

Despite this background, is it possible that Jan might still be considered a feminist?

Contemporary Mormon Feminism

Broadly conceived, a feminist might simply be defined as a person who supports the idea of women's equality with men in all areas of civil and domestic life, especially with regard to the rights and responsibilities of human authority and decision making. More narrowly defined, we might specify that a feminist is one who not only supports the idea of equal rights for women but also actively contributes to the advancement of feminist causes that have been a significant part of the historical transformation of social institutions in modern societies. These definitional differences suggest a wide spectrum of lived experience within which individuals can be considered feminists, ranging from passive supporters to feminist activists and everything in between. They also allow for the possibility of an individual's own changing feminist attitudes and actions over time. Today, Jan espouses liberal political values, but in her unswerving pursuit of scholarly objectivity in Mormon Studies, she has always leaned toward the passive rather than activist side of the feminist continuum.

When we asked Jan if she regards herself to be a feminist, she demurred and said, "I've never been an out-front feminist." First and foremost, she thinks of herself as an *individual*: "I've never called myself a feminist, just a person." She says she greatly appreciates the accomplishments of women in the face of gender discrimination, but she is not personally agitated about women's authority issues in the LDS Church. In contrast to Mormon feminists, she claims she has never personally experienced institutional sexism in the Methodist Church. "I understand the priesthood voice. I grew up in the Southern Methodist Church, and preachers have priesthood voices too. Never have I had any feeling that any person has put on a priesthood voice with me." Jan has always worked closely with men in her scholarly work. In fact, her capacity for effectively engaging in male camaraderie with male colleagues was striking to us in our interviews with Jan. She was welcomed into "the club" of male historians at the Mormon History Association, from whom she only experienced support and praise. As a member and officer of both the Mormon History Association and John Whitmer Historical Association, she never has been confronted with the kind of self-abnegation or frustration that many active LDS women experience in their church service roles as auxiliaries to the male priesthood. In her informal status as esteemed inside-outsider, with privileged access to many Mormon priesthood authorities, she has not been subjected to institutional discrimination because of her gender.

In her marriage, we have noted a consistent pattern of Jan outwardly adhering (but only up to a point) to many traditional gender roles that both she and Tony grew up with. But from Jan's perspective, she never felt that she and Tony were not on the same page, managing as equal partners the affairs of their household and marriage (even though following certain taken-for-granted gender norms in doing so). Jan says that she and Tony "shared child rearing tasks, were respectful of each other's needs, and, in general, worked as a team." Her commitment to her family trumped all others, and because of this she felt she "was needed at home" on a regular basis to fulfill her legitimate portion of their marriage partnership.

Thus, even though trained as a "Big Picture" historian and religious studies scholar, Jan personalizes the issue of priesthood authority for women in terms of her own experience. As a Methodist, the ordination of women has never surfaced for Jan as a personal concern (the United Methodist Church has ordained women to its clergy since 1968), and her personal experiences with Mormon scholars and ecclesiastical officials have been virtually discrimination free. Jan has never embraced the role of critic or reformer in behalf of other women. Instead she is staunchly committed to the principle of detached scholarship in which she separates her gender and liberal political views from her scholarly work.

Today, of course, there is a significant generational difference between Jan and most contemporary Mormon feminists who did not grow up in the same world of taken-for-granted gender inequities that shaped Jan's attitudes as a student and young wife and mother. In recent years, Ordain Women, an activist Mormon group, has gained headlines by its willingness to publicly challenge the exclusion of women from the Mormon priesthood. This has included publishing a website to host personal profiles of Church members who openly support the ordination of women, lining up at the Mormon Tabernacle in Salt Lake City to individually request women's admission to the Church's semi-annual (now annual) all-male priesthood meeting, and circulating photos and texts online of what it would look like to have women officiating in LDS priesthood ordinances. In concert with other Mormon feminists, Ordain Women activists have also sought to bring out of the doctrinal closet Mormonism's controversial and theologically underdeveloped belief in a Heavenly Mother.[7] The Church acknowledges that its doctrine embraces belief in "heavenly parents," but like Protestant evangelicals who

---

7. See, for example, Janice Allred, *God the Mother: And Other Theological Essays*.

cite the biblical example of Jesus teaching his disciples how to pray, it insists that members should pray only to God the Father.

In a book related to Ordain Women that we co-edited with Lavina Fielding Andersen (*Voices for Equality: Resurgent Mormon Feminism*), we quote Jan when she was asked by a press reporter to comment on the excommunication of Ordain Women's most prominent leader, Kate Kelly. Reminiscent of Sonia Johnson's 1980 excommunication, Jan observed, "It does more than excommunicate Kelly. It warns everybody." Jan went on to conclude that LDS leaders were implementing "boundary maintenance," using Kelly and other dissidents as examples to demonstrate how far Church members could go in questioning their faith's practices.[8] While giving a concise, professional response to a reporter's question concerning the significance of Kelly's excommunication, Jan did not volunteer personal support for Ordain Women's goal of priesthood ordination, nor, as we already mentioned, is she personally acquainted with any of the group's current leaders or founders, including Kelly.

Jan is not in the least opposed to Mormon women being ordained to the priesthood. However, given her understanding of Mormon history and theology of family life that requires priesthood temple endowments for families to be eternally "sealed," she is dubious about LDS women gaining the priesthood anytime soon. It's "going to be tough," she told us. It would not work in the same way that women achieved ordination rights in Methodism, for example, which has a very different conception of priesthood—one that is not linked to beliefs concerning the connection between priesthood ordinances and the afterlife.

Jan does agree that contemporary feminist activism has influenced the thinking of some LDS Church authorities in the direction of modest changes in Church policy: "There is no doubt that Mormon women activists are having some impact" on certain LDS authorities, she told us, at least with regard to reexamining and advocating modification of some long-held Victorian assumptions about women and their status in the world, the family, and the Church. But priesthood ordination for LDS women would require a fundamental change in theology and an official revelation issued by the Church President and Quorum of the Twelve Apostles. This, it should be noted, is precisely what Ordain Women activists hang their hopes on.[9] We should also

---

8. Gordon Shepherd and Gary Shepherd, "Conflict and Change in Closed and Open Systems: The Case of the LDS Church," 28.

9. Ordain Women board member, Debra Jenson, summarizes the group's highly publicized Temple Square gathering to dramatize its faithful pleas to LDS authorities for priesthood recognition: "On Saturday, April 5, 2014, more than 400 women and men gathered in a park in Salt Lake City, Utah, to sing hymns and pray for courage. These individuals carried with them the names of 500 more souls who could

note that in 1984 Community of Christ authorities proclaimed an official revelation granting women the priesthood.[10] But, as Jan points out, their views of the afterlife differ significantly from that in Latter-Day Saint theology, which, among other things, requires priesthood temple endowments.

For believing Latter-day Saints, contemporary revelation trumps theology, and whatever theological complications might ensue from a new priesthood revelation could presumably be ironed out. But realistically, Jan contends that for the LDS Church to authorize a revelation giving priesthood to women, older general authorities need to be replaced by younger, more liberal-minded apostles. Here again, however, we encounter the essential dilemma of the LDS seniority system in the ecclesiastical hierarchy. It is a system that functions to maintain institutional stability and continuity with the past but, generally speaking, also militates against contemporary flexibility and adaptive innovation.

As an academic historian whose Mormon "watching" has extended over six decades, Jan is not optimistic that progressive LDS leadership changes will take place soon. Pessimism regarding the likelihood of priesthood ordination for LDS women is not, of course, tantamount to opposition to such a trans-

---

not make the trek to the Beehive State but shared the same desire: to see women ordained to priesthood authority in the Church of Jesus Christ of Latter-day Saints. We lined up, hoping to gain admission to the men-only priesthood session of general conference; we walked to Temple Square, the symbolic home of Mormonism and the LDS Church. We saw ourselves as faithful members of the Church. Overwhelmingly, these men and women were faithful members of the Church. Our internal survey showed that more than 70 percent of those who participated in Ordain Women Actions attended church at least two to three times a month. Long before the general conference, we had asked for tickets to attend this meeting. Denied because of our gender, we next informed our leaders of our intention to wait in the standby line. Again we were rebuffed and invited to stand in the "Free Speech Zone" with anti-Mormon protestors. These same protestors, to whom our leaders had compared us, saw us as Mormons and yelled offensive things at us as we walked quietly by. We were too Mormon for them—but we were not Mormon enough for the General Authorities of the LDS Church . . . The question of whether Ordain Women supporters are faithful members of the LDS Church or on the road to apostasy is key to understanding the progress the group has made so far. It is the same question of inside/outsider status that impacts all social movements in the effort to create change but is particularly important in faith-based movements." Debra Jenson, "From the Kotel to the Square: The Rhetoric of Religious Feminism," 377.

10. This controversial change caused much conflict within the RLDS membership and resulted in significant membership decline as a result. See Robin Kinkaid Linkhart, "Ordination of Women: The Community of Christ Story," 185. The negative organizational consequences of such a change occurring in the LDS Church would presumably be far more severe.

Jan Shipps, 2010.

formative event, but for activists, passive support on the part of knowledgeable people of good will is insufficient, and they project a moral imperative on scholars like Jan to add their respected voices to the cause of women's equality.

Proto-Feminism

For her time and place, Jan was exposed to relatively strong female role models who encouraged her educationally, but her orientation growing up was primarily traditional and practical. Her attraction to academic scholarship only came later in life, and it was both stimulated and channeled by her husband's career. Jan never viewed herself as a feminist scholar doing feminist scholarship. Neither, we might add, did Fawn Brodie or Junita Brooks, whom we have selected for purposes of comparison. Older than Jan, both Brodie and Brooks likewise held traditional views of gender roles, marriage, and the priority duties of motherhood. All three, in fact, were well past the stage of forming their academic and personal identities when second-wave feminism virtually exploded as a mass cultural phenomenon in the 1960s and 1970s. Nonetheless, many Mormon feminist scholars today would agree that both Brody and Brooks should be considered as "proto-feminists."

In what particular ways might we justify describing women scholars of the past century as feminists or proto-feminists who did not themselves adopt these labels? Attaching the modifier "proto" to feminist is a way to define women who lived in a time or place dominated by male preoccupations but whose work anticipated or helped lay the groundwork for future feminist outlooks. Most importantly in the cases of Brooks and Brodie as Latter-day Saint women, their books *challenged* the official religious narrative of the LDS Church that was forcefully defended by male authorities. A fair question to ask is whether Jan's work in Mormon Studies has contributed to a feminist outlook in this same way. An obviously fair answer must be that the content of her books and scholarly articles has not. But perhaps there are other aspects of her work and legacy for contemporary women that are also important to consider.

If nothing else, contemporary women scholars should be heartened by the singular achievements of these three women. Among other things, all three competed with male scholars of their respective eras in the twentieth century and, in the process, produced innovative, groundbreaking books in fields that were dominated by men. In addition to this salient point, let us consider the more subtle, proto-feminist credentials of the most religiously traditional of these three women scholars: Juanita Brooks. In doing this, we perhaps can also discern some of Jan's parallel credentials, even though her major works do not represent an iconoclastic challenge to the teachings and authority of LDS ecclesiastical officials.

Contemporary Mormon feminist Nancy Ross says that in researching Brooks's correspondence and personal papers housed in Dixie State University Library's special collections, she discovered many "points of crossover with the stories and experiences of more recent Mormon feminists" who have violated Mormon cultural traditions that many Latter-day Saints consider inflammatory (especially in challenging male priesthood authority) and consequently endured shunning by people in one's own religious community.[11] Ross goes on to note:

> Brooks emerged from her correspondence as a thoughtful intellectual and concerned family member, but also as an involved Mormon feminist, though that was not a word that she used to describe herself. The label is appropriately applied to Brooks because of her historical work, the themes that emerge in her public speaking, and especially in the way that she helped other Mormons navigate faith and doubt over historical issues.[12]

---

11. Nancy Ross, "Juanita Brooks and the Practice of Mormon Feminism." Instances of shunning Ordain Women supporters in LDS communities are reported in Gary Shepherd and Gordon Shepherd, "What Ordain Women Profiles Tell Us about Mormon Women's Hopes and Discontents," 356–58.

12. Ross, "Juanita Brooks," 1.

According to Ross's analysis, in her speaking as well as writing, Brooks challenged the Mormon framework of womanhood, encouraged women to value inclusion, demonstrated to others that it was possible to balance faith, doubt, and religious participation on the edges of Mormonism, showed a growing interest toward the end of her life in the history of Mormon women, and was claimed by Second Wave Mormon feminists as an important influence on their work.

Jan is a practicing Methodist who has never experienced any religious shunning due to her historical writings. Like Brooks, however, she also is a woman who honors the religious principles and ethical values of other faith traditions, including those of Mormonism. Unlike Fawn Brodie, whose courage to break from her deeply immersed Mormon upbringing may inspire some contemporary Mormon women who have grave misgivings about their inherited faith, Jan, also like Brooks, demonstrates the possibility of balancing faith, doubt, and religious participation. This is precisely the challenge for contemporary Mormon feminists and scholars who wish to remain attached to their religious tradition. And for both women and men interested in the academic study of Mormonism, Jan exemplifies how to write objectively about Mormon history, without taking sides or substituting moral judgment for detached analysis and historical understanding. Finally, also like Brooks, Jan has freely imparted her support and encouragement to younger researchers and colleagues, both mentoring and collaborating with prominent women scholars like Kathryn Daynes, Kathleen Flake, and Sarah Barringer Gordon. Following in the footsteps of Jan, these women, and many others who have been similarly influenced, have gone on to make their own substantial contributions to the study of Mormon history.[13]

Concluding Reflections on Jan Shipps's Feminism

Finally, to better understand Jan's nuanced views toward contemporary feminism, we might fruitfully compare her intellectual career to younger feminist scholars like Susan A. Ross, past president of the Catholic Theological Society of America and Professor of Theology and a Faculty Scholar at Loyola University, Chicago. Beginning her graduate work in 1975, Ross is

---

13. Today, Kathryn Daynes is a retired associate professor of history at Brigham Young University and is the author of the award-winning *More Wives than One: Transformation of the Mormon Marriage System, 1840–1910*. Kathleen Flake is a director of Mormon Studies at the University of Virginia and the author of the award-winning *The Politics of American Religious Identity: The Seating of Reed Smoot, Mormon Apostle*. Sarah Barringer Gordon is a professor of Constitutional Law and a professor of History at the University of Pennsylvania, and is the author of the award-winning *The Mormon Question: Polygamy and Constitutional Conflict in Nineteenth-Century America*.

Jan's junior by twenty-seven years. She came from a much more advantaged background, was strongly encouraged by academic women mentors, and was exposed to 1970s radical feminism as a student at elite, eastern schools (in glaring contrast to Jan's academic experience). As Ross herself states in an article for the *National Catholic Reporter*, "It would seem that I was a born-and-raised feminist (or 'women's libber,' as we called ourselves then) who knew what sexism was."[14] Her first exposure as a graduate student to May Daly's radical critique of religious misogyny, *Gyn/Ecology: The Metaethics of Radical Feminism*, however, upended everything she thought she knew about her religious faith. Ross recalls, "I began to realize that the religion and culture in which I had been raised—even as a privileged, upper-middle class white woman from the suburbs—were profoundly, deeply and utterly riddled with sexism." By way of contrast, the most radical critique of religion that Jan had read at a comparable stage in her education was Fawn Brodie's *No Man Knows my History*, an exposé of Joseph Smith's prophetic pretensions but scarcely a renunciation of all historical religions as the justificatory centers of male dominance over women.

In continuing the story of her own intellectual development, Ross goes on to say:

> A year or so after I read Daly, I was preparing for my first teaching job, and was assigned two introductory courses in theology and one course of my own choosing. When I told my new department chair that I wanted to teach a course on women and religion, he protested that I was hired to teach systematic theology. I asked Carr [a graduate student mentor] what I should say in response, and she said, "Tell him that feminist theology *is* systematic theology: It asks what difference it makes if women as well as men are taken into consideration."[15]

This point, just as essential to interpreting history as expounding on theology, was, of course, never raised by Jan's male mentors: Everett Cooley, Hal Bridges, or Leonard Arrington.

Reflecting finally on her current situation as an esteemed Catholic theologian, Ross concludes by saying,

> But without righteous anger, there would be no feminism. . . . On occasion, I have found myself labeled a "radical feminist." I am sure that Daly, were she still with us today, would object. I have spent my entire teaching career of more than 35 years in colleges and universities run by religious orders of men. I have learned to get along with them, to befriend some of them, to watch my language, to make compromises. I insist that my students not reject theologians solely because of their views on women. But sexism and misogyny still exist.

---

14. Susan A Ross, "Mary Daly Exposed the Slimy Underbelly of Religion's Treatment of Women."

15. Ross.

Religions still have not done enough to condemn them. And powerful statements against these sins are needed more than ever.[16]

Like Ross, Jan has worked for years with authoritative men, both in the Mormon History Association and the Religious Studies Department of IUPUI. And like Ross, Jan confesses to her share of professional compromises with men in academia. Unlike Ross, however, Jan never imbibed deeply of "righteous anger," was never labeled a radical feminist, and never waged a moral crusade against the misogynous deeds of the religious patriarchy. Can we say today that Jan Shipps was or is a feminist, proto or otherwise? She has not addressed feminist issues per se in her scholarly work and is not integrated into contemporary feminist networks.

But let us be generous in our definitions. In her own independent way she has enthusiastically mentored younger women scholars and contributed her institutional part in the advancement of women toward equality with men in the halls of academe, as well as within the Mormon intellectual community. Above all, Jan Shipps's scholarly work and enduring professional stature should stand as inspirational beacons to aspiring women scholars of the twenty-first century.

---

16. Ross.

EPILOGUE

Concluding Reflections on Jan Shipps's Legacy To Mormon Studies

Beyond the publication of *Mormonism: The Story of a New Religious Tradition*, the most enduring part of Jan Shipps's intellectual legacy is undoubtedly her considerable influence as a non-Mormon scholar in helping to legitimize Mormon Studies as a significant subfield of religious studies in general and the history of the American West in particular. The New Mormon History movement—initiated by academically trained Mormon scholars who sought professional recognition of their work—was materially advanced by Jan's important scholarship and unflagging commitment to promoting Mormon Studies in academic circles beyond the Mormon History Association and the John Whitmer Historical Associastion. As excellent as many of Mormonism's trained academic historians were who spearheaded the New Mormon History in the 1960s and 1970s (such as Leonard Arrington, Richard Bushman, Thomas Alexander, James Allen, Michael Quinn, and RLDS scholars Richard Howard, Paul Edwards, and William Russell), their work on Mormon topics never achieved the same kind of professional approbation outside the Mormon intellectual community as did Jan's work.

In retrospect, it's perhaps fair to say that Mormon Studies *required* a non-Latter-day Saint champion to fully gain academic legitimacy. From the outset we have argued that Jan was not merely in the right time and place to join the surge of heightened professional interest in comprehending Mormonism and its history. She was intellectually and academically prepared to become the right person to champion the acknowledgement of Mormon Studies as a legitimate and important academic enterprise. She was as important to the advancement of Mormon Studies as the beckoning field of Mormon history was to her own scholarly advancement. It is retrospectively difficult to conjure one without the other.

A latent but significant ancillary consequence of Jan's status as an "inside-outsider" in the Mormon intellectual community was her ability to win the confidence of conservative LDS Church leaders in her bona fides as an evenhanded observer and commentator on issues of Mormon history and contemporary operations. This, in turn, enhanced her effectiveness as a go-to expert for members of the press as Mormon-related news stories became increasingly relevant to a national and even international audience. While not an apologist for Mormonism's peculiar religious doctrines or typically conservative policies with regard to contemporary social issues, Jan was trusted by both the media and LDS Church communications department personnel to be objectively fair in her public pronouncements and interviews with the press. She had credibility with the press as an expert on Mormonism not only because of her scholarly reputation but also because she wasn't a Mormon. Her reputation for scholarly integrity similarly gave her credibility with LDS Church public relations professionals and authorities, who saw that she was not a hostile critic looking to produce embarrassing exposés. Jan was able to perform an effective liaison role between the press and the Church because she was trusted by both parties.

Her cordial relationship with LDS ecclesiastical authorities, however, also has provoked criticism from some, especially contemporary feminists, for failing to speak out against the Church's conservative views of women and gender roles and its discriminatory policies with regard to priesthood ordination and ecclesiastical decision-making. This criticism counters Jan's commitment to maintain political and theological neutrality in her scholarship by arguing that a woman of Jan's stature and influence should take a public stand in support of women's causes. For her part, Jan, while privately supporting feminist principles of gender equality in public life and academia, resists calling herself a feminist scholar and acknowledges that issues of gender equality have never been at the forefront of her research agenda.

While not publicly advocating for women's equality, it is also the case that Jan was a pioneer and role model for other women scholars in academic fields and organizations long dominated by men. She was of an older generation than most contemporary Mormon feminists and was imbued with traditional notions of gender, marriage, and family while growing up. This, of course, was also true for Fawn Brodie and Juanita Brooks, whose academic careers differed from but also paralleled Jan's as groundbreaking female historians. In this respect, we maintain that Jan, like Fawn Brodie and Juanita Brooks, also richly deserves recognition for her pioneering legacy to twenty-first century women scholars.

Beyond feminist concerns, Jan Shipps's salient scholarly contributions to the understanding of Mormon history, and her influential role in legitimating Mormon Studies as a significant disciplinary area of inquiry, merit deep appreciation of all contemporary scholars of the religious culture and history of the Latter-day Saints.

APPENDIX

Jan Shipps's *Curriculum Vita*, 2001

We present below an incomplete version of Jan Shipps's *curriculum vitae* (CV)—a traditional academic summary of one's scholarly activities and achievements. This CV is incomplete because the most recent version we were able to locate has not ben updated since Jan's formal retirement in 2001 from Indiana University Purdue University Indianapolis as Professor Emeritus of History and Religious Studies. (Thanks are due Philip Barlow for finding and generously sharing this CV with us.) Jan, however, continued being actively engaged in research, writing, publication, speaking, consulting, mentoring, and a variety of other scholarly endeavors until 2018. We combed through a number of sources trying to track down as many of these additional endeavors as possible and found that records of most of her non-published contributions (e.g. conference presentations, media interviews, professional organizational involvements, book and article refereeing, and the like) could not readily be located, if such records exist at all. We were able to locate a number of published items, however, and these have been included at the end of her CV. This updated list of published work is itself undoubtedly incomplete, but it reflects, however imperfectly, the impressive range and extent of Jan's continued contributions—well into her eighties—to the scholarly study of Mormonism.

Education

Attended Alabama College, 1946–48
BS (History), Utah State University, 1961
MA, University of Colorado, 1962
PhD, University of Colorado, 1965

Academic Appointments

Professor Emeritus of History and Religious Studies, Indiana University Purdue University, Indianapolis (IUPUI), 1995–
Senior Research Associate, The (IUPUI) Polis Center, 1995–2001
Emeritus Professor of Philanthropic Studies, 1999
Professor of History and Religious Studies, IUPUI, 1983–94
Graduate Faculty, Indiana University, 1982–
Director, IUPUI Center for American Studies, 1978–89
Associate Professor of Religious Studies and History, IUPUI, 1976–83
Assistant Professor of History and Religious Studies, IUPUI, 1973–76
Part-time Instructor, IUPUI, 1971–73
Part-time Instructor, University of Colorado, Denver Center, 1965–67

Other Appointments

Columnist, Beliefnet.com, 2000–
Project Coordinator, Institute for Sex Research, Indiana University, Bloomington, 1969–70
Editorial Assistant (part-time), Reed Smoot Diary Project, University of Utah Press, 1965–66
Para-professional social work in Chicago and Detroit, 1952–60

Professional Societies

Organization of American Historians
    Ad Hoc Committee to Review the Editor of the *Journal of American History*
American Society of Church History
    Council member 1985–88, 1991–94
    Program Committee, 1993 Spring Meeting
National Historical Society
    Advisory Board, 1976–
    Bell I. Wiley Prize Committee, 1982–84
Western History Association
    Program Committee, Member, 1978, 1980
    Program Committee, Chair, 1982
    Oscar Winther Prize Committee, 1982, 1983
    Oscar Winther Prize Committee, Chair, 1984
    Ad hoc Committee on the Future of the Association, Chair, 1985–87
    Lifetime Member (honorary), 2000–
Society for Historians of the Early Republic
    Local Arrangements, Chair, 1982
Mormon History Association
    Council Member, 1973–75, 1981
    Program Committee, Member, 1973
    Program Committee, Chair, 1977
    Awards Committee, 1975–78
    Nominations Committee, 1982–84
    Vice President, 1978
    President-Elect, 1979
    President, 1980
    Program Committee, 2002
John Whitmer Historical Association
    Council Member, 1974–77
Utah State Historical Society
Indiana Historical Society
Indiana Association of Historians
    President, 1993–94
American Academy of Religion
Midwest American Academy of Religion,
    Section Chair, 1980–81

Indiana Academy of Religion
    Council Member, 1980–81
    President-Elect, 1982; President, 1983–84
American Studies Association, 1980–90
    Delegate to the Japanese American Studies Association, 1998
Great Lakes Regional American Studies Association
    Council Member, 1980–82

Professional Activities

Founding Co-Editor, *Religion and American Culture: A Journal of Interpretation,* 1990–95
Religion Editor, *Encyclopedia of Indianapolis,* 1989–94
Co-Research Director, History of Religion in Indianapolis Project, 1992–94
Co-Research Director, Projects on Religion and American Culture co-sponsored by the IUPUI Center for American Studies and Religious Studies Department and funded by Lilly Endowment, Incorporated, 1983–89
Editorial Board, *Dialogue: A Journal of Mormon Thought,* 1974–82, 1986–90
Editorial Board, Indiana Magazine of History, 1988–90
Reviewer, National Endowment for the Humanities Panel, for NEH fellowships in Religious Studies, 1988, 1989
Reviewer, book-length manuscripts for University of Illinois Press, Indiana University Press, University of Chicago Press, Yale University Press, Cambridge University Press, Oxford University Press, University of Utah Press, University Press of Utah State University, University Press of Kansas
Reviewer, article manuscripts for *Journal of American History, Pacific Historical Quarterly, Journal of the Early Republic, Western Historical Quarterly, Church History, The Historian, Journal of Social History, Indiana Magazine of History, Sunstone Magazine, Dialogue: A Journal of Mormon Thought, The Smithsonian*
Consultant, Western Trails Museum

Grants And Fellowships

To the IUPUI Center for American Studies *during my tenure as director*

Lilly Endowment, Inc., grant to support a project on Religion and the Independent Sector in American Culture, 1987–90, $422,204
——— Planning grant for development of a proposal for a substantial funding to support a project on Religion and the Independent Sector in American Culture, 1986–87, $93,000
——— Grant to support a project entitled "Revisioning America: Religion and American Life," 1983–85, $72,643
——— Planning grant Religion, Youth, and American Culture, 1986–87, $93,831
Indiana Committee for the Humanities [now Indiana Humanities Council] grant to support Childhood in American Life Conference, 1977–78, $10,270
——— Family in American Life Conference, 1981–82, $18,940
——— Religion in American Public Life Conference, 1984–85, $12,650
——— News Forum on American Religion, 1989, $8,350

Personal

Glenn W. Irwin Scholar, 1989–91. (This, the most prestigious research fellowship awarded by IUPUI, provided the following: research support, a semester off for research, and underwriting to allow the convening of a colloquium on Religion and Ethnicity that was directly connected with my research on modern Mormonism.)
Charles Redd Summer Research Fellowship, 1990
School of Liberal Arts/Project Development Grant, 1988
Center for American Studies (IUPUI) Grant-in-Aid of Research, 1977–78
Indiana University Summer Faculty Fellowship, 1976
LDS Church Historical Department Summer Fellowship, 1975
Indiana University Faculty Grant-in-Aid of Research, 1972–73
AAUW Colorado Cohn Fellowship, 1964–65
Denver Westerners' Scholarship Award, 1963
University of Colorado Graduate Fellowship, 1963–64
University of Colorado Development Fund Fellowship, 1962–63

Honors And Awards

President's Award, University of Montevallo, 2001
Mormon History Association Best Book Award, 2000
John Whitmer Historical Association Best Article Award 2001
Western History Association Lifetime Membership
Mormon History Association Steven F. Christensen Documentary Book Award, 1995
John Whitmer Historical Association Award for Excellence in the Edited Document, 1995
Mormon History Association T. Edgar Lyon Award of Excellence for an Article in Mormon History, 1995
Franklin College Brannigan Scholar, 1994
IUPUI Irwin Scholar, 1989–91
Mormon History Association Grace Fort Arrington Award for Historical Excellence, 1986
IUPUI School of Liberal Arts Distinguished Faculty Award, 1984–85
IUPUI "Experience Excellence Award" (Recognition of Service to IUPUI above and beyond the Call of Duty), 1985

Publications

Books

Sojourner in the Promised Land: Forty Years Among the Mormons. University of Illinois Press, 2000.
Mormonism: The Story of a New Religious Tradition. University of Illinois Press, 1985.
The Journals of William E. McLellin, 1831–1836 [ed. with John W. Welch]. University of Illinois Press and *BYU Studies*, 1994.
Taking Stock and Charting Change: Developments and Reconfigurations in Religion in America since the Sixties (A collection of essays in honor of Robert W. Lynn [edited with David H. Smith]). Privately printed, 1989.

Articles

"Second Class Saints." *Colorado Quarterly* (Autumn 1962): 183–90.
"Utah Comes of Age Politically: A Study of the State's Politics in the Early Years of the Twentieth-Century." *Utah Historical Quarterly* (Spring 1967): 91–111.
"A Little Known Account of the Murders of Joseph and Hyrum Smith." *BYU Studies* (Spring 1974): 389–92.
"The Prophet Puzzle: Suggestions Leading toward a More Comprehensive Interpretation of Joseph Smith." *Journal of Mormon History* (1974): 3–20.
"Working with Historical Evidence: Projects for an Introductory Course." *The History Teacher* (May 1976): 359–77.
"The Public Image of Senator Reed Smoot, 1902–1932." *Utah Historical Quarterly* (Fall 1977): 380–400.
"The Mormons: Looking Forward and Outward" [contribution to a series on "The Churches: Where From Here], *Christian Century*, August 16–23, 1978, 761–66.
"Writing about Modern Mormonism: An Essay Review about Samuel W. Taylor's Latest Book with Some Attention Paid to Other Works on the Same Subject." *Sunstone*, March–April 1979, 43–48.
"Sonia Johnson, Mormonism, and the Media." *Christian Century*, January 2–9, 1980.
"Jan Shipps Responds to Sam Taylor." *Sunstone*, January–February 1980, 6.
[With Larry Porter] "The Colesville, New York, 'Exodus' Seen from Two Documentary Perspectives." *New York History* (April 1981): 201–11.
"Civil War and Reconstruction Special Assignment."*Network News Exchange* (Spring 1981): 23.
"A Question of Wheat and Chaff: Review article on *The Roots of Modern Mormonism* [by Mark Leone]." *Sunstone Review*, September–October, 1981, 18–19.
"The Mormon Past: Revealed or Re-visited?" *Sunstone*, November–December 1981, 55–57.
"History for a New Age." Editorial, *American History Illustrated*, January 1982, 5.
"An 'Inside-Outsider' in Zion." *Dialogue: A Journal of Mormon Thought* (Spring 1982): 139–61.
"Brigham Young and His Times: A Continuing Force in Mormonism." *Journal of the West* (January 1984): 65–77.
"The Principle Revoked: A Closer Look at the Demise of Plural Marriage." *Journal of Mormon History* (1984): 65–77.
"The Salamander and the Saints." *Christian Century*, November 15, 1985.
"Brigham Young." (Short entry) *Encyclopedia of Religion*, edited by Mircea Eliade, et al., 1986.
"Twentieth-Century Mormonism and the Secular Establishment." 1986 Dello G. Dayton Memorial Lecture (Pamphlet published by Weber State College Press, 1988).
"Philanthropy, Religion, and American Culture." *Liberal Education* 74, no. 4 (September-October, 1988): 24–25.
Critical descriptions of one book and ten articles in *Religion and American Life: Resources*, edited by Anne T. Fraker (Urbana: University of Illinois Press, 1989).
"A Profile of the Membership of the American Society of Church History." *Church History* 59, no. 3 (September 1990): 444–52.

"Is Mormonism Christian: Reflections on a Complicated Question, *BYU Studies* 33, no. 3 (1993): 439–65.

"Dangerous History: Laurel Ulrich and Her Mormon Sisters." *Christian Century*, October 20, 1993, 1012–15.

"Knowledge and Understanding." *Sunstone*, November 1993, 11–12.

"Mormon Metamorphosis [or What Mike Wallace Missed]." *Christian Century*, August 14–21, 1996.

"The Church of Jesus Christ of Latter-day Saints." Entry in *Encyclopedia of the American West*.

"Mormonism." Entry in both the print and electronic editions of *Encyclopedia Americana*, 1997, 19:457–60.

[With Philip Amerson and Edward J. Stephenson] "A Decline or Transformation? Another View of Mainline Finances [An Exchange with John and Sylvia Ronsvale]." *Christian Century*, February 5–12, 1997, 144–51.

"Brigham Young." Short entry in *The American Heritage Encyclopedia of American History*

"Mormons." Short entry in *The American Heritage Encyclopedia of American History*

"Mormonism." Short entry in *Oxford Companion to U.S. History*.

"Submission in Salt Lake." *Religion in the News* 1, no, 2 (Fall 1998): 6–8, 23.

"*Exponent II*: Mormonism's Stealth Alternative." *Exponent II* 22, no. 4 (1999): 28–33.

"Mormon Women in the Real World." *Religion in the News* 3, no. 2 (Summer 2000): 20, 24.

"Surveying the Mormon Image, 1960–2001." *Sunstone*, April 2001

"Signifying Sainthood, 1830–2001." Leonard J. Arrington Lecture Series, Pamphlet No. 7, 2002.

"How Mormon is the Community of Christ?" John Whitmer Historical Association 2002 Nauvoo Conference Special Edition, 195–204.

"The Mormons Score a 9.6." *Religion in the News* (Spring 2002).

Chapters in Books

"Politics and the Mormons, 1880–1896." *Denver Westerners' Brand Book*, 1964.

"J. Frank Hanly: Enigmatic Reformer." In *Gentlemen from Indiana: National Presidential Candidates, 1836–1940*, 237–68. Indianapolis: Indiana Historical Bureau, 1977.

"In the Presence of the Past: Continuity and Change in Twentieth-Century Mormonism." In *Mormonism in Sesqui-Centennial Perspective*, 3–35. Salt Lake City: Signature Books, 1983.

"The Latter-day Saints." In *Encyclopedia of the American Religious Experience: Studies of Traditions and Movements*, edited by Charles H. Lippy and Peter W. Williams, 3 vols., 1:649–65. New York: Charles Scribne's Sons, 1988.

"Beyond the Stereotypes: Mormon and Non-Mormon Communities in Twentieth-Century Mormondom." In *New Views of Mormon History: A Collection of Essays in Honor of Leonard J. Arrington*, 342–60. Salt Lake City: University of Utah Press, 1987.

"Creation of a New Social Reality: Mormonism as a Case Study." In *The American Quest for the Primitive Church*, edited by Richard Hughes, 281–95. Urbana: University of Illinois Press, 1988.

"Making Saints—In the Early Days and the Latter Days." In *Contemporary Mormonism: Social Science Perspectives*, edited by Marie Cornwall, Tim B, Heaton, and Lawrence A. Young, 64–83. Urbana: University of Illinois Press, 1994.

"Overview: [the history of] Religion in Indianapolis." *Encyclopedia of Indianapolis*, edited by David J. Bodenhamer and Robert G. Barrows, 170–81. Bloomington: Indiana University Press, 1994.

[With Dean and Cheryll May]. "Sugarhouse Ward: A Latter-day Saint Congregation." In *American Congregations*, edited by James P. Wind and James W. Lewis, 293–348. University of Chicago Press, 1994.

"Teaching the Role of Religion in American History." In *Proceeding of a Symposium Sponsored by the Religious History in the Schools Committee*, 16–18. Indianapolis: Indiana Humanities Council, 1994.

"Joseph Smith." In *Makers of Christian Theology in America*, edited by Mark G. Toulouse and James O. Duke, 210–17. Nashville: Abingdon Press, 1997.

"Mormonism after the Death of Joseph Smith." In *Makers of Christian Theology in America*, edited by Mark G. Toulouse and James O. Duke, 373–78. Nashville: Abingdon Press, 1997.

"Difference and Otherness: Mormonism and the American Religious Mainstream." In *Minority Faiths and Mainstream American Protestantism*, edited by Jonathan Sarna, 81–109. Urbana: University of Illinois Press, 1997.

"Religion and Regional Culture in Modern America." In *Can Charitable Choice Work? Covering Religion's Impact on Urban Affairs and Social Services*, edited by Andrew Walsh, 23–38. Hartford, CT: Leonard E. Greenberg Center for the Study of Religion in Public Life, 2001.

Electronic Articles

"Prophets, Seers, and Revelators: A New Form of Revelation for Mormonism's New Age." Beliefnet, http://www.beliefnet.com.

"Confronting the Mormon Question: How to Turn a Latter-day Saint into a Methodist—and Vice Versa." Beliefnet, http://www.beliefnet.com.

"That 'M' Word." Beliefnet, http://www.beliefnet.com.

"'Mormons' In; 'Mormon Church' Out: The Church of Jesus Christ of Latter-day Saints Alters Its Nomenclature." Beliefnet, http://www.beliefnet.com.

"The Mormon Olympics?" Beliefnet, http://www.beliefnet.com.

Book Forewords and Afterwards

Foreword to *Sisters in Spirit: Mormon Women in Historical and Cultural Perspective*, edited by Maureen Beecher and Lavina Fielding Anderson. Urbana: University of Illinois Press, 1987.

Foreword and Afterword to a new printing of *The Mountain Meadows Massacre* by Juanita Brooks. Norman: University of Oklahoma Press, 1992.

A Foreword to Ronald W. Walker, *Wayward Saints: The Godbeites and Brigham Young*. Urbana: University of Illinois Press, 1998.

Reprinted Articles and Chapters from Books

"The Riddle of Governor Hanley." In *The Hoosier State: Readings in Indiana History. II: The Modern State*, 73–81. Grand Rapids: Erdmanns, 1981.

"The Mormons: Looking Forward and Outward." In *Where the Spirit Leads: American Denominations Today*, edited by Martin E. Marty, 25–40. Atlanta: John Knox Press, 1980.

"History for a New Age." *Indiana Historical Bulletin,* March 1982, 3–7.

"The Prophet Puzzle: Suggestions Leading toward a More Comprehensive Interpretation of Joseph Smith." In *The New Mormon History: Revisionist Essays on the Past*, edited by D. Michael Quinn, 53–74. Salt Lake City: Signature Books, 1992.

"The Genesis of Mormonism." In *Religion and American Culture*, edited by David G. Hackett, 167–84. New York and London: Routledge, 1995.

"Prologue." In *Nineteenth-Century Literary Criticism*, edited by Denise Kasinec. Detroit: Gale Research, Inc., 1996–97.

"The Prophet Puzzle: Suggestions Leading toward a More Comprehensive Interpretation of Joseph Smith." In *The Prophet Puzzle: Interpretive Essays on Joseph Smith*, edited by Bryan Waterman, 25–47. Salt Lake City: Signature Books, 1999.

"Is Mormonism Christian? Reflections on a Complicated Question." In *Mormons & Mormonism: An Introduction to an American World Religion*, edited by Eric A. Eliason, 76–98. Urbana: University of Illinois Press, 2000.

"Beyond the Stereotypes: Mormon and Non-Mormon Communities in Twentieth-Century Mormondom." In *Mormons & Mormonism: An Introduction to an American World Religion*, edited by Eric A. Eliason, 147–63. Urbana: University of Illinois Press, 2000.

Selected Lectures And Papers Presented To Professional Societies

"W. J. Cash and the *Mind of the South*." Rocky Mountain Modern Language Association, annual meeting, Denver, April 1963.

"The Mormons in Politics, 1896–1910." Utah State Historical Society annual meeting, 1963.

"The Mormons in Politics, 1910–1920." Utah State Historical Society annual meeting, 1964.

"From Satyr to Saint: American Attitudes toward the Mormons, 1860–1960." Organization of American Historians annual meeting, Chicago, IL, March 1973.

"The Prophet Puzzle." John Whitmer Historical Association annual meeting, September 1974.

"The Public Image of Senator Reed Smoot, 1902–1932." Symposium on Senator Smoot, Brigham Young University, April 1974.

"Lucy Mack Smith: The Mormon Mother as Model." Restoration Lecture, Graceland College, May 1975.

"The Mormon Experience in the Modern Era." Featured lecture, National Historical Society Assembly, June 1977.

"The Prophet, His Mother, and Early Mormonism: Mother Smith's History as a Passageway Understanding." Mormon History Association annual meeting, 1978.

"In the Presence of the Past: Continuity and Change in Twentieth Century Mormonism." Charles Redd Lecture, Brigham Young University, October 1979.

"Continuity and Change in Mormonism." Indiana Academy of Religion annual meeting, 1980.

"Mormonism's Entry into American Life, 1890–1930." Stewart Lecture, Weber State University, February 15, 1980.

"Using History of Religions Theory in the Study of Mormonism." Conference on Mormon Studies, Cornell University, April 30, 1980.

"Priorities for a Turn-of-the-Millennium Generation." Commencement Address, Graceland College, May 18, 1980.

"Restoration: Divinity's Sphere of Action in Space and Time." Plenary address, Sunstone Theological Symposium, Salt Lake City, 1981.

"The Creation of the Mormon World." Presidential Address, Mormon History Association annual meeting, 1980.

"Reformation and Restoration in Early Mormonism." American Society of Church History spring meeting, 1981.

[Lecture series] "Is Mormonism Christian?" "Restoration: Starting All Over Again." "Mormonism's Human Landscape." Circuit Rider Seminar of the Washington-Eastern Idaho Conference of the United Methodist Church, Boise, April 1982.

"Seer, Prophet, Revelator, President, High Priest, King: Joseph Smith and the Beginnings of Mormonism." Seminar on Mormonism, Bloomington, Indiana, December 1982.

"The Principle Revoked: The Impact of the Manifesto on Polygamous Wives." Mormon History Association annual meeting, 1982.

"Religions in the Making." Indiana Association of Historians annual meeting, 1983.

"Religion in the Making: Mormonism as a Case Study." Presidential Address, Indiana Academy of Religion annual meeting, 1983.

"From Gentile to Non-Member: Mormon Attitudes toward Non-Mormons, 1880–1940." American Society of Church History annual meeting, 1983.

"Brigham Young and His Times: A Continuing Force in Mormonism." Utah State Historical Society/Sons of the Utah Pioneers Lecture Series, Salt Lake City, May 1983.

"A New View of Joseph Smith." Plenary address, Sunstone Symposium, Salt Lake City, August, 1984.

"Non-Mormon Attitudes toward Mormons and Mormon Attitudes toward Non-Mormons: A History." Mormon History Association annual meeting, 1984.

"Magic and Early Mormonism." Society for the Historians of the Early Republic annual meeting, 1984.

"Through the Looking Glass: New Methodological Approaches to the Study of the Mormons." American Society of Church History annual meeting, 1985.

"Two Histories; Two Churches." John Whitmer Lecture Series, Independence, MO, and Lamoni, IA, March 1985.

"Magic, Mormons, and History." Reynolds Lecture, University of Colorado, Boulder, March 1985.

"Magic and What to Think about Mormon Beginnings." Plenary address, Sunstone East Symposium, Washington, DC, May 1985.

"Restoration: Ideal and Reality in Mormonism." A Symposium on the Restoration Ideal in American History, Abilene, TX, July 1985.

"Religion, the Constitution, and American Culture." Symposium on Church and State in America." Chapel Hill, NC, February 1986.

"Twentieth Century Mormonism and the Gentile Establishment." Dello Dayton Lecture, Weber State University, April 1986.

"Mormons and Gentiles: A Peculiar Relationship in the Twentieth Century." Lecture sponsored by the Center for Colorado Plateau Studies, Northern Arizona University, October 1986.

"Salt Lake City: The View According to Picture Postcards." Illustrated lecture, Wasatch Westerners, Salt Lake City, October 1986.

"The Creation of a New Social Reality: Mormonism as a Case Study." Mormon History Association annual meeting, 1986.

"The Impact of the Bureaucratization of the LDS Church on Mormon Culture." Plenary address, Sunstone West Symposium, Berkeley, CA, February 1987.

"Approaching Mormonism from the Perspectives of History, Sociology, and Religious Studies." Departmental Colloquium, Religion Department, University of Washington, February 9, 1987.

"Mormons: A Religious Culture and an Ethnic Group, Reflections on the Canadian Experience." Keynote address for an international conference on The Mormons in Canada, University of Alberta, Edmonton, Alberta, May 7, 1987.

"The Scattering of the Gathering and the Gathering of the Scattered: The Twentieth Century Mormon Diaspora." Juanita Brooks Lecture, presented at an Inaugural Convocation on the Occasion of the Inauguration of Douglas D. Alder as President of Dixie College, St. George, UT, March 12, 1987; a revision of this paper was presented at annual meeting of the Western History Association, Los Angeles, October 1987.

"The Mystery of Nineteenth-Century Mormondom: You Can't Get There from Here." Banquet address at the annual meeting of the Vernacular Architecture Forum, Salt Lake City, May 9, 1987.

"Documents, Historians, and Joseph Smith: A Discussion of What We Have Learned and Where LDS History Goes From Here." Church History and Recent Forgeries: A Symposium, Brigham Young University, August 6, 1987.

"Correlation and the Context of Authority in Twentieth-Century Mormonism." Sunstone Symposium IX, Salt Lake City, August 29, 1987.

"Surveying the Mormons in the Twentieth Century." Symposium on the American West Held at the University of Notre Dame to Inaugurate the Andrew V. Tackes Chair in History, South Bend, IN, September 25, 1987.

"The Constitution and America's Future." Plenary session at the Democracy is Us Conference organized on the occasion of the nation's Bicentennial by the National Conference of Christians and Jews, Philadelphia, August 19–20, 1987.

"Beyond Consensus: What Has Happened since Will Herberg Wrote *Protestant,*

Catholic, Jew?" Presented in a Program Series presented by the Indianapolis Hebrew Congregation, March 30, 1988.

"Seeing Mormonism from the Outside." Anderson College, April 6, 1988.

"Adding Philanthropy to the University Curriculum." Independent Sector Academic Retreat, Indianapolis, June 7, 1988.

"The West in the Religious Imagination." Idaho Endowment for the Humanities Lecture, Harriman State Park, ID, August 12–13, 1988.

"Latter-day Saints and Jehovah's Witnesses: Beliefs, Practices, and Ethics." Medical Ethics Seminar, IU Poynter Center and Methodist Hospital Corporation, February 10, 1989.

"Saints and Christians: Where the Differences Begin—and End." Taylor University, Upland, IN, March 16, 1989.

"Religion and Rural Life." Idaho Endowment for the Humanities Lecture, Harriman Park, ID, August 1989.

"Making Saints in the Early Days and the Latter Days." Plenary address, annual meeting, Society for the Scientific Study of Religion, Salt Lake City, October 26, 1989; also presented as a public lecture, Brigham Young University, October 25, 1989.

"The Church Office Building as a Symbol of Success and Growth." Plenary address, annual Sunstone symposium, Salt Lake City, August 1990.

"From Peoplehood to Church Membership." Mormon History Association annual meeting, Claremont, CA, June 1991.

"Remembering, Recovering, and Inventing What Being the People of God Means: Reflections on Method in the Scholarly Writing of Denominational History." Denominational History Conference, Chapel Hill, NC, October, 1991.

"The Mormon Mission in the Modern World." Mormon History Association annual meeting, 1992.

"Is Mormonism Christian?" Plenary Address, Mormon History Association annual meeting, May 1993.

"Searching for Connections: The Place of Literature, History, and Social Science in the Creation and Preservation of Community." Indiana Humanities Council Twentieth Anniversary Lecture Series, Terre Haute, IN, September 1993.

"Communities of Memory: The Importance of History in the K–12 Curriculum." Indiana State Teachers Association, October 1993.

"Being Mormon: The Latter-day Saints since World War II." Western History Association annual meeting, Tulsa, OK, October 1993.

"Promising Trends in the Recent Writing about American Religion." Keynote Address for a Symposium on Teaching the Role of Religion in American History, Christian Theological Seminary, January 1994.

"The Religious Marketplace in Ante-bellum America." Presidential Address, Indiana Association of Historians, February 1994.

"Understanding Mormonism: A Non-Mormon Scholar's View." Brannigan Address, Franklin College, April 1994.

"The Difficult Problem of Maintaining Balance between Center and Periphery in an Expanding Church." Plenary session, Sunstone Symposium, Salt Lake City, August, 1994.

"Teaching about Religion outside the American Mainstream." New England Colloquium on American Religion, Yale University, December 1994.

"My Life as an Alien, or Some Things I've Learned as an Inside-Outsider in Zion." Keynote Address, Seventy Years of Western History at CU: A Center for the American West Conference. University of Colorado, October 1995.

"Explaining Mormon Theology." Jessie DuPont Ball Seminar on The Hebrew Bible in Cultural Context. National Humanities Institute, Research Triangle, NC, June 1996.

"Congregations in the American City." IUPUI Senior Academy Lecture, Co-sponsored by the IUPUI Polis Center and the Alban Institute Center on Congregations, Indianapolis, April 1997.

"Mormonism and the American Religious Mainstream." American Studies Center, University of Tokyo, June 1997.

"Religion in Urban America." Japanese American Studies Association, Nagoya, Japan, June 1997.

"The Latter-day Saints since World War II." Colorado State University, June 1997.

"The Center Place as Urban Space." Concluding plenary session, Sunstone Symposium, Salt Lake City, August 1997.

"A Religion in Providence in Comparative Perspective." Conference on Rhode Island History, Brown University, Providence, RI, November 1997.

"Patterns of Urban Congregational and Denominational Life in Comparative Perspective." Organization of American Historians, Indianapolis, April 3, 1998.

"Surveying the Mormon Image Since 1960." Sunstone Symposium, Salt Lake City, July 1998.

"Church Adherence Patterns in Mid-size American Cities." The Urban Institute, Washington, DC, July 28, 1998.

"Sojourning in the Land of Promise." University Lecture, Brigham Young University, Spring 1999.

"Fellow Traveling with the Latter-day Saints, 1960–1999." Sunstone Symposium, Salt Lake City, July 1999.

"Measuring the Impact of Religion on Civic Culture in America's Mid-size Cities." American Society of Church History, Washington, DC, January 1999.

"Religion and Culture in Urban America." Religion in the News Conference, Leonard E. Greenberg Center for the Study of Religion in American Life, Trinity College, June 25, 2000.

"Using the 'M' Word Today." Sunstone Symposium, Seattle, September 23, 2000.

"Religion and Culture in Urban America." Conference on Religion and Delivery of Social Services in Urban America, Leonard E. Greenberg Center for the Study of Religion in American Life, Trinity College, February 4, 2001.

"Gentle Gentile among the Mormons: A Non-Mormon Scholar as Inside-Outsider." Utah Valley State College, Orem, UT, February 14, 2001.

"From Difference to Otherness and Back Again: The Strange Odyssey of Mormonism in America." David E. Miller Lecture, University of Utah, February 15, 2001.

"Religion in Five American Cities." Chicago Area Group for the Study of Religious Communities, De Paul University, March 3, 2001.
"Finding My Own Voice." Women's History Group, Indiana Historical Society, Indianapolis, March 10, 2001.
"Dueling Renditions of Mormonism in a Visual Age." Organization of American Historians Annual Meeting, Los Angeles, April 28, 2001.
"A Sojourner's Adventure." Sunstone Symposium, Washington, DC, May 5, 2001.
"Placing Religion in Indianapolis in Context." Religion and Urban Culture Project Capstone Conference, Indianapolis, June 19, 2001
"The Persisting Establishment Pattern in Salt Lake City." Sunstone Symposium, Salt Lake City, August 10, 2001
"Religion in Five American Cities." Fulbright Seminar, Indianapolis, July 25, 2002.
"How Mormon is the Community of Christ?" John Whitmer Historical Association annual meeting, September 27, 2002.
"Creating Centers and Institutes in the Late 20th Century Academic Environment." Conference of Directors of Centers and Institutes convened by the Center for the Study of Religion and American Culture (IUPUI), Indianapolis, October 25, 2002.
"Mormonism Today and Yesterday: Getting Here from There." Keynote Address, Conference on Saints and Others: Mormonism in the North American West, University of Montana, November 15, 2002
"Mormonism in Global Perspective." Forum Lecture, Brigham Young University—Idaho, February 20, 2003.
"Locating Mormon Theology on the American Landscape." God, Humanity, and Revelation: Perspectives from Mormon Philosophy and History, Yale University Divinity School, March 29, 2003.

Notes: An extended section on the historical work of Jan Shipps is included in Davis Bitton and Leonard Arrington, *Mormons and Their Historians* (Salt Lake City: University of Utah Press, 1989).

Jan Shipps has often appeared in extended interviews on local radio and television programs. She has also appeared in interviews as a specialist on radio talk shows on national and regional stations all across the United States. On NPR, these include "Talk of the Nation," the "Diane Rehm Show," "All Things Considered," and "Morning Edition." On several occasions, she has been interviewed on radio shows on BBC (London) and BBC (Sydney, Australia). She has also served as a "talking head" on shows presented on the History Channel, PBS, and on ABC News. Besides that, Shipps has been quoted in countless articles in the print media, including (among many others) *Newsweek*, *Time Magazine*, the *New York Times*, the *Los Angeles Times*, the *Denver Post*, and *USA Today*.

Partial List of Published Writings After 2001

"Dean L. May, April 1930–May 2003." *Journal of Mormon History* 29, no. 2 (2003): vi.

"Spinning Gold: Mormonism and the Olympic Games." *Dialogue: A Journal of Mormon Thought* 36, no. 1 (Spring 2003): 133–50.

Religion and Public Life in the Mountain West: Sacred Landscapes in Transition [edited with Mark Silk]. Altamira Press, 2004.

"American Massacre: The Tragedy of Mountain Meadows." Review in *Journal of American History* 91, no. 2 (2004): 632–33.

"Joseph Smith and the Making of a Global Religion." *BYU Studies* 44, no. 4 (2005): 293–305.

"Mormon Communities Around the World." In *The Oxford Handbook of Global Religions*, 389–98. New York: Oxford University Press, 2006.

"Prophets and Prophecy in the Mormon Tradition(s)." *John Whitmer Historical Journal* 26 (2006):1–16.

"Black and Mormon." Review in *Western Historical Quarterly* 37, no. 4 (2006): 520–21.

"Polygamy Returns." *Religion in the News* 9, no 2. (2006): 7–10.

"Reflections on the Relationship Between Biography and History: What Val Might Have Said." *John Whitmer Historical Journal* 27 (2007): 65–74.

"Richard Bushman, the Story of Joseph Smith and Mormonism, and the New Mormon History." *Journal of American History* 94, no. 2 (2007): 498–516.

"Romney and the Mormon Movement." *Religion in the News*, 10, nos. 1–2 (2007): 5

"From Peoplehood to Church Membership: Mormon Trajectory Since WW II." *Church History* 76, no. 2 (2007): 241–61.

"Non-Mormon Views on Mormonism." In *Mormonism: A Historical Encyclopedia*, edited by W. Paul Reeve and Ardis E. Parshall, 377–82. Santa Barbara, CA: ABC-CLIO, 2010.

"The Saints Come Marching In." *Religion in the News* 14, no. 2 (2012): 2–4.

"Mormons." In *Encyclopedia of Global Religions*, edited by Mark Juergensmeyer and Wade Clark Rook, 2:82–89. Thousand Oaks, CA: Sage Publications, 2012.

"In Heaven as It Is on Earth: Joseph Smith and the Early Mormon Conquest of Death." Review in *Journal of American History* 100, no. 2 (2013): 509–10.

"An Interpretive Framework for Studying the History of Mormonism." In *Oxford Handbook of Mormonism*, edited by Terryl Givens and Philip Barlow, 7–23. New York: Oxford University Press, 2015.

"Fatal Convergence in the Kingdom of God: The Mountain Meadows Massacre in American History [with Sarah Gordon Barringer]." *Journal of the Early Republic* 37, no. 2 (2017): 307–47. [Winner of the Arrington-Prucha Prize for Best Essay of the Year on Religious History in the West.]

Bibliography

Ahlstrom, Sydney. *A Religious History of the American People*. New Haven: Yale University Press, 1972.
Alexander, Thomas G. "Historiography and the New Mormon History: A Historian's Perspective." *Dialogue: A Journal of Mormon Thought* 19, no. 3 (Fall 1986): 25–49.
Allen, James B., Ronald J. Walker, and David Whittaker, eds. *Studies in Mormon History: An Indexed Bibliography*. Urbana: University of Illinois Press, 2000.
Allen, Judith. *The Kinsey Institute: The First Seventy Years*. Bloomington: Indiana University Press, 2017.
Allred, Janice. *God the Mother: And Other Theological Essays*. Salt Lake City: Signature Books, 1997.
American Psychological Association, Inc. "Intelligence: Knowns and Unknowns." *American Psychologist* 51, no. 2 (February 1996): 77–101.
Armes, Ethel. *The Story of Coal and Iron in Alabama*. Leeds, AL: Beechwood Books, 1987.
Arneson, Rosemary H. "University of Montevallo." Encyclopedia of Alabama. Last updated January 20, 2017. http://www.encyclopediaofalabama.org/article/h-1827.
Arrington, Leonard J. *Adventures of a Church Historian*. Urbana: University of Illinois Press, 1998.
———. *Great Basin Kingdom: An Economic History of the Latter-day Saints, 1830–1900*. Cambridge: Harvard University Press, 1958.
———. "Scholarly Studies of Mormonism in the Twentieth Century." *Dialogue: A Journal of Mormon Thought* 1, no. 1 (Spring 1966): 15–32.
Arrington, Leonard J., Reid L. Neilson, and Ronald W. Walker. *Reflections of a Mormon Historian: Leonard J. Arrington on the New Mormon History*. Glendale, CA: The Arthur H. Clark Company, 2006.
Bagley, Will. *Blood of the Prophets: Brigham Young and the Massacre at Mountain Meadows*. Norman: University of Oklahoma Press, 2002.
Barlow, Philip. "Jan Shipps and the Mainstreaming of Mormon Studies." *Church History* 73, no. 2 (June 2004): 412–26.
Bennett, Jim. "Ever Wonder What Happened to Birmingham's Forgotten Colleges?" Al.com. June 22, 2016. https://www.al.com/opinion/2016/06/birminghams_forgotten_colleges.html.
Berger, Peter. *The Sacred Canopy: Elements of a Sociological Theory of Religion*. New York: Doubleday, 1967.
Bergera, Gary James, ed. *Confessions of a Mormon Historian: The Diaries of Leonard J. Arrington*. Salt Lake City: Signature Books, 2018.
Bitton, Davis. "Taking Stock: The Mormon History Association after Twenty-Five Years." *Journal of Mormon History* 17 (1991): 1–27.

———. "Ten Years in Camelot: A Personal Memoir." *Dialogue: A Journal of Mormon of Mormon Thought* 16, no. 3 (Autumn 1983): 11–35.
Bowman, Matthew. "Eternal Progression: Mormonism and American Progressivism." In *Mormonism and American Politics*, edited by Randall Balmer and Jana Riess, 53–70. New York: Columbia University Press, 2016.
Bridges, Hal. *American Mysticism: From William James to Zen*. New York: Harper and Row, 1970.
———. *Lee's Maverick General: Daniel Harvey Hill*. Lincoln: University of Nebraska Press Bison Books, 1991.
Bringhurst, Newell G. *Fawn McKay Brodie: A Biographer's Life*. Norman: University of Oklahoma Press, 1999.
———. *Saints, Slaves, and Blacks: The Changing Place of Black People Within Mormonism*, 2nd ed. Salt Lake City: Greg Kofford Books, 2018.
Brodie, Fawn McKay. *The Devil Drives: A Life of Sir Richard Burton*. New York: Norton, 1967.
———. *No Man Knows My History: The Life of Joseph Smith*. New York: Alfred A. Knopf, 1945.
———. *Richard Nixon: The Shaping of His Character*. New York: Norton, 1981.
———. *Thaddeus Stevens: Scourge of the South*. New York: Norton, 1959.
———. *Thomas Jefferson: An Intimate History*. New York: Norton, 1974.
Brooks, Juanita. *John D. Lee: Zealot, Pioneer Builder, Scapegoat*. Glendale, CA: Arthur H. Clark, 1972.
———. *The Mountain Meadows Massacre*. Palo Alto: Stanford University Press, 1950. 3rd edition, first paperback printing, Norman: University of Oklahoma Press, 1991.
———. *Quicksand and Cactus: A Memoir of the Southern Mormon Frontier*. Logan: Utah State University Press, 1992.
Brown, Samuel M. "Early Mormon Adoption Theology and the Mechanics of Salvation." *Journal of Mormon History* 37, no. 3 (Summer 2011): 3–52.
Bryant, J. C. "Mercer University." Encyclopedia of Georgia. December 1, 2006. http://www.georgiaencyclopedia.org/articles/education/mercer-university.
Bush, Lester E. Jr., and Armand Mauss. *Neither White Nor Black: Mormon Scholars Confront the Race Issue in the Universal Church*. Salt Lake City: Signature Books, 1984.
Bushman, Richard L. *Joseph Smith: Rough Stone Rolling*. New York: Alfred A. Knopf, 2005.
Chambers, John. *The Metaphysical World of Isaac Newton: Alchemy, Prophecy, and the Search for Lost Knowledge*. Rochester, Vermont/Toronto, Canada: Destiny Press, 2018.
Church of Jesus Christ of Latter-day Saints, The. "Canada's Brigham Young: The Life of Charles O. Card." Church History. May 17, 2012. https://history.lds.org/article/biographical-sketch-charles-card.
Clark, Daniel A. "The Two Joes Meet—Joe College, Joe Veteran: The G. I. Bill, College Education, and Postwar American Culture." *History of Education Quarterly* 38, no. 2 (June 1998): 165–89.
Daly, Mary. *Gyn/Ecology: The Metaethics of Radical Feminism*. Boston: Beacon Press, 1978.
Dart, John. "Mormons Ponder 1830 Letter Altering Idealized Image of Joseph Smith." *Los Angeles Times*, August 25, 1984.

Davis, David Brion. "Secrets of the Mormons." *The New York Review of Books*, August 15, 1985.

Daynes, Kathryn M. *More Wives than One: Transformation of the Mormon Marriage System, 1840–1910*. Urbana: University of Illinois Press, 2001.

Dex, Shirley. *Women's Occupational Mobility: A Lifetime Perspective*. New York: St. Martin's Press, 1987.

Dlouhy, Katja, and Torsten Biemann. "Path Dependence in Occupational Careers: Understanding Occupational Mobility Development Throughout Individuals' Careers." *Journal of Vocational Behavior* 104, no. 1 (February 2018): 86–97.

Dobay, Clara V. "Intellect and Faith: The Controversy Over Revisionist Mormon History." *Dialogue: A Journal of Mormon Thought* 27, no. 1 (Spring 1994): 103–16.

Douglas, Susan J. *Where the Girls Are: Growing Up Female with the Mass Media*. New York: Three Rivers Press, 1994.

Downs, Mathew L. "Great Depression in Alabama." Encyclopedia of Alabama. Last updated April 21, 2015. http://www.encyclopediaofalabama.org/article/h-3608.

Dulaney, Liz. "Jan Shipps." Paper presented October 14, 2017, in Washington, DC, at the annual meeting of the Mormon Social Science Association. Copy in authors' possession.

Durkheim, Emile. *The Elementary Forms of the Religious Life*. Cambridge: Cambridge University Press, 1968.

Edwards, Paul M. *Our Legacy of Faith: A Brief History of the Reorganized Church of Jesus Christ of Latter Day Saints*. Independence, MO: Herald Publishing House, 1991.

Flake, Kathleen. "The LDS Intellectual Tradition: A Study on Three Lives." Lecture given April 11, 2014, as the University of Utah Tanner Humanities Center McMurrin Lecture on Religion and Culture. Accessed February 1, 2018. https://thc.utah.edu/lectures- programs/past-lectures/Flake.php

——— . *The Politics of American Religious Identity: The Seating of Reed Smoot, Mormon Apostle*. Chapel Hill: The University of North Carolina Press, 2004.

Flanders, Robert. "Some Reflections on the New Mormon History." *Dialogue: A Journal of Mormon Thought* 9, no. 1 (Spring 1974): 34–41.

Gary, Shannon. "Tuskegee University." Encyclopedia of Alabama. Last updated November 16, 2017. http://www.encyclopediaofalabama.org/article/h-1583.

Gillon, Steve. *Boomer Nation: The Largest and Richest Generation Ever, and How It Changed America*. New York: Free Press, 2004.

Godfrey, Audrey M. "Logan, Utah." Utah History Encyclopedia. Accessed September 22, 2018, https://www.uen.org/utah_history_encyclopedia/l/LOGAN.shtml.

Goode, Erich. *Justifiable Conduct: Self-Vindication in Memoir*. Philadelphia: Temple University Press, 2013.

Gordon, Sarah Barringer. *The Mormon Question: Polygamy and Constitutional Conflict in Nineteenth-Century America*. Chapel Hill: The University of North Carolina Press, 2002.

Gottlieb, Robert, and Peter Wiley. *America's Saints: The Rise of Mormon Power*. New York: Putnam, 1984.

Gray, Ralph D., ed. *Indiana History: A Book of Readings*. Bloomington: Indiana University Press, 1995.

———. *IUPUI: The Making of an Urban University*. Bloomington: Indiana University Press, 2003.

Hansen, Klaus J. "The Long Honeymoon: Jan Shipps among the Mormons." *Dialogue: A Journal of Mormon Thought* 37, no. 3 (Fall 2004): 1–28.

———. "Reflections on *The Lion of the Lord*." *Dialogue: A Journal of Mormon Thought* 5, no. 2 (Summer 1970): 105–11.

Head, William. "History of Warner Robins, Georgia." Robins Air Force Base. November 1, 2010. https://www.robins.af.mil/About-Us/Fact-Sheets/Display/Article/377484/history-of-warner-robins-georgia/.

Heath, Harvard, ed. *In the World: The Diaries of Reed Smoot*. Salt Lake City: Signature Books, 1997.

Herrnstein, Richard J., and Charles Murray. *The Bell Curve: Intelligence and Class Structure in American Life*. New York: Free Press, 1994.

Hill, Marvin. "The 'New Mormon History' Reassessed in Light of Recent Books on Joseph Smith and Mormon Origins." *Dialogue: A Journal of Mormon Thought* 21, no. 3 (Autumn 1988): 115–27.

Holbrook, Kate, and Matthew Bowman, eds. *Women and Mormonism: Historical and Contemporary Perspectives*. Salt Lake City: The University of Utah Press, 2016.

Homer, Michael W. *Joseph's Temples: The Dynamic Relationship Between Freemasonry and Mormonism*. Salt Lake City: University of Utah Press, 2014.

Howard, Richard P. *The Church Through the Years*. Independence, MO: Herald Publishing House, 1992.

Howlett, David, John Hamer, and Barbara Walden. *Community of Christ: An Illustrated History*. Independence, MO: Herald Publishing House, 2010.

Irwin, Douglas A. *Peddling Protectionism: Smoot–Hawley and the Great Depression*. Princeton: Princeton University Press, 2011.

Jenson, Debra Elaine. "From the Kotel to the Square: The Rhetoric of Religious Feminism." In *Voices for Equality: Ordain Women and Resurgent Mormon Feminism*, edited by Gordon Shepherd, Lavina Fielding Anderson, and Gary Shepherd, 377–95. Salt Lake City: Greg Kofford Books, 2015.

John, Oliver P., Richard W. Robins, and Lawrence A. Pervin. *Handbook of Personality: Theory and Research*, 3rd ed. New York: Guilford Press, 2008.

Johnson, Sonia. *From Housewife to Heretic*. New York: Doubleday, 1981.

Kaledin, Eugenia. *Mothers and More: American Women in the 1950s*. New York: Twayne Publishers, 1984.

Kohli, Martin. "Generational Change." In *The Blackwell Encyclopedia of Sociology*. Accessed September 22, 2018, https://doi.org/10.1002/9781405165518.wbeosg031.pub2.

Kuhn, Thomas. *The Structure of Scientific Revolutions*. Chicago: University of Chicago Press, 1962.

Larson, Stan, and Samuel J. Passey, eds. *The William E. McLellin Papers, 1854–1880*. Salt Lake City: Signature Books, 2008.

Launius, Roger D. "The 'New Social History' and the 'New Mormon History': Some Reflections." *Dialogue: A Journal of Mormon Thought* 27, no. 1 (Spring 1994): 109–27.

Levine, Susan. *School Lunch Politics: The Surprising History of America's Favorite Welfare Program*. Princeton: Princeton University Press, 2008.

MacKinnon, William P. *At Sword's Point, Part 1: A Documentary History of the Utah War to 1858*. Norman, OK: The Arthur H. Clark Company, 2008.

Mauss, Armand L. *The Angel and the Beehive: The Mormon Struggle with Assimilation*. Urbana: University of Illinois Press, 1994.

May, Dean L., and Reid L. Neilson with Richard Lyman Bushman, Jan Shipps, and Thomas G. Alexander. *The Mormon History Association's Tanner Lectures: The First Twenty Years*. Urbana: University of Illinois Press, 2006.

May, Elaine Tyler. *Homeward Bound: American Families in the Cold War Era*. New York: Basic Books, 2008.

McCartney, Laton. *The Teapot Dome Scandal: How Big Oil Bought the Harding White House and Tried to Steal the Country*. New York: Random House, 2009.

McClelland, David C. *The Achievement Motive*. New York, Appleton-Century-Crofts, 1953.

———. *The Achieving Society*. New York: The Free Press, 1961.

———. *Talent and Society: New Perspectives in the Identification of Talent*. New York: D. Van Nostrand Company, 1959.

McCombs, Brady. "Mormon Church Excommunicates Women's Group Founder." AP News. June 23, 2014, https://apnews.com/7f3789ccb0c64cf1b1a3b2fe7337f95c.

McMurrin, Sterling M. *The Theological Foundations of the Mormon Religion*. Salt Lake City: The University of Utah Press, 1965.

———. "Jack Newell Interviews Sterling McMurrin." Sunstone Symposium, Salt Lake City, 1993. Accessed September 22, 2018. http://www.lds-mormon.com/newell_mcmurrin.shtml.

Merrill, Milton R. *Reed Smoot: Apostle in Politics*. Logan: Utah State University Press, 1990.

Merton, Robert K. *Social Theory and Social Structure*. Glencoe, IL: Free Press, 1957.

Mills, C. Wright. *The Sociological Imagination*. New York: Oxford University Press, 1959.

Moore, R. Lawrence. "Prophets in Their Own Country." *New York Times Book Review*, July 21, 1985.

Morgan, Dale L. *The Humboldt: Highroad of the West*. New York: Farrar & Rinehart, 1943.

———. *Jedediah Smith and the Opening of the West*. Indianapolis: The Bobs-Merrill Company, 1953.

———, ed. *Overland in 1846: Diaries and Letters of the California-Oregon Trail*. Jersey City, NJ: Talisman Press, 1963.

———. "A Prophet and His Legend." *Saturday Review of Literature*, November 24, 1945, 7–8.

Mormon History Association. "About Us." Mormon History Association. Accessed February 12, 2018. https://mormonhistoryassociation.org/about.

"Mormon History Association Awards for 1976." *Journal of Mormon History* 3, no. 1 (1976): 2, 84.

Neuhaus, Jessamyn. "The Way to a Man's Heart: Gender Roles, Domestic Ideology, and Cookbooks in the 1950s." *Journal of Social History* 32, no. 3 (Spring 1999): 529–55.

Nelson, Megan Kate. "Stop Calling Me 'Independent Scholar.'" *The Chronicle of Higher Education*, October 8, 2017, https://www.chronicle.com/article/Stop-Calling-Me-Independent/241376.

Newell, Jackson, L. "Remembering Sterling McMurrin." *Sunstone* 103 (September 1996): 10–11.

Newell, Linda King, and Valeen Tippetts Avery. *Mormon Enigma: Emma Hale Smith, Prophet's Wife, Elect Lady, Polygamy's Foe, 1804–1879*. New York: Doubleday, 1984.

Nibley, Hugh. *No, Ma'am, That's Not History*. Salt Lake City: Deseret Book, 1946.

Nicolson, Adam. *God's Secretaries: The Making of the King James Bible*. New York: Harper Collins Publishers, 2005.

Nicholson, Virginia. *Perfect Wives in Ideal Homes: The Story of Women in the 1950s*. New York: Viking/Penguin, 2015.

Nielsen, François. "Achievement and Ascription in Educational Attainment: Genetic and Environmental Influences on Adolescent Schooling." *Social Forces* 85, no. 1 (September 2006): 193–216.

O'Dea, Thomas. *The Mormons*. Chicago: University of Chicago Press, 1957.

Ostling, Richard, and Joan K. Ostling. *Mormon America: The Power and Promise*. New York: Harper Collins, 2007.

Peterson, Levi S. *A Rascal by Nature, A Christian by Yearning: A Mormon Autobiography*. Salt Lake City: University of Utah Press, 2006.

———. *Juanita Brooks: The Life Story of a Courageous Historian of the Mountain Meadows Massacre*. Salt Lake City: University of Utah Press, 2011.

Pieschel, Bridget Smith. "The History of Mississippi University for Women." Mississippi History Now. March 2102. http://mshistorynow.mdah.state.ms.us/articles/379/the-history-of-mississippi-university-for-women.

Pomerance, Benjamin. "Strings of History." Meadowmount School of Music. Accessed September 24, 2018, http://www.meadowmount.com/inner.php?pageid=120.

Prince, Gregory A. *David O. McKay and the Rise of Modern Mormonism*. Salt Lake City: University of Utah Press, 2005.

———. *Leonard Arrington and the Writing of Mormon History*. Salt Lake City: University of Utah Press, 2016.

Quinn, D. Michael. "Biographers and the Mormon 'Prophet Puzzle.'" *Dialogue: A Journal of Mormon Thought* 32, no. 2 (Summer 2006): 226–45.

———. *Early Mormonism and the Magic World View*. Salt Lake City: Signature Press, 1998.

———. "LDS Church Authority and New Plural Marriages, 1890–1904." *Dialogue: A Journal of Mormon Thought* 18, no.1 (Spring 1985): 9–105.

———. *The New Mormon History: Revisionist Essays on the Past*. Salt Lake City: Signature Books, 1992.

RAAC IUPUI. "About." The Center for the Study of Religion & American Culture. Accessed April 10, 2019, https://raac.iupui.edu/about/who-we-are/.

Robinson, Chris. "Occupational Mobility, Occupation Distance and Specific Human Capital." *The Journal of Human Resources* 53, no. 2 (Spring 2018): 513–51.

Roper, William L., and Leonard Arrington. *William Spry: Man of Firmness, Governor of Utah*. Salt Lake City: The University of Utah Press, 1971.

Ross, Alex. "Josef Gingold, 85, Violinist And Influential Teacher, Dies." *New York Times*, January 13, 1995, https://www.nytimes.com/1995/01/13/obituaries/josef-gingold-85-violinist-and-influential-teacher-dies.html

Ross, Nancy. "Juanita Brooks and the Practice of Mormon Feminism." Paper presented October 23, 2016, at the annual conference of the Western Historical Association. Copy in authors' possession.

Ross, Susan A. "Mary Daly Exposed the Slimy Underbelly of Religion's Treatment of Women." *National Catholic Reporter*, December 25, 2016, https://www.ncronline.org/blogs/ncr-today/mary-daly-exposed-slimy-underbelly-religions-treatment-women.

Russell, William. "History of JWHA." John Whitmer Historical Association. Accessed February 12, 2018. https://www.jwha.info/history-of-jwha.

Saunders, Richard L. "The Strange Mixture of Emotion and Intellect: A Social History of Dale L. Morgan, 1933–42." *Dialogue: A Journal of Mormon Thought* 28, no. 4 (Winter 1995): 39–58.

———, ed. *Dale Morgan on the Mormons: Collected Works, Part 1, 1939–1951*. Norman, OK: The Arthur H. Clark Company, 2012.

———, ed. *Dale Morgan on the Mormons: Collected Works, Part 2, 1949–1970*. Norman, OK: The Arthur H. Clark Company, 2013.

Scamehorn, H. Lee. *Albert Eugene Reynolds: Colorado's Mining King*. Norman: University of Oklahoma Press, 1995.

———. *Mill and Mine: The CF&I in the Twentieth Century*. Lincoln: University of Nebraska Press, 1992.

Shepherd, Gordon. "Memoir Construction." *The Oakland Journal* 16 (Winter 2009): 44–65.

Shepherd, Gordon, and Gary Shepherd. "Conflict and Change in Closed and Open Systems: The Case of the LDS Church." In *Voices for Equality: Ordain Women and Resurgent Mormon Feminism*, edited by Gordon Shepherd, Lavina Fielding Anderson, and Gary Shepherd, 27–48. Salt Lake City: Greg Kofford Books, 2015.

———. *A Kingdom Transformed: Early Mormonism and the Modern LDS Church*. Salt Lake City: The University of Utah Press, 2015.

———. *A Kingdom Transformed: Themes in the Development of Mormonism*. Salt Lake City: The University of Utah Press, 1984.

Shepherd, Gordon, Lavina Fielding Anderson, and Gary Shepherd, eds. *Voices for Equality: Ordain Women and Resurgent Mormon Feminism*. Salt Lake City: Greg Kofford Books, 2015.

Sherrill, Rowland A. *The Prophetic Melville: Experience. Transcendence, and Tragedy*. Athens: University of Georgia Press, 1979.

———, ed. *Religion and the Life of the Nation: American Recoveries*. Urbana: University of Illinois Press, 1990.

Shipps, Anthony W. *The Quote Sleuth: A Manual for the Tracer of Lost Quotations*. Urbana: University of Illinois Press, 1991.

Shipps, Jan. "An 'Inside-Outsider' in Zion." *Dialogue: A Journal of Mormon Thought* 15, no. 1 (Spring 1982): 138–61.

———. Forward to *The Mountain Meadows Massacre*, by Juanita Brooks, v–ix. Norman: University of Oklahoma Press, 3rd edition, first paperback printing, 1991.

———. *Mormonism: The Story of a New Religious Tradition*. Urbana: University of Illinois Press, 1985.

———. Oral History. Interviewed by Gordon Irving, May 6, 1986. The James Moyle Oral History program, Historical Department, The Church of Jesus Christ of Latter-day Saints, Salt Lake City, Utah.

———. Oral History. Interviewed by Maureen Ursenbach Beecher, October 15–16, 1983. The James Moyle Oral History program, Historical Department, The Church of Jesus Christ of Latter-day Saints, Salt Lake City, Utah.

———. "The Prophet Puzzle: Suggestions Leading Toward a More Comprehensive Interpretation of Joseph Smith." *Journal of Mormon History* 1 (1974): 3–20.

———. "Richard Lyman Bushman, the Story of Joseph Smith and Mormonism, and the New Mormon History." *Journal of American History* 94, no. 2 (September 2007): 498–516.

———. "Second Class Saints." *Colorado Quarterly* 10, no. 3 (Autumn 1962): 183–90.

———. *Sojourner in the Promised Land: Forty Years Among the Mormons*. Urbana: University of Illinois Press, 2000.

———. "Sonia Johnson, Mormonism, and the Media." *Christian Century* 97 (January 2, 1980): 5–6.

Shipps, Jan, and John W. Welch, eds. *The Journals of William E. McLellin, 1831–1836*. Urbana: University of Illinois Press and Provo: BYU Studies, 1994.

Sillitoe, Linda, and Alan Dale Roberts. *Salamander: The Story of the Mormon Forgery Murders*. Salt Lake City: Signature Books, 1988.

Smith, George D. *Nauvoo Polygamy: But We Called It Celestial Marriage*. Salt Lake City: Signature Books, 2011.

Stoet, Gijsbert, and David C. Geary. "The Gender-Equality Paradox in Science, Technology, Engineering, and Mathematics Education." *Psychological Science* 29, no. 4 (February 2018): 581.

Stark, Rodney, and Reid L. Nielson. *The Rise of Mormonism*. New York: Columbia University Press, 2005.

Stevenson, Russell M. *For the Cause of Righteousness: A Global History of Blacks and Mormonism, 1830–2013*. Salt Lake City: Greg Kofford Books, 2014.

Swick, Joe Steve, III, and Cheryl L. Bruno. *Method Infinite: Freemasonry and the Mormon Restoration*. Salt Lake City: Greg Kofford Books, 2020.

Tam, Tony, and Jin Jiang. "The Making of Higher Education Inequality: How Do Mechanisms and Pathways Depend on Competition?" *American Sociological Review* 79, no. 4 (July 2014): 807–16.

Toobin, Jeffery. "The Legacy of Lynching, On Death Row." *The New Yorker*, August 22, 2016, https://www.newyorker.com/magazine/2016/08/22/bryan-stevenson-and-the-legacy-of-lynching.
Treiman, Donald J. "Occupational Mobility." In *The Blackwell Encyclopedia of Sociology*. Accessed October 26, 2015. https://onlinelibrary.wiley.com/doi/10.1002/9781405165518.wbeoso003.pub2.
Turley, Richard E. *Victims: The LDS Church and the Mark Hofmann Case*. Urbana: University of Illinois Press, 1992.
Turner, Ralph H., and Lewis M. Killian. *Collective Behavior*, 3rd ed. New York: Prentice Hall, 1987.
UC Denver. "University History." University of Colorado Denver. Accessed February 12, 2018. http://www.ucdenver.edu/about-us/history/Pages/default.aspx.
Van Wagoner, Richard S. *Mormon Polygamy: A History*. Salt Lake City: Signature Books, 1989.
Walker, John Phillip, ed. *Dale Morgan on Early Mormon History: Correspondence and a New History*. Salt Lake City: Signature Books, 1986.
Walker, Ronald W., Richard E. Turley, and Glen M. Leonard. *Massacre at Mountain Meadows*. New York: Oxford University Press, 2008.
Wasserman, Stanley, and Katherine Faust. *Social Network Analysis: Methods and Applications*. Cambridge: Cambridge University Press, 1994.
Weber, Max. *The Protestant Ethic and the Spirit of Capitalism*. Translated by Talcott Parsons. London and New York: Routledge, 2001.
Weinberg, Martin S., and Alan P. Bell. *Homosexuality: An Annotated Bibliography*. New York: Harper and Row, 1972.
Whipple, Maurine. *The Giant Joshua*. Boston: Houghton Mifflin, 1942.
Whittaker, David J. "The Hofmann Maze: A Book Review Essay with a Chronology and Bibliography of the Hofmann Case." *BYU Studies* 29, no. 1 (Winter 1989): 67–124.
Wiley, Bell Irvin. *Confederate Women: Beyond the Petticoat*. Baton Rouge: Louisiana State University Press, 1975.
———. *The Life of Johnny Reb: The Common Soldier of the Confederacy*. Baton Rouge: Louisiana State University Press, 1943.
———. *The Plain People of the Confederacy*. Baton Rouge: Louisiana State University Press, 1943.
———. *The Road to Appomattox*. Baton Rouge: Louisiana State University Press, 1956.
Wood, Gordon S. *The Creation of the American Republic, 1776–1787*. Chapel Hill: University of North Carolina Press, 1969.
———. *The Radicalism of the American Revolution*. New York: Random House, 1991.

Index

A

Abrams, Milton, 34
abstracted empiricism, 122
abstract thinking, 121–24
academia. *See* Shipps, Jan, career of
activism, 9, 198–202
Ahlstrom, Sydney, 64
Alabama College for Women, 15–17
alcoholism, 10–11, 126, 188–89
Alder, Doug, 73–77, 84, 132–33
Alexander, Thomas, 48, 63, 77, 93, 192–93
 at MHA meetings, 65, 77
 relationship with Shipps, 67–68, 84, 133
 review of Mormonism, 105
Allen, James, 48, 59
American Academy of Religion (AAR), 91
American History Association, 59–60
American History Illustrated, 69, 70
"Answers to Queries" (T. Shipps), 58, 106
apologetics, 36, 60, 75, 103, 143, 190
Arrington, Leonard, 34, 38, 40, 46, 123
 as Church Historian, 59, 76, 94, 197
 and MHA, 64–65
 as Shipps mentor, 48, 54, 64, 131–32
 and Spry biography, 59, 61
Aunt Sue, 3, 21, 125, 128
authorial credit, 57, 110
Avery, Val, 93

B

Baker-Fancher party, 148
Barlow, Philip, 90
Barnett, Bernard, 12
Barnett, Billy, 6, 12
Barnett, Jo Ann. *See* Shipps, Jan
Barnett, Sue, 2–13, 15–17
 relationship with Shipps, 3, 23, 117, 128–29, 161–62

Barnett, Thalia Jenkins Bell, 1–13, 20–22, 40–41
 career, 2, 156
 influence on Shipps, 116–17, 119, 125–29, 161, 185–86
Barnett, William McKinley, 1–13, 20
 career, 3, 7–8, 11–12
 influence on Shipps, 116–17, 119, 125–29, 161, 185–86
 racial tolerance of, 7–8, 12–13
Beecher, Maureen Ursenbach, xi, xiii, 192–93
Bell, Alan, 57, 84
Bible, King James, 192
biological factors, 114–15
Birmingham, Alabama, 1–2
Bitton, Davis, 59, 65
blacks, 6–8, 12–13, 15, 119. *See also* racial prejudice
 Mormon, 46, 96–97
Bloomington, Indiana, 51–58, 138–39
Book of Mormon, 192
Boulder, Colorado, 40–50
boundary maintenance, 200
Bridges, Hal, 41–42, 46–47, 123, 132, 190, 193
Brimhall, Fawn, 156–62
Brodie, Bernard, 162–64, 167–69
Brodie, Fawn, ix–x, 91–92, 97, 190–91. *See also No Man Knows My History*
 achievements noteworthy, 167, 183–84
 age and regional history, 152–54, 163–66
 career comparison with Juanita Brooks and Jan Shipps, 143–84
 domestic disruptions to work, 165–67, 183
 as independent scholar, 178–84
 as inside-outsider, 149, 154–55
 intelligence and education, 157, 160–61, 169–72, 178–79

marriage and motherhood, 162–69
modest Mormon upbringing, 155–60
parent and sibling influence, 159–62
as proto-feminist, 202–4, 208
as woman, 152–53, 182
Brooks, Juanita, ix–x, 168–69. *See also Mountain Meadows Massacre, The*
achievements noteworthy, 150–51, 167, 182–84
age and regional history, 152–54, 158–59, 163
as believer, 149, 154, 161
career comparison with Fawn Brodie and Jan Shipps, 143–84
domestic disruptions to work, 165–66, 183
as independent scholar, 149, 178–84
as inside-outsider, 154–55, 181
intelligence and education, 157, 160–61, 169–72, 178–79
marriage and motherhood, 162–69
modest Mormon upbringing, 155–60
parent and sibling influence, 158–62
as proto-feminist, 202–4, 208
as woman, 152–53, 162–69, 182
Brooks, Will, 162–64, 167–69
Bush, Alfred, 48, 54, 65, 74, 77, 92
Bushman, Claudia, 91, 93–94, 196
Bushman, Richard, 98, 109, 133
and *Rough Stone Rolling*, 146–47, 191
at conferences, 48, 54, 64, 65, 91, 93–94
BYU Studies, 109–10

C

Cahill, Jerry, 95–97, 105
capabilities, primary, 115–25
Card, Charles O., 39
Case Western Reserve, 70
Catholicism, 18, 204–5. *See also* Christianity
Center for American Studies, 92–94, 140
Chicago, Illinois, 23–26
chicken coop dancing, 5–6
Christensen, Steven, 107–8
Christianity, 101–2, 186–87, 193, 194
Church Historical Department (LDS), 109

Church History Department (LDS), 59, 63, 94
and Hofmann case, 107–8
and McLellin diaries, 109–10
Church of Jesus Christ of Latter-day Saints, 143, 148, 194–95
controversial issues in, 144–45, 149–52, 180–81
cultural norms in, 33–34, 36, 84, 119
intellectual ferment in, x, 59–60
and media, 97, 110–11, 207–8
Shipps approval from leaders in, 95–97, 197, 207–8
theology of, 199–201
Civil War, 36, 44, 79
Clark, Roger, 98
Colorado Quarterly, 46
Community of Christ (formerly Restored Church of Jesus Christ of Latter Day Saints [RLDS]), 59, 61–62, 194–95, 200–201. *See also* John Whitmer Historical Association (JWHA)
and the LDS Church, 61–63, 72–77.
comparative analysis. *See* Shipps, Jan, methodology of
comparative imagination, 121–24
competitive-cooperator relationships, 128–29
Compton's Pictured Encyclopedia, 7
contingency factors, 114–15, 136
Conventicle, The, 187–88, 194
Cooley, Everett, 177–78
mentoring Brodie and Brooks, 175–76
mentoring Shipps, 34, 38–42, 47–49, 118–19, 131–32, 172, 193
cow milking, 11
Crawford, Vesta, 175
curiosity. *See* Shipps, Jan, traits and talents of

D

Daly, May, 205
Dart, John, 107–8
Davis, David Brion, 102–3
deism, 186–90, 194
feminine, 199–200
DePillis, Mario, 64, 91

Deseret News, 144–45
Detroit, Michigan, 26–29
Dialogue: A Journal of Mormon Thought, xi, 56, 60, 77–78, 193
Divine. *See* deism
domesticity, female, 21, 162, 195
Dulaney, Liz, 94–95, 98, 110
Durham, Reed, 75–76
Durkheim, Emile, 187

E

Edmunds–Tucker Act, 39
Edwards, Paul, 61, 74–77, 98, 132–34
Ellsworth, George, 38, 48
Equal Rights Amendment, 196–97
eschatological history, 101–2
Esplin, Ron, 65
excommunication, 144–45, 181, 200
Exponent II, 60, 196
external contingencies. *See* contingency factors

E

feminism, modern, x, 196–206. *See also* gender equality, LDS Church; proto-feminism
Flanders, Robert, 61, 77
Fletcher, Peggy, 107
"From Satyr to Saint: American Attitudes toward the Mormons, 1860–1960," 75–67, 139–40

G

Gantry, Elmer, 191
gender equality, LDS Church, 195–206
gender roles. *See* domesticity, female
Genealogical Society, 39
genetic inheritance, 116–25
gentiles, 33–36
Georgia College for Women, 22
gerontocracy, 195, 201
Gingold, Josef, 52
grand theory, 122
Great Basin Kingdom, 34, 131–32
Great Depression, 1–10, 48, 153, 155

H

Hansen, Klaus
  at conferences, 48, 54, 65–68, 74, 77
  review of Shipps's work, 54, 56, 98, 105
  as Shipps mentor, 132–33
Hill, Marvin, 71–73, 75
Hinckley, Gordon B., 96
Hirshson, Stanley P., 54
historiography, 79–80
history. *See* eschatological history; naturalistic history; Mormon history; New Mormon history; Western history
Hofmann, Mark, 73–74, 96–97, 107–10
Holifield, E. Brooks, 105
Homosexuality: An Annotated Bibliography, 57, 110
Howard, Richard, 61
Hueytown, Alabama, 1–13

I

ideographic studies, 79–80
Indiana University Press, 97–99
Indiana University-Purdue University Indianapolis (IUPUI), 57–78, 66, 83
  colleagues' reception of Shipps's book, 104–5
industriousness, 156–57
inside-outsider. *See* Shipps, Jan, identity of
"'Inside-Outsider' in Zion, An," 193
insider, academic, 180–81. *See also* Shipps, Jan, identity of
ironing set up, 166
Irving, Gordon, xi, xiii

J

Jack Mormons, 33–34
James, Henry, 26
Jesse, Dean, 65
Johnson, Robert, 27, 29
Johnson, Sonia, 196–97, 200
John Whitmer Historical Association, 69–74
  Shipps service with, 69–72, 90–91, 124, 198–99

Josephine (Barnett home worker), 4, 7–8, 13
Joseph Smith: Rough Stone Rolling, 146–47, 191
Journal of Mormon History, 60, 71
Judaism, 163, 193–94

K

Kelly, Kate, 200
Kimball, Heber, 94
Kimball, Stanley, 54, 94
Kinsey Institute for Sex Research, 54–58, 66, 84, 110
    Shipps employment as turning point event, 139, 140
Kinzer, Donald, 57
Knopf Literary Fellowship, 146

L

LDS Church. *See* Church of Jesus Christ of Latter-day Saints
Leavitt, Charity, 162
Leavitt, Henry, 155–59
Leavitt, Mary Hafen, 155–59
Lee, John D., 148–50, 169
Leone, Mark, 91
Lilly Endowment, Inc., 92–93
Lion of the Lord, The, 54, 56
Logan, Utah, 31–40, 119, 137
Los Angeles Times, 107–8
"Lucky," (Shipps boyfriend), 10
Lynn, Robert, 93

M

Macon, Georgia 17–22
Madsen, Brigham, 48
Marrs, Ross, 82, 135, 194
Martin, David, 105
Marty, Martin, 66, 69, 91, 98, 105
masonry, 75–76
May, Dean, 92
McKay, David O., 144
McKay, Flora, 162
McKay, Thomas E., 144, 155–56, 159–61
McKiernan, Mark, 71–73
McLellin, William E., diaries, 108–10
McMurrin, Sterling, 48, 97, 105, 133–34
mentoring, 172–78. *See also* Arrington, Leonard; Cooley, Everett; Hansen, Klaus; Morgan, Dale; Shipps, Jan, relationships of
Merton, Robert K., 84
Methodism, 1, 8–9, 34–35. *See also* Shipps, Jan, life experiences of
Mills, C. Wright, 122–24
miscarriage, 164
missionary work, 33, 158
Mississippi State College for Women, 2
Moore, Lawrence, 103
Morgan, Dale, 146, 176–78, 182
    mentoring Brodie, 165, 172–73
    mentoring Brooks, 172, 174–75
Mormon Church. *See* Church of Jesus Christ of Latter-day Saints
Mormon exceptionalism, 103
Mormon history, 143, 180–82. *See also* Mormon History Association; Mormon Studies; New Mormon History
Mormon History Association, 60–78, 151
    conferences, 53–54, 58–63, 74–78
    informal hotel meetings at, 64–65
    Shipps service with, 68, 70, 90–92, 124, 182, 196, 198–99
    Shipps reconnection with, 139
    women attending as wives, 62, 65, 77, 175
Mormonism: The Story of a New Religious Tradition, ix–x, 82, 95–111, 141
    compared to Brodie's and Brooks's books, 178–84
    and Mills's Sociological Imagination, 122–24
Mormon Moment, 110
"Mormons in Politics, 1839–1844, The," 42
"Mormons in Politics: The First Hundred Years, The," 49–50, 54
Mormon Social Science Association, 60

Mormon Studies, 60, 92–111. *See also*
Mormon history; New Mormon History
Shipps legitimizing of, ix–xi, 77, 82–83, 125, 181, 207–8
"Shippsification of," 90–92
motherhood, 164–69. *See also* Brodie, Fawn; Brooks, Juanita; Shipps, Jan, life experiences of
Mountain Meadows Massacre, 147–52
Mountain Meadows Massacre, The, 36, ix–x, 147–52, 174–75
Shipps's foreword and afterword, 151, 174
compared to Shipps's and Brodie's books, 178–84
Mullin, Theodore "Ted," 81–82, 135
mysticism, 41, 132, 190–93

N

naturalistic history, 101–2, 143, 155, 181, 184
Nauvoo Temple, 71–75
New Mormon History, 48, 60, 62, 102, 181, 197
New York Review of Books, The, 102–3
New York Times, 45, 58, 66–67
New York Times Book Review, The, 102–3
Nibley, Hugh, 145
Noall, Claire, 175
"No Ma'am, That's Not History," 145
No Man Knows My History, ix–x, 36, 92, 144–47, 190–91
compared to Shipps's and Brooks's books, 178–84
nomothetic studies, 79–80, 143
Notes and Queries, 45

O

Oak Grove, Alabama, 10
occupational mobility, 113–16, 136
Ordain Women, 110, 199–200
Organization of American Historians, 65–70, 91–92
outsider, academic, 180–81

P

Pacific Historical Review, 59, 61
Packer, Boyd, 195
Pearson, S. C., 105
"Personal Voices," xi
Peterson, Levi, 151
pioneer heritage, 155–56
Pittsview, Alabama, 22–23
polemics, 36, 143, 161, 190
polygamy, 67, 72
Poole's Index to Periodical Literature, 66
prayer, 189–90
Presbyterianism, 35
priesthood, 148, 150
exclusion for blacks, 96–97
exclusion for women, 110, 152, 195–98
progressivism, American, 44, 153
"Prophet Puzzle: Suggestions Leading toward a More Comprehensive Interpretation of Joseph Smith, The," 71, 74, 191
proto-feminism, 202–4. *See also* feminism, modern
Pulsipher, Ernest, 163, 171

Q

Quicksand and Cactus, 169
Quinn, Michael, 65
Quorum of the Twelve Apostles, 195, 200
Quote Sleuth: A Manual for the Tracer of Lost Quotations, The, 106

R

racial prejudice, 6, 13, 46, 119
Reader's Guide to Periodical Literature, 66
religious dimension, 189–91, 194
Religious History of the American People, A, 64
religious studies, 80–83, 101–2. *See also* Shipps, Jan, Mormon scholarship of
religious tradition, new, 193–94. *See also* Shipps, Jan, Mormon scholarship of
Restored Church of Jesus Christ of Latter Day Saints. *See* Community of Christ
Ricks, Joel, 38

Ridge, Martin, 91
role sets, 84
Romney, Mitt, 110
Ross, Nancy, 203
Ross, Susan A., 204–6

S

Salamander Letter, The, 107–8
Scamehorn, Lee, 44, 47–48, 63, 132
"Second Class Saints," 46
sexism. *See* Shipps, Jan, life experiences of; *see also* gender equality, LDS Church
Sheets, J. Gary, 108
Sheets, Kathy, 108
Sherrill, Rowland Anthony "Tony," 81, 87–88, 93, 124, 135
Shipps, Jan, career of, 127–28. *See also* American History Illustrated, Shipps service with; Mormon History Association; John Whitmer Historical Association
   academia influence on, 178–98
   achievements, 167, 182–84
   comparisons to Fawn Brodie and Juanita Brooks, 143–84
   delays to, 51–58, 182
   domestic disruptions to, 44, 165–66, 172, 183
   joint IUPUI religious studies and history professorship, 70, 79–83, 134–35, 140, 179
   as teacher, 16, 80–81, 88
Shipps, Jan, education of, 16–17, 22, 169–72, 178–79
   college major switch from music to history, 37, 137–38
   early, 10, 44
   example of women's, 3, 15, 117, 127.
   historiography course, 79, 118–19
   self-, 80–81, 119, 121, 123–24, 130–31
   teaching certificate, 38, 40
   at Utah State University, 35–40
   at University of Colorado, 40–50, 121, 138
Shipps, Jan, identity of
   as academic insider, 45, 180–82
   as inside-outsider, 62, 65, 77–78, 97, 154–55, 184, 197–99
   as liaison between LDS Church and press, 97, 110–11, 207–8
   as non-Mormon, 62, 68–69, 77, 114
   own reconstruction of, 83–90
   as proto-feminist, 202–8
   as respected scholar, 43, 62, 68–69, 95–97, 207–8
   as wife and mother, 56, 166
   as woman, 62–63, 65, 68–69, 77, 82, 152–53, 182
Shipps, Jan, life experiences of
   birth and early life, 1–13, 52, 153
   improbable story, ix–xi, 136
   images of, 5, 85, 100, 130
   loneliness/unhappiness, 53–58, 139
   marriage and motherhood, 162–69, 179
   Methodism as adult, 82, 119, 154, 161, 185–89, 194
   Methodism of youth, x, 8–9, 22–23, 34–35, 185–86
   modest upbringing, 6, 10, 155–56
   of sexism, 198–202, 208
   of sexual harassment, 43
Shipps, Jan, methodology of
   comparative analysis, 44, 99, 134, 143
   detached, non-political approach, 196–97, 204, 208
   historiographical methods, 38–40, 44, 56
   practice of everyday religion, 73, 79–80, 119
   survey research methodology, 55–56, 66–68
Shipps, Jan, Mormon scholarship of, 33–35, 44, 63, 77, 119, 143. *See also* Mormon Studies
   and Christian primitivism, 99, 101, 123, 143, 193–94
   devout/Jack/non-, 35–37, 119
   as new religious tradition, 82, 99, 101, 123, 125, 193–94

in religious studies/Western history, 63–65, 82–83, 99, 101, 193–94
nineteenth- v. twentieth-century, 97–99, 135, 141, 194
Shipps, Jan, relationships of
with IUPUI colleagues, 121, 127–28, 134–35, 194
mentoring women, 88, 204
with Mormon intellectuals, 9, 65, 77, 132, 194, 198–99
with own mentors, 131–35
with scholars, 65, 77, 121, 124–25, 127–28, 134–35
with students, 80–81
Shipps, Jan, traits and talents of
confidence, 37, 42, 71–72, 123–24
curiosity, 118–20, 193
empathy, 6, 127
independence, 4, 7–8
intelligence, 160–61, 169–72, 178–79
morality, 8–9, 186–88
piano playing, 3–5, 12, 15, 21, 117, 127
practical learning/talents, 4
racial equality belief, 6, 9, 12–13, 15
reading, 9–10, 28, 44, 117, 127, 166
tolerance, 118–20
writing, 123–24, 135
Shipps, Stephen (Jan's son), 86, 104, 123, 164
childhood, 24–25, 32, 34–35
violin playing, 41, 45–46, 52–53, 56
trips with Jan, 54, 166
religiosity, 187–89
Jan's piano accompanying, 52–53, 139
Shipps, Stephen (Tony's brother), 18
Shipps, Teri, 86, 189
Shipps, Tony, 17–29, 87–88, 123
career, 19, 21–22, 26–29, 40–51
college, 19, 21, 23–29
colon cancer, 85–89
family insecurities, 20, 23–24, 129
interest in Mormons, 119, 130–31
religiosity of, 187–89
Shipps, Tony, relationship with Jan Shipps, 129–31, 137
commitment to traditional, 45, 56, 88–89, 129–31, 137–38
courtship and marriage, 19–20, 24–25, 45, 137
equally managing, 86, 199
Jan as Tony's research assistant, 26, 28, 31, 130
Jan asking Tony for permission, 42–43, 139
Jan subordinating to a point, 88–89, 199
family ties in, 20, 23–24
leaving South, 24–25, 154, 163–66
and parenting, 86–90, 127–28
parenting at-risk girls, 26–28, 81, 119, 164
Tony's career over Jan's, 31, 44–45, 50–51, 129, 137–38, 164
Tony's support of Jan, 53, 83, 104, 106, 167–69
turning points in, 83–90, 121, 140
Smith, Joseph, 72. *See also Rough Stone Rolling*; *No Man Knows My History*
Shipps on, 71, 74, 102–3, 107–8, 190–93
Smith, Timothy, 91
smoking, 27–28, 41
Smoot, Reed, diaries, 48–49
Smoot–Hawley Tariff Act, 48
Sociological Imagination, The, 122–24
Sojourner in the Promised Land, xi, 67
Southerland, Harrold, 18
Southern Illinois University, 53–54
Spry, William, 59, 61
Stanford University Press, 147
Stark, Rodney, 91
Stephenson, Ed, 188
Stout, Hosea, diaries, 175–76
Sunstone, xi, 60, 107

T

Tanner Lectures, 49, 91
Taylor, Joseph, 79–80, 93, 140
teaching, 80–81, 88, 172
Teapot Dome scandal, 49
temples, 34, 39, 71–75
testimony, 193

Theological Foundations of the Mormon Religion, 133–34
theoretical analysis, 134–35
Thomas Jefferson, 92
translation of sacred texts, 192
Turley, Richard, 109
turning point events, 114–15, 135–41

U

Ulrich, Laurel Thatcher, 196–97
University of Colorado, 39–40. *See also* Shipps, Jan, education of
history department factions, 47, 132
library at, 40–50
University of Colorado Denver Center, 51
University of Illinois Press, 94–95, 98–99, 110
University of Utah Press, 49
Utah Historical Quarterly, 175–77
Utah State Archives, 47
Utah State Historical Society, 47–48, 175
Utah State University, 29, 31–40, 73–74
Utah War, 36

U

wagon wheel analogy, 186–87
Warner Robins, Georgia, 11–12
Wayne University, 26–29
Weber, Max, 79, 190
Weinberg, Martin, 57, 84
Welch, John, 109–10
Western history, 90–91
Western History Association, 63–65
Wiley, Bell, 58, 63, 69, 140
William, Russel, 77
Williams House, 27–28
Wimberly, Mary, 18
Wimberly, Olin, 18
Wood, Gordon, 69, 91
Woodruff, Wilford, 192–93
Works Progress Administration, 2, 174
World War II, 10–13, 153

Y

Young, Brigham, 102–3, 148, 150. *See also Lion of the Lord, The*

Also available from
GREG KOFFORD BOOKS

On the Road with Joseph Smith: An Author's Diary

Richard L. Bushman

Paperback, ISBN 978-1-58958-102-9

After living with Joseph Smith for seven years and delivering the final proofs of his landmark study, *Joseph Smith: Rough Stone Rolling* to Knopf in July 2005, biographer Richard Lyman Bushman went "on the road" for a year, crisscrossing the country from coast to coast, delivering addresses on Joseph Smith and attending book-signings for the new biography.

Bushman confesses to hope and humility as he awaits reviews. He frets at the polarization that dismissed the book as either too hard on Joseph Smith or too easy. He yields to a very human compulsion to check sales figures on Amazon. com, but partway through the process stepped back with the recognition, "The book seems to be cutting its own path now, just as [I] hoped."

For readers coming to grips with the ongoing puzzle of the Prophet and the troublesome dimensions of their own faith, Richard Bushman, openly but not insistently presents himself as a believer. "I believe enough to take Joseph Smith seriously," he says. He draws comfort both from what he calls his "mantra" ("Today I will be a follower of Jesus Christ") and also from ongoing engagement with the intellectual challenges of explaining Joseph Smith.

Praise for *On the Road With Joseph Smith*:

"The diary is possibly unparalleled—an author of a recent book candidly dissecting his experiences with both Mormon and non-Mormon audiences . . . certainly deserves wider distribution—in part because it shows a talented historian laying open his vulnerabilities, and also because it shows how much any historian lays on the line when he writes about Joseph Smith."
        -Dennis Lythgoe, *Deseret News*

"By turns humorous and poignant, this behind-the-scenes look at Richard Bushman's public and private ruminations about Joseph Smith reveals a great deal—not only about the inner life of one of our greatest scholars, but about Mormonism at the dawn of the 21st century."
        -Jana Riess, co-author of *Mormonism for Dummies*

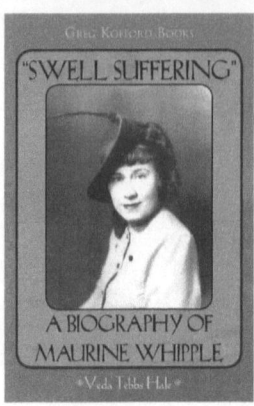

"Swell Suffering": A Biography of Maurine Whipple

Veda Tebbs Hale

Paperback, ISBN: 978-1-58958-124-1
Hardcover, ISBN: 978-1-58958-122-7

Maurine Whipple, author of what some critics consider Mormonism's greatest novel, *The Giant Joshua,* is an enigma. Her prize-winning novel has never been out of print, and its portrayal of the founding of St. George draws on her own family history to produce its unforgettable and candid portrait of plural marriage's challenges. Yet Maurine's life is full of contradictions and unanswered questions. Veda Tebbs Hale, a personal friend of the paradoxical novelist, answers these questions with sympathy and tact, nailing each insight down with thorough research in Whipple's vast but under-utilized collected papers.

Praise for *"Swell Suffering"*:

"Hale achieves an admirable balance of compassion and objectivity toward an author who seemed fated to offend those who offered to love or befriend her. . . . Readers of this biography will be reminded that Whipple was a full peer of such Utah writers as Virginia Sorensen, Fawn Brodie, and Juanita Brooks, all of whom achieved national fame for their literary and historical works during the mid-twentieth century"
—Levi S. Peterson, author of *The Backslider* and *Juanita Brooks: Mormon Historian*

Hugh Nibley: A Consecrated Life

Boyd Jay Petersen

Hardcover, ISBN: 978-1-58958-019-0

Winner of the Mormon History Association's Best Biography Award

As one of the LDS Church's most widely recognized scholars, Hugh Nibley is both an icon and an enigma. Through complete access to Nibley's correspondence, journals, notes, and papers, Petersen has painted a portrait that reveals the man behind the legend.

Starting with a foreword written by Zina Nibley Petersen and finishing with appendices that include some of the best of Nibley's personal correspondence, the biography reveals aspects of the tapestry of the life of one who has truly consecrated his life to the service of the Lord.

Praise for *A Consecrated Life*:

"Hugh Nibley is generally touted as one of Mormonism's greatest minds and perhaps its most prolific scholarly apologist. Just as hefty as some of Nibley's largest tomes, this authorized biography is delightfully accessible and full of the scholar's delicious wordplay and wit, not to mention some astonishing war stories and insights into Nibley's phenomenal acquisition of languages. Introduced by a personable foreword from the author's wife (who is Nibley's daughter), the book is written with enthusiasm, respect and insight. . . . On the whole, Petersen is a careful scholar who provides helpful historical context. . . . This project is far from hagiography. It fills an important gap in LDS history and will appeal to a wide Mormon audience."
       —Publishers Weekly

"Well written and thoroughly researched, Petersen's biography is a must-have for anyone struggling to reconcile faith and reason."
       —Greg Taggart, Association for Mormon Letters

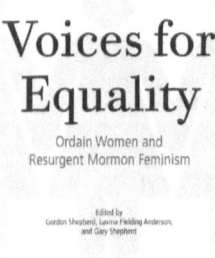

Voices for Equality: Ordain Women and Resurgent Mormon Feminism

Edited by Gordon Shepherd, Lavina Fielding Anderson, and Gary Shepherd

Paperback, ISBN: 978-1-58958-758-8

Praise for *Voices for Equality*:

"Timely, incisive, important—this book teaches us that our sometimes very personal struggles with gender and equality in Mormonism have profound and far-reaching significance. In these pages, some of Mormonism's finest researchers and thinkers bring a richness of historical and scholarly perspective and a powerful new survey of tens of thousands of Mormon people to bear on headline-making issues like women's ordination, sister missionaries, church discipline, the internet and faith, and change in the LDS church. They offer us a rare and precious opportunity to grasp the full significance of this moment. This book is a much needed mirror for our time."

— Joanna Brooks, co-editor of *Mormon Feminism: Essential Writings* and author of *The Book of Mormon Girl: A Memoir of an American Faith*

"*Voices for Equalty: Ordain Women and Resurgent Mormon Feminism* is a very important contribution to the discussion of Mormon feminism and the struggle for the ordination of women to the priesthood in the LDS Church. Anyone interested in this subject, any library concerned to be up-to-date on these issues, needs to have this book."

— Rosemary Radford Ruether, world-renowned feminist scholar and Catholic theologian, author of *Sexism and God-Talk: Toward a Feminist Theology* and *Women-Church: Theology* and *Practice of Feminist Liturgical Communities*

www.ingramcontent.com/pod-product-compliance
Lightning Source LLC
Chambersburg PA
CBHW031642170426
43195CB00035B/348